Critical practice with children and young people

Edited by Martin Robb and Rachel Thomson

The Open University

First published in 2010 by

The Policy Press • University of Bristol
Fourth Floor • Beacon House
Queen's Road • Bristol BS8 1QU, UK

Tel +44 (0)117 331 4054 • Fax +44 (0)117 331 4093
e-mail tpp-info@bristol.ac.uk • www.policypress.org.uk

North American office:
The Policy Press • c/o International Specialized Books Services (ISBS)
920 NE 58th Avenue, Suite 300 • Portland, OR 97213-3786, USA
Tel +1 503 287 3093 • Fax +1 503 280 8832
e-mail info@isbs.com

in association with

The Open University, Walton Hall, Milton Keynes, MK7 6AA, United Kingdom,
www.open.ac.uk

British Library Cataloguing in Publication data
A catalogue record for this book is available from the British Library

Library of Congress Cataloging-in-Publication Data
A catalog record for this book has been requested.

ISBN 978 1 84742 682 6 (hardback)
ISBN 978 1 84742 681 9 (paperback)

Typeset by The Policy Press
Cover design: Qube Associates, Bristol
Front cover: image kindly supplied by www.istock.com
Printed and bound in Great Britain by TJ International, Padstow

FSC
Mixed Sources
Product group from well-managed
forests and other controlled sources
Cert no. SGS-COC-3482
www.fsc.org
© 1996 Forest Stewardship Council

Contents

Acknowledgments

This book was produced for The Open University module, 'Critical practice with children and young people' (K802), which is part of the Masters in Childhood and Youth. Many people contributed to its production and the collaborative nature of the book needs to be acknowledged. Not only are we appreciative of the contributions of all our authors, but we would also like to thank those who put in a great deal of work and effort behind the scenes.

Jo Dawson as course manager played a key role in coordinating production, with support from Val O'Connor as course team assistant. Our external assessors, Gill Frances and Simon Bradford, provided valuable feedback on outlines and drafts, as did our team of critical readers. We would also like to acknowledge the contribution of the practitioners from a wide range of backgrounds who took part in the consultative process that helped shape the book.

Finally, we would like to thank Gill Gowans, Copublishing Executive at The Open University, and the team at The Policy Press, in particular Karen Bowler and Jo Morton, for all their help.

Notes on the contributors

Jane Aldgate is Professor of Social Care at The Open University, Honorary Professor of Social Work at Queen's University Belfast and Honorary Professorial Fellow at the University of Edinburgh. Her recent work includes studies on kinship care and child well-being for the Social Work Inspection Agency's review of looked-after children in Scotland, *Extraordinary Lives* (2006), which she co-authored. Recent co-edited books include *The Developing World of the Child* (2006), and *Enhancing Social Work Management: Theory and Best Practice from the UK and the USA* (2007) both for Jessica Kingsley Publishers. Jane is currently seconded to the Scottish government's *Getting it Right for Every Child* team as professional adviser and is patron of the charity, Kinsfolk Carers Edinburgh. She was awarded the OBE in 2007 for services to children and families.

Lisa Arai is Senior Lecturer in Children and Young People in the School of Health & Social Care at Teesside University. She has special interests in child health and well-being, adolescent health, evidence-based policy and practice and methodological innovation in the public health sciences. Her book *Teenage Pregnancy: The Making and Unmaking of a Problem* was published by The Policy Press in 2009.

Janet Batsleer is Principal Lecturer and Head of Youth and Community Work at Manchester Metropolitan University. Her longstanding professional engagement with youth and community work is informed by a strong theoretical engagement with women's studies and cultural studies. She contributes regularly to the professional and academic debates in these areas. Recent contributions include *Informal Learning in Youth Work* (Sage Publications, 2008) and the editorship, with Keith Popple, of the Learning Matters series Empowering Youth and Community Work Practice. She remains active in youth work in Manchester, as a volunteer with The Blue Room (a project using creativity as a means of engagement with vulnerable young men in the city centre) and as a member of the board of trustees of 42nd Street, a community-based resource for young people experiencing stress.

Maria Eriksson is Associate Professor in Sociology and Senior Lecturer in Child and Youth Studies at Uppsala University, Sweden. Her special field of research is gender, violence, parenthood and children, in particular policy and welfare practice in relation to these issues. Recent publications include 'Girls and boys as victims: social workers' approaches to children exposed to violence', *Child Abuse Review* (2009, vol 18, no 6, pp 428–45), 'Participation in family law proceedings for children whose father is violent to their mother' (with Elisabet Näsman, *Childhood*, 2008, vol 15, no 2, pp 259–75) and *Tackling Men's Violence in Families: Nordic Issues and Dilemmas* (edited with M. Hester, S. Keskinen and K. Pringle, The Policy Press, 2005).

Jane Franklin is a Project Coordinator and Researcher in Social Policy at new economics foundation (nef). She is a policy analyst and political sociologist, whose work has focused on critical engagement with the politics of community, social capital, the third way and a risk society. More widely, her research interests include the dynamic between theory, policy and practice; late modernity and social change; equality and social justice in contemporary societies; and feminist theory and politics. She has also worked at the Institute for Public Policy Research, London South Bank University and The Young Foundation.

Val Gillies is Reader and Director of the Families and Social Capital research group at London South Bank University. She has researched and published in the area of family and social class, producing various journal articles and book chapters on parenting and social policy, young people's family lives, family and social change, as well as qualitative research methods. Her book *Marginalised Mothers: Exploring Working Class Parenting* was published in 2007 by Routledge.

Sue Higham is Lecturer in Nursing – Child Health and Generic Pathways at The Open University. Having spent 15 years as a clinical children's nurse in the fields of neonatal care and acute in-patient care, Sue has worked in a variety of roles in pre- and post-qualification children's nursing education. Her research interests include how children, young people and their families experience and manage illness and hospitalisation.

Barry Luckock is Senior Lecturer in Social Work and Social Policy at the University of Sussex, where he is currently the Programme Director for the MA in Social Work. He has experience as a schoolteacher, social worker and guardian *ad litem* and has served as an elected member for a local authority. His research interests include child and family policy, adoption support and social work with children in care as well as integrated children's services. His recent publications include *Developing Adoption Support and Therapy: New Approaches for Practice* (with A. Hart, Jessica Kingsley Publishers, 2004) and *Direct Work: Social Work with Children and Young People in Care* (edited with M. Lefevre, BAAF, 2008).

Jane Martin is Professor in Social History of Education at the Institute of Education, University of London. She is the author of *Women and the Politics of Schooling in Victorian and Edwardian England* (Leicester University Press, 1999) and has just completed a typescript with the title *Making Socialists: Mary Bridges Adams and the Fight for Knowledge and Power, 1855-1939* (Manchester University Press, 2009). She is vice-president of the UK History of Education Society.

Heidi Safia Mirza is Professor of Equalities Studies in Education and Director of the Centre for Rights, Equalities and Social Justice at the Institute of Education, University of London. She established the Runnymede Collection, an archive documenting the history of the civil rights struggle for a multicultural Britain. She is author of several books including *Race, Gender and Educational Desire: Why Black Women Succeed and Fail* (Routledge, 2009).

Michael Murphy is currently a Senior Lecturer at the University of Salford, where he teaches on the post-qualifying childcare award. Michael trained as a social worker and a counsellor and has been involved in childcare for 30 years. Michael's research interests include interagency collaboration in childcare, partnership working, substance misuse and family life and stress in social care. Michael has published widely in all four areas.

Eileen Oak is Assistant Head of Department in the Faculty of Health and Social Care at The Open University. She has been a social work academic and researcher for seven years and a qualified childcare social worker for over 20. Her specialist interests include looked-after children, interagency working, social exclusion and issues pertaining to children's agency. She has recently published *Social Work and Social Perspectives* (Palgrave Macmillan, 2009).

Lindsay O'Dell is a Lecturer in the Children and Young People group in the Faculty of Health and Social Care at The Open University. Her key area of teaching and research interest focuses on children who are in some way 'different', including sexually abused children, children with a visible difference, children with autism and working children. She has published widely and is currently adjunct professor at the Royal University of Phnom Penh, Cambodia.

Jayne Osgood is Reader in Early Childhood Education at London Metropolitan University. She has a background in critical feminist approaches to early childhood education and has research interests in critical discourse analysis; autobiographical narrative methods; and theorising identity construction. She has published widely on these issues and publications include *Professional and Social Identities in the Early Years: Narratives from the Nursery* (Routledge, 2010) and 'Childcare workforce reform and the "early years professional": a critical discourse analysis', *Journal of Education Policy* (2009, vol 24, no 6, pp 733-51).

Keith Pringle is Professor in Sociology at Uppsala University, Sweden, and holds a chair in Social Policy and Social Work at London Metropolitan University. His research fields include: masculinities/men's practices; comparative welfare analysis; and the sociology of social work. Among his publications are five books as author or co-author and six as co-editor, including the *International Encyclopaedia of Men and Masculinities* (Routledge, 2007), *European Perspectives on Men and Masculinities* (Palgrave Macmillan, 2006), *A Man's World: Changing Men's Practices in a Globalised World* (Zed Books, 2001) and *Children and Social Welfare in Europe* (Open University Press, 1998).

Andy Rixon is a Lecturer in the Children and Young People group in the Faculty of Health and Social Care at The Open University. He has a background in social work practice and in training and development in children's services. Contributions to publications include *Youth in Context: Frameworks, Settings and Encounters* (Sage Publications, 2007) and co-editor of *Connecting with Children: Working and Learning Together* (The Policy Press, 2008). He is particularly interested in the development of post-qualifying education for social workers.

Martin Robb is a Senior Lecturer in the Faculty of Health and Social Care at The Open University. Before joining the university he managed a range of community education projects for socially disadvantaged groups. His research interests include fatherhood, masculinity and childcare, and young people, identity and relationships. He is the author of *Youth Policy and Practice* (Palgrave, forthcoming), editor of *Youth in Context: Frameworks, Settings and Encounters* (Sage

Publications, 2007) and co-editor of *Communication, Relationships and Care: A Reader* (Routledge, 2004).

Yvonne Robinson is Senior Research Fellow in the Families and Social Capital research group at London South Bank University. Her background is in Human Geography and her broad research interests are in 'race', ethnicity and youth studies, education and the arts.

Mary Robson is Associate for Arts in Health and Education at the Centre for Medical Humanities, Durham University. She has held a three-year Fellowship with the National Endowment for Science, Technology and Arts (NESTA) to explore her own working practice in the light of community, ethics and excellence, empathy and ritual. Mary has 20 years' experience of directing arts in health projects. Her particular interest is in working with children, teaching staff and families to nurture social and emotional development. Using the arts, she helps foster new traditions that put children in the driving seat of cultural change. She is an experienced facilitator and trainer in workforce development, focused conversation and reflective practice. She is director of an NHS-funded project at Chickenley Community Junior Infant and Nursery School in West Yorkshire that uses the arts to encourage social and emotional development.

Anna Souhami is Lecturer in Criminology at the School of Law, University of Edinburgh. Her main research interests are in the sociology of criminal justice professions and policy, in particular in relation to questions of the organisation and culture of contemporary youth justice. She has a particular interest in ethnographic methodologies and has conducted and published ethnographic research in the fields of both youth justice and policing. She is the author of *Transforming Youth Justice: Occupational Identity and Cultural Change* (Willan, 2007).

Rachel Thomson is Professor of Social Research in the Faculty of Health and Social Care at The Open University. Her research interests include youth transitions, generation and changing gender identities. Recent publications include *Researching Social Change: Qualitative Approaches* (with J. McLeod, Sage Publications, 2009), *Unfolding Lives: Youth, Gender and Change* (The Policy Press, 2009) and *Making Modern Motherhoods* (with M.J. Kehily *et al.*, The Policy Press, forthcoming).

Introduction

Martin Robb and Rachel Thomson

These are interesting and challenging times for those who work with children and young people. The past decade has seen a number of significant policy developments, as well as important changes in the organisation of services. The introduction of *Every Child Matters* in England and *Getting it Right for Every Child* in Scotland, for example, have signalled a new emphasis on improving outcomes for children. At the same time, the development of a 'common core' of knowledge and skills for those working with children and young people is driving changes in the structure and delivery of services. As well as a renewed emphasis on outcomes and targeting provision, recent government policy in the UK has been aimed at breaking down barriers between services and encouraging the development of integrated practice. There has also been an increasing drive towards professionalisation at all levels, from early years through to youth work.

In this rapidly changing context there is a need for experienced practitioners with the knowledge, understanding, skills and motivation to take leading roles in increasingly integrated services for children and young people. These advanced professionals will need a critical understanding of recent policy developments, an awareness of the impact of organisational change and how to manage it, and the ability both to develop their own practice and to enable others to do the same. This collection aims to contribute to the process of developing a critical and reflective practice that is able to help shape change, in the interests of children and young people, rather than simply responding to it.

The book is aimed primarily at experienced practitioners who wish to progress professionally and academically, but it should also be of interest to anyone concerned with the future direction of services for children and young people. It has been designed to be relevant to a wide range of practice settings, including education, social work, healthcare, nursing, youth work and youth justice, and covers the whole age range, from early years to young adulthood. Rather than commissioning chapters that focus on a single age group or professional context, we have attempted to assemble a collection that addresses issues of relevance to *all* practitioners, whatever their setting or background. Authors have been invited to draw on their particular area of expertise, but at the same time to bear in mind the needs and interests of a wide range of potential readers.

The book brings together authors from diverse backgrounds in research, teaching and practice, with many combining experience and expertise in more than one of these fields. The chapters, too, are diverse in form, with theoretical and political argument sitting alongside analysis of everyday practice, and findings from research being complemented by more personal reflections. Divided into three parts, exploring different facets of practice, the chapters share a common purpose of stimulating critical reflection that will lead to changes in practice and improved outcomes for children and young people.

Part One: Conceptual context

Part One is concerned with the ways in which ideas about children and young people shape practice, and in the opening chapter Lindsay O'Dell challenges some widely shared notions about children and their welfare. Adopting a social constructionist approach, she argues that, rather than being universal and timeless, many of the ideas that inform work with children and young people have their roots in specific social and historical contexts. In particular, the chapter takes issue with the enormously influential ideas of developmental psychology, and argues for a 'critically informed practice' in which 'it is important to understand how knowledge about children is produced, and becomes taken for granted as the facts about children's lives'.

Lisa Arai's chapter continues the theme, exploring the ways in which particular ideas assume the status of 'common sense' and help to shape policy and practice. Taking teenage pregnancy and motherhood as a focus, she challenges media representations of the issue, suggesting that they often provide misinformation about the realities of young people's lives. Where the previous chapter used theory to interrogate popular assumptions, this chapter argues for the importance of research in developing a more critical practice. In making the case for evidence-based practice, Lisa Arai warns practitioners against assuming that what counts as 'evidence' is necessarily straightforward. Echoing Lindsay O'Dell's argument for critically informed practice, Lisa Arai calls for research-literate practitioners and a stronger 'research–practitioner' partnership.

Building on the previous two chapters, Heidi Safia Mirza provides a powerful demonstration of the way particular sets of ideas become embedded in public policy, and how this can lead to the needs of some

children and young people being overlooked or distorted. Her chapter
argues that a discourse of 'liberal multiculturalism' has informed
welfare practice in a way that disadvantages young ethnicised women,
especially those who are the victims of so-called 'honour' crimes.
Like Lisa Arai, Heidi Safia Mirza explores the role of the media in
shaping public perceptions, and thus indirectly influencing practice. As
with Lindsay O'Dell's chapter, this contribution prompts the difficult
question as to whether there are any universal values underpinning
work with children and young people, or whether all such ideas are
culturally relative.

The second group of chapters in Part One explores another way
in which different ideas result in different kinds of practice, as they
examine the role of political priorities and structures in determining
policies relating to children and young people. Taking the experience
of children who are victims of domestic violence as their focus,
Maria Eriksson and Keith Pringle discuss some of the key differences
between the UK and Sweden, challenging common assumptions
about policy and practice in the two countries. At the heart of their
chapter is a concern with the extent to which children's voices are
taken account of in the framing of policies that affect their lives. Jane
Aldgate's chapter continues the theme of geographical and political
diversity, comparing Scottish policy towards children with the rest
of the UK, particularly since devolution. She suggests that thinking
about children's welfare has developed in quite distinctive ways in the
different jurisdictions, with Scotland adopting a more holistic and
child-centred approach. Anticipating a key theme in Part Two, the
chapter also examines the increasingly important issue of integrated
practice, and particularly the challenge for agencies that work with
children of finding a common language.

If the previous two chapters provided clear demonstrations of how
approaches to children's welfare differ according to space and place,
then the final chapter in Part One shows how policy and practice
change over time, and how they might take on a different direction
in the future. Jane Franklin provides a useful thumbnail sketch of
changes in welfare policy in the UK. However, the main thrust of
her chapter is forward-looking, offering a distinctive, radical vision
of how work with children and young people might develop in the
future, under the influence of 'green' ideas. The discussion of 'co-
production', exemplified by two case studies, provides a link with the
emphasis, which has run through the whole of Part One, on the vital
importance of involving children and young people in decisions about
policy and practice that affect their lives.

Part Two: Organisational context

If Part One provided some widely divergent examples of how ideas influence practice with children and young people, then Part Two offers a closer, critical analysis of some recent developments in practice. The first three chapters in this section explore aspects of the move towards integrated practice across the field of services for children and young people. The first two chapters focus particularly on the impact of interagency collaboration on children themselves as the users of services. Barry Luckock's chapter begins by describing some of the advantages of integration, but then moves on to assess the reality on the ground against the rhetoric of policy, posing the question as to whether joint working means real change for children. He draws on two case studies to suggest some of the problems arising from the aspiration to provide holistic services, and discusses the risks associated with attempts to 'blur the boundaries between the specialist expertise of different professionals'. Michael Murphy and Eileen Oak continue this debate in their chapter, which examines 'the enduring challenge of achieving increased interagency collaboration in childcare'. The emphasis here is on safeguarding vulnerable children and young people, and the authors look at the impact on statutory work of greater interagency cooperation. Their survey of the historical and social policy context of integrated practice complements the accounts of policy development in Part One of the book, showing how similar issues and tensions have recurred in attempts to develop joined-up working in children's services.

Anna Souhami continues the exploration of multi-agency work, but switches the focus to its impact on practitioners, and the ways in which attempts at developing integrated practice can affect professional identities. Again, this contribution sets out some of the benefits of interprofessional working, but also explores some of the conflicts between professional cultures, and the tensions that can result between generalism and specialist expertise. Making extensive use of data from a study of professionals in a Youth Offending Team (YOT), Anna Souhami views multi-agency practice in the context of the new managerialism and an increasing emphasis on effectiveness and outcomes. Andy Rixon takes up the theme of practitioner identities as he explores the ways that recent developments in practice are altering notions of professionalism. This chapter draws on interviews with social workers about their experience of continuing professional development and (echoing other chapters in Part Two) raises important questions about the relative importance of different kinds of experience and expertise in practice with children and young people.

One aspect of professionalism that has never been more in demand, especially in the context of widespread organisational change, is the skill of leadership, and particularly the ability to motivate and inspire practitioners. Mary Robson's chapter offers a personal reflection on her experience of receiving and giving supervision, drawing on her work in the arts in health and education. She offers an illuminating account of how the skill of reflective practice can be developed both with practitioners and with children and young people. The final chapter in Part Two maintains the focus on practitioners but turns its attention to the composition of the workforce, and particularly to attempts at redressing the gender imbalance in services for children and young people. Continuing the critical questioning of policy developments that runs through the first two sections of the book, Martin Robb asks why there has been so much emphasis in recent years on recruiting more men to work with children, and offers a critical examination of the 'male role model' discourse that has been influential in debates around this issue. In calling for a more critical understanding of how masculinity comes into play in work with children, the chapter anticipates the focus on gender issues in many of the chapters in the final section of the book.

Part Three: Personal and professional contexts

The final part of the book explores the interface between the professional identities of people working with children and young people and their personal lives. The idea of a 'vocation' has a long tradition in this area, associated mostly clearly with nursing and teaching, and bearing traces of the roots of these professions in maternal, religious and political practices.

The historical development of particular formations of professional identity is addressed in several of the chapters. Jane Martin explores how teaching identities developed over the course of the 20th century, alongside a series of different welfare settlements that have reconstituted the meaning of education and the relationship between the teacher, pupils and the curriculum. What is remarkable about the picture that she paints, drawing on archives and oral histories, is the extent to which teachers of different generations provide a relatively consistent account of the qualities that make up a 'good teacher', while at the same time expressing considerable regret about changes that they have witnessed in their careers and disappointment with the new generation of professionals around them. The difficulties involved in intergenerational conversations between professionals are explored in detail by Janet Batsleer, who describes an initiative in youth work called Feminist Webs, which has brought together different generations of feminist youth workers. She shows how a common identification with a collective political project such as feminism can facilitate difficult conversations and enable the sharing of expertise, experience and insight. Both Janet Batsleer and Jane Martin point to the significance of a political reflexivity that goes beyond the individual project of improving one's own practice to include an awareness of the broader collective, the forms of governance that pertain at a particular historical moment and the significance of social divisions.

What it means to be a professional must always be made sense of in relation to the concrete conditions of practice. This is brought to life in Jayne Osgood's account of early years workers in nurseries, showing how professional expertise is co-produced. Her research details how workers in a private nursery were neither recognised nor valued by middle-class parents, yet equally qualified workers were treated as esteemed experts in a statutory nursery serving a mixed community and a voluntary sector nursery serving a predominantly working-class community. Osgood shows how the drive towards professionalisation of early years workers is entangled with the promotion of a set of middle-class cultural values, making this predominantly working-class workforce vulnerable to media attack and exploitation.

The attempt to rid professional identities of any vestiges of personal life or of informal or lay knowledge needs to be understood in relation to the considerable fight involved in claiming professional status for practices that have traditionally been marginalised as 'women's work'. Sue Higham's account of children's nursing demonstrates the complexity of a professional identity that seeks to both include and exclude a model of maternal care. So although teaching, nursing, youth and social work are all informed by familial-type relationships and models of care, the marker of professionalism in these roles is the ability to resist the seductions of these identifications. As both Sue Higham and Rachel Thomson point out, such professionalism can be troubled by the experience of parenthood. The evidence in Thomson's account of teachers becoming mothers suggests that there are times when people working with children and young people want and need to create boundaries between their working and personal lives, where being the object and the subject of expertise is just 'too much'. Yet both her account and Sue Higham's suggest that the heightened reflexivity brought about through a collision of personal experience and professional obligation can be productive.

In different ways, each contribution to Part Three explores how we might enrich our understanding of reflective practice to include an often uncomfortable acknowledgement of inequalities of power, conflicts of interests and emotional investments. The contribution by Val Gillies and Yvonne Robinson helps move our attention from the personal/professional biography towards understanding the professional from the outside, as part of a wider institutional and social landscape. The authors provide a vivid account of the situations that professionals must survive, giving a sense of the defensive function of professional identities, helping workers to bear the limits of their power to improve the lives of children and communities. Their account of a tough school under pressure also reveals something of the relationship between the emotional life of a school and the ways in which such feelings are formalised through curricula and other formal techniques. The curriculum on emotional literacy bears little relation to the emotional volatility of classroom practice, nor the creative and sometimes desperate strategies of teachers to maintain some control. Val Gillies and Yvonne Robinson take us on their research journey, modelling a capacity to describe honestly, to observe and record feelings, and to reflect on these productively.

In compiling this collection we have sought to provide readers with a set of resources that will enable them to think beyond the specificities of their own practice experience. We also hope to encourage the development of a critical perspective on policy and practice, which includes a sense of the historical and cultural contexts of current debates about the well-being of children and young people. Ideally readers will also gain a sense of possibility, imagining ways of interrogating, enriching and remaking their own practice with children and young people.

Part One
Conceptual context

Part One
Conceptual context

One

Theorising development, constructing 'normal' childhoods

Lindsay O'Dell

Introduction

This chapter explores a social constructionist approach to understanding child development. This theoretical approach is used to scrutinise our understandings of how children develop and to demonstrate how taken-for-granted ideas about development can be seen not as natural abilities but as part of specific bodies of knowledge and theory. The commonsense view of development as a progressive accumulation of skills through childhood and into adulthood sets up a number of implications that are discussed in relation to a critically informed practice.

Social constructionist theory emphasises that, rather than documenting a natural process, developmental theory *produces* particular kinds of children at particular geo-temporal locations. It argues that all knowledge is tied to particular historical, cultural and spatial contexts, thus making it difficult to sustain a universal view of childhood and child development. Implicit within this theoretical position is scepticism of developmental psychology's generation of universal laws and theories of development. Martin Woodhead (1999) and others have argued that psychology produces knowledge from a particular cultural (and historical) location, typically from North America, which is taken as universal knowledge about child development.

Historical and cultural context of 'development'

Development as progression through time

Theorists working from a critical or social constructionist stance, such as Erica Burman (2008a) and Nikolas Rose (1990), have argued that the view of development as a progression through the lifespan arose out of a particular set of cultural circumstances at a specific place in time. Cultural and scientific movements of the 19th century, including evolutionary theory and changes in Judeo-Christian theology, produced an understanding of 'development' as progression (Vandenberg, 1993). Vandenberg argued that in European theology during the Victorian era there was a move from seeing life as cyclical, and possibly degenerate, to one in which life on earth was seen as a way to progress towards a more godly life with the possibility of ascent to heaven. Evolutionary theory proposed the orderly progression of species moving from simplified to more complex organisms. The Child Study Movement (a precursor to modern-day developmental psychology; see Morss, 1990) drew on evolutionary theory to argue that human development occurred in a similar way, but through an individual's lifespan rather than over millions of years, from simplified organisms (children) through to evolved complex organisms (adults). This is illustrated below in a quote from Professor James Sully, a member of the Child Study Movement:

> Comparison between child, prehistoric man (sic) and "savage" presupposes a concept of development, of individual and of evolutionary progress, as unilinear, as directed steps up an ordered hierarchy. (cited in Burman, 1994: 11)

The implicit assumption within this dominant view is that development is a cumulative acquisition of skills, moving from undeveloped, less sophisticated and immature childhood to the endpoint of adulthood. Thus childhood is seen as a state of natural immaturity, vulnerability and dependence.

Welfare for the developing child

In the 19th century philanthropic work in British society demonstrated an urge to save children from the harsh, oppressive world of (what was beginning to be constructed as) adult life and the world of work. The theoretical perspective of the Child Study Movement (and later developmental psychology) was drawn on to emphasise the differences between children and adults. Zelizer (1985) charted a cultural transformation in the meaning of childhood from a pre-Victorian view of a child as an active economic agent, to the image of a child as someone with no economic worth but who was emotionally priceless (a view much in evidence today). The assumption was that children's lack of cognitive (and other) skills made participation in adult life difficult and often dangerous. Therefore children were excluded from economic engagement and positioned as unable to be active participants in the (newly constructed) adult world of work.

The newly emergent 'child' as separate from adult life drew to itself new measures of welfare and surveillance in which practice and policy directed towards families became focused on the welfare of the child (Rose, 1985). Alongside new child welfare professionals the introduction of compulsory schooling provided an arena through which to check children's development and a mechanism for assessing parental engagement with their children (Rose, 1990). Thus the role of Victorian practitioners was to 'save' children from the harsh realities of adult life, to work to ensure 'normal' developmental trajectories and to educate children to become rational (or at least, reasonable) subjects and citizens. Within the Child Study Movement and early developmental psychology there was a focus on the nature of individual children (Walkerdine, 2009). By understanding habit and nature, scientists could understand changes in childhood and produce knowledge of typical or 'normal' development.

Normal development and 'stolen' childhoods

The task of 19th-century practitioners working with children and their families was to document development, track progression and be alert to the possibility of deviation from a 'normal' trajectory (Rose, 1990), with the aim of returning the child to a 'normal' path of development (Mayall, 2005). This practice was underpinned by theoretical knowledge produced by psychological science, initially the Child Study Movement and later developmental psychology, which implicitly constructed 'normal' development as a series of developmental stages and theories.

The notion of 'normal' childhoods is still commonly drawn on in our understandings of child development, particularly for younger children and babies, being embedded within policies such as the 1989 UK Children Act and within concepts such as 'significant harm'. It is also drawn on in media concerns about individual child victims of abuse, war and other damaging events. 'Lost children' and 'stolen childhood' are common images of children both domestically and 'abroad' in the western media. In these instances a (fictional) universal child is invoked against which 'different' children are judged to have lost out on childhood. This is also seen in commentaries produced about the issues faced by these children, for example, in a key early publication about young carers entitled 'The lost children' (Aldridge and Becker, 1983). While I am not dismissing the very real harmfulness of childhood abuse and trauma, I am concerned with the way in which an assumed loss of childhood stigmatises and further marginalises children who are already in difficulty. This notion of 'normal' childhoods also produces a simplified version of the life of, in this instance, child carers, which may not represent the lived experience of the children themselves (O'Dell *et al.*, forthcoming).

A series of advertising campaigns run by Barnardo's provides an excellent example of this and of issues covered more broadly in this chapter. The advertisements have been subject to critique from a number of authors including Burman (2005), Kehily and Montgomery (2003) and myself (O'Dell, 2008). The series of advertisements ran over a number of years and were used very powerfully to illustrate a direct link between childhood difficulties and damaged adulthood. In each advertisement a fictitious child is portrayed in a scene of danger and difficulty. The timeline of each scene has been disrupted. In the first set of advertisements, the individual is seen as a small child but placed in a scene from their future life with accompanying text writing their adult future:

> Kim Vale age 24: neglected as a child, it was always
> possible Kim would be an easy victim for pimps.
>
> With Barnardo's help, an unhappy childhood
> need not mean an empty future.

In the second set of advertisements, the juxtaposition of time is inverted, so that the adult is seen in the image but the text places them in their earlier difficult childhood:

> Barry Stark. Died: Age 2 years.
> THEY need your help. MAKE a donation.

The campaigns evoke powerful feelings in the viewer. The children are obviously in situations that are not part of a 'normal' childhood, and one of the powerful feelings elicited from the images is an urge to 'save' the child from the hazardous situation in which they are depicted. As such they have been very powerful and highly successful advertisements.

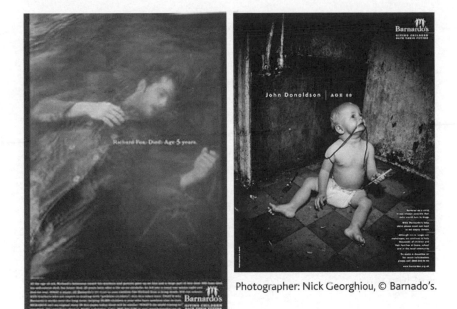

Photographer: Nick Georghiou, © Barnado's.

Photographer: Nadav Kander, © Barnado's.

Images used in Barnardo's advertising campaign.

The construction of the child as developing, being in a state of 'becoming' adult, is drawn on to make a powerful point about the need to act to save children from long-term harm. While this may seem unproblematic and self-evident, I have concerns about the implications of this view. From this perspective a key aspect of our concern for children relates to what we imagine will be their future: we protect children, in part to prevent the development of damaged adults (Kitzinger, 1990; O'Dell, 2003; Mayall, 2005). Along with other commentators, I have argued that in acknowledging the long-term harmfulness of abuse (and other forms of trauma) it is also important to recognise and work with the child's immediate concerns. The construction of the child as progressively developing through time can, in some instances, be an unhelpful way to understand children in difficulty:

> The construction of children as passive dependents
> – as not adults and therefore lesser beings than
> adults – enables adults to discount and marginalize
> children's knowledge. (Mason, 2005: 96)

The Barnardo's advertising campaigns were extremely successful because they drew on a particular view of childhood, portraying a singular developmental trajectory from damaged, lost childhood to problematic adulthood. The experience of abuse is seen in the form of a deterministic link between childhood difficulty and damaged adulthood. A key issue here is the singularisation of experience, in that traumatic events in childhood are depicted as automatically leading to damaged adults. However, psychological research has stressed the importance of various factors that mediate the long-term impacts of abuse (such as a child's temperament, the presence of a supportive context for the child and the possibility of school providing a safe and protective environment). In addition, research from adult survivors of abuse also emphasises individual factors that play a part in how abused children develop into adults (O'Dell, 2003). In critically informed practice it is important to understand how knowledge about children is produced, and becomes taken for granted as the facts about children's lives.

Constructing developmental psychology

From theory to evidence

The view of development as a cumulative progression through time, which arose through the 19th century, appears to be a self-evident truth. However, as has been discussed, a critical view argues that development as progression is a product of a particular temporal and cultural location rather than a natural characteristic of childhood. Developmental psychology has drawn on the notion of development as progression in the theoretical work of the discipline, which informs our everyday understandings of childhood and practice with children (Mayall, 2005).

A social constructionist perspective argues that all research evidence arises from theoretical underpinnings. Even when researchers do not articulate a theoretical position, they are drawing on dominant, taken-for-granted views of child development. It is important to note that each aspect of developmentalist theory, such as Jean Piaget's ideas, which are seen as 'the archetype of development theories' (Walkerdine, 2009: 116), has been extensively critiqued and questioned. For example, Piaget theorised that children needed to have developed to the concrete operations stage (at approximately seven years old and upwards) to be able to distinguish reality from fiction. However, there is increasing evidence that the context in which children make these distinctions makes a significant difference to their ability to distinguish reality (Lightfoot et al., 2008). Concepts from Piaget's theory such as egocentricity and the difficulty children have in distinguishing facts from fiction remain part of our everyday understandings. This has implications for practice with children where, for example, understandings of intent and the ability to be a competent witness are key.

However, while the ideas of developmental psychologists such as Piaget have become part of our everyday understandings of childhood, these remain a product of a particular cultural and temporal context. In addition, it can be argued that the theory itself is an interpretation. Valerie Walkerdine (2009) questions the link between accomplishment of an experimental task and what is seen as 'development', arguing that:

> The task itself is part of a theoretical framework which makes certain assumptions about the nature of mind, childhood, evolution, a pre-given subject changed through adaptation to a physical world, and so on. (2009: 116)

Different theoretical understandings of the developing child

Burman (2008a) argued that developmental psychology produces different understandings of childhood when examined in different historical periods. She suggests that developmental psychology draws on contemporary (physical, biological and medical) scientific knowledge in order to understand the child. For example, as already discussed, in the 19th century a biological theory of development influenced by the theory of evolution was dominant (Morss, 1990). In the 1920s behaviourist psychologists saw children in terms of how they could be trained, viewing the child as a *tabula rasa* or a blank slate, and therefore as a passive agent in their own development. However, Walkerdine points out that the view of biology drawn on here is a partial one: 'Indeed, the natural itself is a very specific reading of the relation of a biology, understood evolutionarily, to a psychology' (2009: 116).

By the 1960s, psychology had begun to be informed by the new sciences of technology and computing. There was a shift to viewing children in a far more active role, seeing them as information gatherers and processors. Since the 1990s the development of neuroscience has been used within developmental psychology to address how aspects of a child's environment can produce particular patterning and development of the brain's structure. Thus the emphasis has been on the neurological underpinnings of developmental tasks such as attachment. A newly emergent biologicised view of development, based on neurological functioning, has become widespread in psychology as a discipline and in the way it has been used in popular culture. Examples in children's media include television programmes such as Brain-Jitsu and 'brain training' computer games.

Different technologies to study children's development

In addition to employing different theoretical understandings of children's abilities and capabilities, Burman (2008a) noted that at different periods psychology has drawn on advances in technology to theorise and provide mechanisms for studying child development. For example, cognitive developmental psychology often uses IT and information from debates in artificial intelligence to provide theoretical insights and technological methods of investigation. Similarly, the neuroscientific knowledge currently produced by developmental psychologists relies heavily upon advances in CT scanning to provide methods of understanding children and mapping their abilities.

From a social constructionist perspective, technology is not a neutral aspect of the environment but is itself part of the constructed world we inhabit, produced by technicians who are part of the culture. I would argue that it is important for critically informed practitioners to resist the urge to assume that technology can 'speak for itself', that the CT mapping or computer programmes stand outside of the realm of interpretation. To illustrate this further, I will move outside of the disciplinary concerns of psychology to provide an example from child protection work carried out in the 1960s (see Parton 1985). At this time the new technology was the developing science of radiography used to diagnose bone fractures. This important advance in medical science was drawn on by paediatricians, psychologists and radiographers to allow them to 'see' children's bodies in a new way and to gather evidence of abuse. The technology was instrumental in highlighting a medicalised view of child abuse that came to the attention of the public and significantly changed attitudes, policy and practice. A key issue for my argument here is that X-rays of children's bones need interpretation: they do not speak for themselves. Practitioners very quickly became aware that a fuller examination of the circumstances leading up to a child's broken bones was needed to be able to satisfactorily intervene in appropriate ways. Similarly, CT mapping requires interpretation and contextualisation. Research that uses CT scans to generate hypotheses about brain development and the effect of particular family circumstances is open to debate and interpretation. Reducing children's development to a neurological basis simplifies many complex social issues. In addition, drawing on neuroscientific theoretical understandings provides a powerful explanation for children's development that is difficult to counter (particularly for those who are not familiar with the fine grain detail of neuroscientific theory and research), thus silencing alternative explanations. While it is obviously important to draw on recent advances in technology and science in our work with children, it is also vital that we remain aware of the dangers in relying on one source of evidence to make judgements about families and children.

Different understandings of the vulnerability and resiliency of the child

Changing understandings of childhood through time are also evident in debates about the resiliency or fragility of children. In the 1970s Rutter and his colleagues produced theoretical and empirical work on resiliency. Their view was that some limited exposure to stressful events could help a child learn to develop coping strategies to deal with adverse life events in the future (Rutter, 1990). In popular culture, the dominant understanding of childhood during this time was the notion that children could 'bounce back' from adversity. Rutter and others postulated that resiliency was in part due to a child's characteristics and in part due to their environment, thereby explaining how some children can be more affected by trauma than others. The view from the beginning of the 21st century is a different one in which child development is framed in terms of risk, vulnerability and problems for individual children (Caputo, 2007). The focus on *individual* children is evident in everyday concerns about children. For example, Morrow (2007) argues that studies of western children focus on individualised risks of problems such as obesity. Burman (1994) examined how this illustrated the western focus of developmental theory where risks of obesity and eating disorders (assumed to be universal concerns) were discussed in developmental textbooks in relation to the risks for individual children. The cultural production of obesity as part of a particular geo-temporal context was not examined: the risk of obesity only existed in contexts where children had access to enough or too much food.

Culturally different children

In addition to accounting for temporal variations in understandings of childhood and child development, social constructionist theory also suggests that childhood is produced within particular cultural contexts (Woodhead, 1999; Burman, 2008b). In theorising development as a process experienced by all children, childhood is abstracted from the contexts in which children live (Gordo Lopez and Burman, 2004). Cultural contexts for children can be seen in terms of geographical location (childhood is experienced differently in different parts of the world), but also in other aspects of cultural identity such as a child's ethnicity, gender, (dis)ability and socioeconomic status. Walkerdine argues that universalised understandings of childhood are at best unhelpful and can occlude other power dynamics:

> It also means that we can only see the relation of exploitation between the First World and the Third as one in which the Third-World children are being denied a childhood or are underdeveloped. If the First-World child exists, in a sense, at the expense of the Third, the complex economic relation is being lost in the developmental explanation. (Walkerdine, 2009: 118)

Current mainstream psychological theories of development have (to some limited extent) engaged with issues of 'culture', but largely by exclusion or by treating difference in highly simplified ways (Chua and Bhavnani, 2001). Thus in understanding children in their particular geo-political contexts 'culture' is often operationalised as simplified 'independent variables' such as gender or 'race', where children are tested to see if there are gender differences, for example, in a particular skill or attribute. Therefore one axis of a child's cultural context is emphasised and made amenable to testing. However, other aspects of the child's context are left unexamined. If we take an example of children's achievement in primary school tests in the UK, there has been much debate and discussion about gendered differences in achievement. Christine Griffin (2000) has critically examined the 'boys' underachievement' debate to argue that it is framed as a moral panic where girls' superiority is seen as unfair and boys' poor performance is seen as victimisation. However, the debate focuses on gender as the key analytic with which to understand the achievement of children, while other aspects of children's cultural context are left unexamined or are shifted into different debates.

The focus on gender does not fully engage with an understanding of socioeconomic status, echoing a concern of critical academics that there is little consideration of class within psychological literature and research (Holt and Griffin, 2005). The focus on gender has also not fully taken into account concerns about ethnicity, particularly the educational achievement of black boys. Broader issues relating to achievement and educational experience, such as the feminisation of early years and a broader, societal concern with masculinity in 'crisis', are left unaddressed. The multiple intersections of 'race', culture, class, gender and other aspects of a child's identity are also absent from consideration of these issues.

Conclusion

> It seems perverse to suggest that, prior to the early
> twentieth century, children did not 'develop'. Surely
> their growth from infancy to maturity has always
> been obvious to any with eyes to see. Yet it was by
> no means self-evident that a systematic knowledge
> of childhood should be grounded in the notion that
> their attributes should be linked along the dimension
> of time in a unified sequence. (Rose, 1990: 141)

In this chapter I have argued for a social constructionist understanding of child development to demonstrate that decisions about children's development are not straightforward. As Rose notes in the above quotation, this is not to argue that children do not develop. However, I am arguing that the ways in which we see development shift through historical and cultural contexts. This is not to advocate a form of cultural relativism but to stress the contested nature of development, and to argue that developmental processes are not natural or universal. In claiming to speak for all children, and to produce universal knowledge about child development, developmental psychology speaks for a particular set of children who occupy positions of relative privilege in the developed world (Woodhead, 1999; Burman, 2008b). Benchmarks and other forms of measurement of children's development are not a neutral technology but are part of a theory and knowledge base that produces particular kinds of children as the norm and others as deviant from this.

There is an obvious tension between acknowledging the constructed nature of childhood and the challenges of everyday practice. However, Garland (1990) argues that theory is necessary in order to allow us to think differently about our practice; it enables us to think of alternative solutions and actions. By engaging with theoretical understandings of child development we are producing a form of practice, one in which we become aware that theories of development arise from particular times and places to describe and construct particular kinds of children. At a theoretical level all developmental psychological work is disputed, researched and debated. It is important for critical practitioners to have the confidence to challenge particular views of development, and to be aware of the basis on which they are making claims. Informed critical work can draw on the notion of 'standpoint' so that, having assessed all the competing 'truth claims', practitioners make a stand and speak from an informed position, aware that there are alternative viewpoints but confident in their view of the situation.

Rather than 'throwing the baby out with the bathwater', as Burman (2008b) and Lee (2001, cited in Walkerdine, 2009) have noted is often the case with some critiques of developmental psychology, I would argue that there is a need for psychology – but *different* psychology – to address how children become subjects within specific understandings of childhood and how these are enacted to produce 'particular configurations of subjectivity' (Walkerdine, 2009: 121). Walkerdine (2009) and others (such as Orellana *et al.*, 2003 and de Abreu and Cline, 2003) suggest that a way forward for a psychology of childhood is to look at how childhood is situated within specific and particular local practices, and to examine how children change through time but without assuming a universal trajectory that can be studied and understood from outside of the child. A sociocultural psychology can produce an understanding that involves the culture of practices to be learned:

> 'Development' is about the acquisition of particular
> cultural skills and tools that are adaptive to a particular
> socioeconomic context and historical epoch, not about
> a once-for-all universal process. (Woodhead, 1999: 10)

References

Aldridge, J. and Becker, S. (1993) 'The lost children', *Community Care*, March, p 23.

Burman, E. (1994) *Deconstructing Developmental Psychology*, London: Routledge.

Burman, E. (2005) 'Childhood, neoliberalism and the feminization of education', *Gender and Education*, vol 17, no 4, pp 351-67.

Burman, E. (2008a) *Deconstructing Developmental Psychology* (2nd edn), London: Routledge.

Burman, E. (2008b) *Developments: Child, Image, Nation*, Hove and New York, NY: Routledge.

Caputo, V. (2007) '"She's from a good family": performing childhood and motherhood in a Canadian private school setting', *Childhood*, vol 14, pp 173-92.

Chua, P. and Bhavnani, K.K. (2001) 'From critical psychology to critical development studies', *International Journal of Critical Psychology*, vol 1, no 1, pp 62-78.

de Abreu, G. and Cline, T. (2003) 'Schooled mathematics and cultural knowledge', *Pedagogy, Culture and Society*, vol 11, no 1, pp 1-30.

Garland, D. (1990) *Punishment and Modern Society*, Oxford: Oxford University Press.

Gordo Lopez, A. and Burman, E. (2004) 'Emotional capital and information technologies in the changing rhetorics around children and childhoods', *New Directions for Child and Adolescent Development*, no 105, pp 63-80.

Griffin, C. (2000) 'Discourses of crisis and loss: analyzing the "boys' underachievement" debate', *Journal of Youth Studies*, vol 3, no 2, pp 167-88.

Holt, M. and Griffin, C. (2005) 'Students versus locals: young adults' constructions of the working class other', *British Journal of Social Psychology*, vol 44, no 2, pp 241-67.

Kehily, M.J. and Montgomery, H. (2003) 'Innocence and experience', in M. Woodhead and H. Montgomery (eds) *Understanding Childhood: An Interdisciplinary Approach*, Chichester and Milton Keynes: Open University and John Wiley, pp 221-65.

Kitzinger, J. (1990) 'Who are you kidding? Children, power and the struggle against child abuse', in A. James and A. Prout (eds) *Constructing and Reconstructing Childhood*, London: Falmer Press, pp 161-86.

Lightfoot, C., Cole, M. and Cole, S.R. (2008) *The Development of Children*, New York, NY: Worth Publishers.

Mason, J. (2005) 'Child protection policy and the construction of childhood', in J. Mason and T. Fattore (eds) *Children Taken Seriously in Theory, Policy and Practice*, London: Jessica Kingsley Publishers, pp 91-7.

Mayall, B. (2005) 'The social condition of UK childhoods: children's understandings and their implications', in J. Mason and T. Fattore (eds) *Children Taken Seriously in Theory, Policy and Practice*, London: Jessica Kingsley Publishers, pp 79-90.

Morrow, V. (2007) 'At the crossroads', *Childhood*, vol 14, no 1, pp 5-10.

Morss, J.R. (1990) *The Biologising of Childhood: Developmental Psychology and the Darwinian Myth*, Hillsdale, NJ: Lawrence Erlbaum Associates Limited.

O'Dell, L. (2003) 'The "harm story" in childhood sexual abuse: contested understandings, disputed knowledges', in S. Warner and P. Reavey (eds) *New Feminist Stories of Child Sexual Abuse*, London: Routledge, pp 131-47.

O'Dell, L. (2008) 'Representations of the "damaged" child: "child saving" in a British children's charity advertising campaign', *Children and Society*, vol 22, no 5, pp 383-92.

O'Dell, L., Crafter, S., de Abreu, G., Cline, T. and Crafter, S. (forthcoming) 'Constructing "normal childhoods": young people talk about young carers', *Disability & Society*.

Orellana, M.F., Reynolds, J., Dorner, L. and Meza, M. (2003) 'Cultural diversity research on learning and development: conceptual, methodological and strategic considerations', *Educational Researcher*, vol 32, no 5, pp 26-32.

Parton, N. (1985) *The Politics of Child Abuse*, Basingstoke: Palgrave Macmillan.

Rose, N. (1985) *The Psychological Complex: Psychology, Politics and Society in England 1869-1939*, London: Routledge.

Rose, N. (1990) *Governing the Soul: The Shaping of the Private Life*, London: Routledge.

Rutter, M. (1990) 'Psychosocial resilience and protective mechanisms', in J. Rolf, A.S. Masten, D. Ciccetti, K.H. Nuechterlein and S. Weintraub (eds) *Risk and Protective Factors in the Development of Psychopathology*, New York, NY: Cambridge University Press, pp 181-214.

Vandenberg, B. (1993) 'Developmental psychology, God and the good', *Theory and Psychology*, vol 3, no 2, pp 191-205.

Walkerdine, V. (1993) 'Beyond developmentalism', *Theory and Psychology*, vol 3, no 4, pp 451-69.

Walkerdine, V. (2009) 'Developmental psychology and the study of childhood', in M.J. Kehily (ed) *An Introduction to Childhood Studies*, Milton Keynes: Open University Press, pp 112-23.

Woodhead, M. (1999) 'Reconstructing developmental psychology – some first steps', *Children and Society*, vol 13, no 1, pp 3-19.

Zelizer, V.A.R. (1985) *Pricing the Priceless Child*, Princeton, NJ: Princeton University Press.

Two

Meeting the needs of pregnant and parenting teenagers using research: pointers for practice

Lisa Arai

Introduction

This chapter was written to provide pointers as to how research might be used by practitioners working to prevent teenage pregnancy or to improve outcomes for pregnant and parenting teenagers. It draws on findings from an exploratory scoping review of the literature on teenage pregnancy and has four sections. The first provides background information about pregnant and parenting teenagers and describes policy initiatives. In the second section evidence-based approaches to practice (EBP) are briefly described. The scoping review itself and its main findings are presented in the third section. These are summarised in the fourth concluding section.

Although the focus here is on practitioners who work with pregnant and parenting teenagers, or teenagers who may become pregnant, the issues raised about good practice will have a resonance for practitioners working with children and young people more generally.

Teenage pregnancy and teenage parents

> ### Pregnant at 11 and "happy to be a mum"
> A 12-year-old girl will become Britain's youngest mother when she gives birth next month. She became pregnant at the age of 11 when she lost her virginity to a 15-year-old boy during a drunken night out. Police said yesterday that the boy had been charged with rape.... The girl ... has insisted she is ready for motherhood. "I didn't think I'd get pregnant because it was my

first time, but I'm really excited and looking forward
to being a mum," she said. (*Daily Telegraph*, 2006)

This newspaper extract is typical of the coverage of teenage pregnancy
in the British press. Without specifically referring to it, the 'underclass',
with its dark and dangerous attributes – drunkenness, sexual ignorance,
criminal behaviour – is strongly evoked. Sensational reporting of
teenage pregnancy contributes to the perception that conceptions
at this very young age are increasing. However, it is in respect of
maternal age that the newspaper story is most unusual. Of the 101,900
conceptions to under-20s in England and Wales in 2005, 59,701
(nearly 60%) were to those aged 18 or 19. In the same year, there were
327 girls under 14 who became pregnant. Of these, 132 continued
with the pregnancy (ONS, 2005).

There is a 'myth-reality' gap in relation to teenage pregnancy that
affects large sections of the population (Arai, 2009). Analysis of social
attitudes data has shown that the public over-estimate the proportion
of the population that are teenage parents (Clarke and Thomson,
2001), and dubious motivations are often ascribed to young women's
reproductive behaviour for which there is little or no evidence (a
common one being that young women become pregnant to secure a
council flat; see Allen *et al.*, 1998). These perceptions contribute to the
ongoing demonisation of pregnant and parenting teenagers.

Trends in teenage pregnancy and fertility

As noted above, most people over-estimate the proportion of the
population who have babies as teenagers, and imagine that rates
of youthful pregnancy in the UK are 'soaring' (Arai, 2009). In fact,
teenage fertility (that is, birth) rates have been declining since the
1970s; see Table 2.1.

Teenage fertility rates in England and Wales were at their highest
in 1971, at nearly 51 per 1,000, and, by 2005, had almost halved, to
around 26. Even with some fluctuation, the overall trend in early
childbearing is downwards. The situation in England and Wales is
similar to that in the other UK nations, as well as other developed-
world countries, where a similar decline in youthful childbearing has
occurred (UNICEF, 2001).

Childbearing in the teenage years is believed to cause poor health
and socioeconomic outcomes for mothers and their children and
is regarded as a cause of social exclusion. In relation to the former,
teenage childbearing is held responsible for school drop-outs, welfare

dependency and reduced job opportunities. Many of the poor health outcomes associated with early fertility relate to pregnancy and birth itself, with teenage mothers considered to be at greater risk than older mothers of experiencing anaemia in pregnancy and higher rates of premature birth, for example. There is a long-standing debate about the degree to which age itself rather than socioeconomic and other background factors is responsible for some of the poor outcomes associated with young motherhood. Despite extensive research, no consensus has yet been reached on this issue (for an overview see Arai, 2009).

Eight of 28 OECD (Organisation for Economic Co-operation and Development) countries are (or recently have been) intervening to reduce youthful conception, and a further 12 countries consider teenage pregnancy to be a minor concern (UNICEF, 2001). The English approach to teenage pregnancy – the Teenage Pregnancy Strategy (TPS), implemented since 1999 – is concerned with a relatively large section of the teenage population (under-18s) and is being implemented over a long time period (initially to 2010). Other UK nations have developed their own initiatives to tackle teenage pregnancy; the Northern Irish approach was described in a report published by the Department of Health, Social Services and Public Safety (DHSSPS) soon after the introduction of the TPS in England (DHSSPS, 2000).

Table 2.1: Teenage (under 20) fertility rates, England and Wales: various years, 1966-2005

Year	Rate
1966	47.7
1971	50.6
1976	32.2
1981	28.1
1986	30.1
1991	33.0
1995	28.5
1999	30.9
2000	29.3
2001	28.0
2002	27.0
2003	26.8
2004	26.9
2005	26.3

Source: Data taken from ONS (2006, Table 3.1). Rates are per 1,000 females aged under 20

Drawing on international evidence about 'what works', the TPS has described the factors likely to lead to a reduction in conception rates, the first aim of the strategy. These include: the engagement of partners (in health, education, social services); a senior champion to oversee the local implementation of the TPS; prioritisation of school-based sex and relationships education (SRE); a focus on targeted interventions; and a well-resourced youth service. These activities run alongside others aimed at countering social exclusion among teenage mothers (the second aim of the TPS) and which are largely focused on providing education or training.

The success of the TPS depends on the work of practitioners. Whether it is in the coordination of services, the delivery of SRE or the forging of links with colleagues in other sectors, experienced, knowledgeable practitioners are paramount to the attainment of TPS targets. And the TPS – as an evidence-based strategy that utilises high-quality research – needs those implementing it to be evidence-based in their practice with young people.

Using research in practice settings

Evidence-based movement

There is not the scope here to fully describe the history of the evidence-based movement. Briefly, it can be traced back to Archie Cochrane's advocacy of the rigorous evaluation of the effectiveness of healthcare interventions (Cochrane, 1971). This idea was refined by Sackett and colleagues, who articulated a much-used definition of evidence-based medicine as '... the conscientious, explicit, judicious use of current best evidence in making decisions about the care of individual patients' (Sackett *et al.*, 1996). These beginnings led to the Cochrane Collaboration devoted to producing systematic reviews of healthcare interventions, and the Campbell Collaboration that uses Cochrane-style methodology to produce systematic reviews of social care interventions. The Campbell Collaboration defines a systematic review as one that uses: '... transparent procedures to identify, assess, and synthesize results of research on a ... topic. These procedures are explicit, so that others can replicate the review, and are defined in advance of the review...' (www.campbellcollaboration.org/what_is_a_systematic_review/index.php).

The theoretical underpinnings of the evidence-based movement – which now encompasses many fields beyond medicine – have not been uncontested. There is, for example, a long-running debate about what constitutes 'evidence' in the context of a systematic review, and concerns about the reliability of findings generated by the synthesis of diverse kinds of evidence (Nutley *et al.*, 2003). MacLure (2005) maintains that systematic review methodology cannot live up to its own high standards, and that the rigidity of the review process – with its reduction of scholarship to screening, data extraction and synthesis – leads to '… tiny dead bodies of knowledge disinterred by systematic review' (p 394). In addition, there are limits about the extent to which a systematic review can offer a 'take home' message about 'what works' (Petticrew, 2003). Despite these criticisms, systematic reviews can be useful in providing busy practitioners with a robust, concise and comprehensive overview of research in their field, thus allowing them to make informed decisions about the care of their patients and clients.

Practitioners and EBP

Practitioners working with pregnant and parenting teenagers are not immune to negative representations of teenage pregnancy. Yet practitioners are in a unique position not only to challenge stereotypes but also to have their own perceptions informed by their work with young people. Insights gained through education, training as well as interaction with colleagues can reinforce this. Using research findings in practice settings can be part of this process. Importantly, different types of research can be used: the findings of systematic reviews, the primary studies used in systematic reviews or the findings of mapping or scoping reviews. The latter provide an overview of research or service activity, usually in a short space of time, and are often undertaken at an early stage in the systematic review process.

Practitioners can utilise research to inform their practice or in the development of services so that better outcomes are achieved for client groups. There are other benefits to be gained from greater practitioner research literacy. Practitioners might achieve satisfaction and confidence from becoming research literate, and service users (and the general public, who are often quick to criticise practitioner 'failings') can be reassured that practitioners' work is based on research evidence.

Yet practitioners – even those fresh from education or training – may not know how to locate, assess and use research evidence effectively. This, and the difficulties of trying to 'do' EBP in the face of organisational, financial and time constraints, can mean that practitioners are not always able to utilise research effectively (Marks, 2002; Stevens and Liabo, 2005). Other factors might also impede this process, including a reluctance to learn about research (or a fear of doing so).

In a review of the literature on social care practitioners' use of research, one of the findings was the belief that research is often '... producer driven and distant from their own local needs' (Walters *et al.*, 2004). This is unfortunate given that practitioners are now *expected* to engage in EBP. To this end, there have been a number of initiatives developed to promote EBP or, relatedly, practice founded on 'research literacy' and 'research awareness'. Whatever the distinction between these terms, these all have as a central aim the greater use of research evidence by practitioners in the expectation that this will translate into better outcomes for service users. Key initiatives include: 'Making research count at UEA' (www.uea.ac.uk/swp/research/mrc); Research in Practice (rip: www.rip.org.uk/); the Research Mindedness Virtual Learning Environment for social workers (www.resmind.swap.ac.uk/); and the Research Unit for Research Utilisation (RURU: www.ruru.ac.uk). 'What Works for Children' (www.whatworksforchildren.org.uk) was set up in 2001 to explore barriers and levers to the use of research evidence among practitioners working with children (Liabo, 2005). There has been research undertaken on how to foster EBP in practice settings. A SCIE review of the use of research by practitioners described three models of the use of research in social care settings (see Box 2.1).

These simplified models are believed to reflect what is currently happening in the UK and each has its own strengths and limitations. The first relies heavily on practitioner knowledge and capacity, for example, whereas the second may impede practitioner development. These models say little about how to actually 'do' EBP. A recent systematic review (Walter *et al.*, 2005) condensed the process of EBP into five stages: effective dissemination; the forging of positive interaction by creating collaborations; influencing (and being influenced by) peers and experts; the facilitation of EBP by technical and financial means; and its reinforcement through use of rewards and/or controls.

In summary, EBP (in one form or another) is now a requirement of work in many sectors. Despite the growth of literature on EBP, and the development of initiatives to foster it, there may be a reluctance to embrace EBP among individual practitioners. Alongside insights gained from work with young people, the use of research evidence in practice settings has the potential to improve outcomes for young people as well as benefit practitioners. Here, the focus is on pregnant and parenting teenagers, or those at risk of early pregnancy. The rest of this chapter describes findings from exploratory, scoping work on research on good practice with these groups of young people.

Box 2.1: Three models of research use in social care

Research-based practitioner model
- It is the role and responsibility of the practitioner to keep up with research and ensure it is used to inform practice.
- The use of research is a linear process of accessing, appraising and applying research.
- Practitioners have the autonomy to change practice based on research.
- Education and training are important in enabling research use.

Embedded research model
- Research use is achieved by embedding research in the systems and processes of social care (its standards, policies, procedures and tools).
- Responsibility for ensuring research use lies with policy makers and service delivery managers.
- The use of research is linear and instrumental and research is translated directly into practice change.
- Funding, performance management and regulatory regimes are used to encourage the use of research-based guidance and tools.

Organisational excellence model
- The key to use of research lies with social care delivery organisations (their leadership, management etc).
- Research use is supported by developing an organisational culture that is 'research-minded'.
- There is local adaptation of research findings and ongoing learning within organisations.
- Partnerships with local universities and other organisations are used to facilitate the creation and use of research knowledge.

Source: Adapted from Walter *et al.* (2004)

Findings from an exploratory scoping review

A search of the academic and other literature was undertaken to identify research items that might be useful for practitioners working with teenagers who might become pregnant or those already pregnant or parenting.[1] The review had two main aims: to provide pointers for work with this group; and to demonstrate the utility of a scoping review. The search was not systematic or comprehensive. In its 'purest' form, EBP is based on the selection and use of 'best' evidence (considered to be that arising from systematic reviews, especially those measuring the effectiveness of interventions). The intention here is not to explore the 'best' kinds of evidence, but to provide pointers from the research base that are practice-relevant.

Overview of the research

Around 1,100 abstracts were scan-read. All of these are potentially of use to practitioners although only a few might be described as practice-relevant. No judgement was made about methodological quality since no critical appraisal was undertaken and, in most cases, abstracts only were read.

There is a relatively large body of research on teenage pregnancy and parenthood. Research crosses disciplinary boundaries and (as might be expected) there are many items from the nursing and health-related literature on (in particular) the prevention of teenage pregnancy. The (former) Health Development Agency's (HDA) *Review of Reviews* (Swann *et al.*, 2003) on what works in teenage pregnancy prevention and in improving outcomes for young mothers was used extensively. This review summarised systematic and other review evidence and, while not specifically practitioner-oriented, its findings do have relevance for practice.

Prevention of teenage pregnancy

Many of the items focused on the prevention of teenage pregnancy are concerned with the provision of sexual health and contraceptive services or SRE. Importantly, the literature on SRE is often not practice-oriented but seeks to establish effectiveness (of SRE) and usually sees teenage pregnancy as always (or mostly) undesirable. This position is not accepted by all commentators on youthful reproduction, many of whom have described the positive aspects of young motherhood (for example, Phoenix, 1991). However, given that one of the aims of the TPS is to *prevent* early pregnancy, provision of sexual health services and SRE are, therefore, important aspects of the strategy.

In relation to services, some authors consider issues of access to 'enhanced' services for adolescents. That is, services that are improved particularly in respect of offering increased levels of confidentiality to users, fostering a non-judgemental approach among staff, overcoming physical and geographical issues of access and promoting the service through publicity (Sykes and O'Sullivan, 2006). Enhanced service development can also be informed by the views of young people

(Meldrum and Pringle, 2006). Ensuring that these factors – assurance of confidentiality, a non-judgemental approach, ease of access, publicity and consultation with service users – are in place is consistently flagged up in the literature as leading to good practice. The characteristics of service providers can also be important determinants of the services that young people receive. In one study, the authors observe that younger and female GPs were more likely to prescribe contraception than older or male GPs (Bethea *et al.*, 2007).

In the HDA's *Review of Reviews*, evidence on the prevention of teenage pregnancy also centres on SRE and provision of contraception and sexual health services. The authors conclude that SRE can be effective, although they do acknowledge that a systematic review of interventions to reduce teenage pregnancy (DiCenso *et al.*, 2002), and which found little evidence that SRE could reduce pregnancy rates, led to a change in consensus about the effectiveness of SRE. It is true that there is little 'hard' evidence that SRE leads to a reduction in teenage conceptions, although it can improve sexual health knowledge and have other positive outcomes, such as boosting self-esteem.

There are many suggestions in the research on SRE about what can be useful for practitioners working in this area. In one document on the delivery of SRE in further education (FE) settings, the authors argue that SRE not only leads to a reduction in conception rates but can lead to higher FE retention rates. In addition, practitioners delivering SRE are asked to have a non-judgemental approach, to forge links with other service providers and to respect confidentiality (as noted earlier, an important issue with this age group) (DfES, 2007).

Some of the work on SRE explores its limitations. The wider determinants of sexual and reproductive behaviour are often not explored within standard SRE, for example. Bonell and colleagues (2007) describe school ethos as an important influence on sexual behaviour, and in a systematic review of interventions aimed at preventing social exclusion, the authors concluded that the reduction of social exclusion was likely to have a greater impact on teenage pregnancy than SRE (Fletcher *et al.*, 2008). Coleman (2002) observes that most interventions are mono-focused (that is, on pregnancy reduction) and do not explore other risk factors, such as alcohol or drug consumption, despite evidence that adolescents might demonstrate a constellation of risky health behaviours. This has implications not only for the design of interventions but also for everyday work with young people who may need assistance from different kinds of practitioners (Tripp and Viner, 2005).

Government departments have issued guidance documents aimed at practitioners working with young people 'at risk' of early pregnancy. These provide advice to practitioners as well as insights from case studies. In one of these, and alongside discussion of legal, ethical and social aspects of sexual health work with young people, the authors repeat a common refrain when they observe that:

> Advice to young people should always be in the context
> of helping them to resist pressure to have unwanted sex
> and to delay first sex until they feel ready and confident
> to make safe and responsible choices. (DfES, 2005: 6)

Pregnant and parenting teenagers

Good practice with pregnant teenagers is built on at least two major organising principles. The first relates to the kinds of services offered to them. These might be described as 'mainstream, but additional'. For example, pregnant teenagers need access to high-quality antenatal services, and, in this respect, they are no different to older pregnant women, but they might also need help with their nutritional needs, for example, so they do not become anaemic, or assistance to help stop smoking to counter the increased risk of low birth weight in this group (Cunnington, 2001). Apart from antenatal care, pregnant teenagers might need help to complete their education, or to enter a training scheme, or help to stay in the family home. This assistance may be needed beyond the post-partum period.

The second relates to the manner in which services are delivered: pregnant teenagers are acutely aware of how they are perceived by those around them (Whitley and Kirmayer, 2008). They want confidentiality and non-judgemental treatment from practitioners and service providers and they need services that are non-stigmatising and appropriate (de Jonge, 2001).In the HDA's *Review of Reviews* some of these issues are discussed, although the authors observe that there is less evidence about what works with pregnant or parenting teenagers to improve outcomes than there is on what works in relation to teenage pregnancy prevention. Here, a relatively small number of practice-relevant items were found describing initiatives to address the needs of pregnant and parenting teenagers.

In the antenatal period, interventions aimed at teenagers are designed to help them access antenatal services and engage in healthier behaviour during pregnancy (Derbyshire, 2007). Some practitioners endorse the establishment of dedicated teenage antenatal clinics as a way of dealing with young mothers' own anxieties about how they are perceived by others.

A number of guides, or 'toolkits', have been written to aid practitioners in the implementation of teenage-friendly initiatives. One of these, 'Getting maternity services right for pregnant teenagers and young fathers', is aimed at midwives and other healthcare workers. This guide describes the background to the TPS and the reasons why teenage pregnancy is considered problematic. A distinction is made between generic services and specialist support. Where the latter is not available, the standard service needs to be accessible, be clear about confidentiality and child protection issues, treat young people with respect, include young fathers, provide support to prevent further unplanned pregnancies and be staffed by practitioners trained to work with young people. Tips are offered from midwives already working with young mothers; staff are encouraged to make the clinic young-person friendly by putting up posters depicting teenage mothers, for example. The trust of pregnant young women can be secured through appropriate use of body language and avoidance of patronising language. There is also a section on including young fathers. To endorse the messages provided in guidance on teenage pregnancy, and to provide networking opportunities for healthcare workers, practitioners set up the National Teenage Pregnancy Midwifery Network (www.rcm.org.uk/cillege/standards-and-practice/national-teenage-pregnancy-midwifery-network).

In the period after birth, teenage parents may need a variety of support services, but there are at least three main areas where additional help may be needed: breastfeeding, parenting skills and help to re-enter employment or education. Some of the research on breastfeeding among young mothers (who traditionally have low rates of breastfeeding; see Dewan et al., 2002) has relevance for practice. In one study (Dykes et al., 2003), qualitative data were analysed and five themes related to experiences emerged: feeling watched and judged, lacking confidence, tiredness, discomfort and sharing accountability. A further five themes were developed to describe the support needs of parenting teenagers. These fell into emotional, esteem, instrumental, informational and network categories. Key supporters identified were the teenager's mother, her partner and the midwife.

Support is also the focus of Furey's (2004) review of parenting programmes for teenage parents. She found that only one systematic review explored interventions aimed at teenage parents and their children, and that social support and parenting interventions could improve maternal–child interaction and child cognitive development but had little impact on birth weight, the risk of stillbirth or neonatal death. In a systematic review (Macdonald *et al.*, 2007) of home visiting support for teenage mothers, just five studies (with 1,838 participants) were included in the review and little evidence was found for the effectiveness of home visiting as a way to improve maternal and child outcomes.

The second aim of the TPS is to counter social exclusion among young mothers and there is a growing body of work on the education of pregnant and parenting young women. However, as Shaw and Woolhead (2006) note in their analysis of qualitative data, in some locations there are currently no standard procedures or practices in place for tracking the participation of teenage parents in employment, education or training. But these authors do observe that practitioners have a good understanding of the needs of young parents.

Conclusion

In summary, there is a myth-reality gap on teenage pregnancy, and pregnant and parenting teenagers are still demonised. Practitioners are in a unique position to counter stereotypes about pregnant and parenting teenagers. Standing at the interface between teenagers and policy, they come to their practice with varying degrees of knowledge (and their insights can, in turn, inform the development of knowledge and be fed back into practice). Whatever stage of their career practitioners are at, greater research awareness can be beneficial for them and young people, and EBP is a requirement of work in many sectors. Research awareness might involve using findings from a systematic review, or from primary studies or scoping reviews.

Specific items of practice-relevant research have been briefly discussed here. A thread that runs through the research is the recognition that pregnant and parenting teenagers are a stigmatised group and that services aimed at them should be non-judgemental or young mothers will not engage with them. Confidentiality, access and the provision of a safe, welcoming environment is paramount. Practitioners working to prevent teenage pregnancy typically implement SRE. However, the evidence base shows that SRE is largely ineffective in reducing teenage pregnancy. Importantly, however, young people receiving SRE often report positive attitudes to it, even though it may not lead to outcomes such as reduced pregnancy. There are fewer practitioner-oriented items exploring the macro-level determinants of early reproduction (possibly because these are seen to be beyond individual practitioners' abilities) although research does suggest that these may be more important than standalone SRE. In many respects, it is important not to treat pregnant and parenting teenagers as wholly different to the general population, although they may have additional needs, and services need to be tailored appropriately. There is some debate about whether antenatal clinics should be generic with additional teenage-friendly components or be specialist. Clearly, cost and other constraints affect to what extent the latter can be achieved. In addition, teenage mothers have specific support needs in the early years of their child's life and the education and training needs of young mothers are a policy priority and education services have been set up especially for pregnant teenagers or those already parenting.

In conclusion, three points about practice with pregnant and parenting teenagers are briefly made here. First, the TPS is still in place, although its focus may change in light of evidence that English teenage pregnancy rates are not declining fast enough to meet TPS targets (Arai, 2009). And the Family–Nurse Partnership, a programme founded in the US and with home visitation of young mothers by trained nurses at its core, has been introduced in 10 English areas (DCSF, 2009). Practitioners working with pregnant young women or teenage mothers on these, or similar, programmes may find that new skills and competencies are required as the focus of initiatives change, or new programmes (with new targets and aims) are introduced. Given this, 'keeping up' with the research literature will become even more of a priority for practitioners.

Second, in many practice areas (for example, in delivery of SRE), there is a danger that practitioners might become disheartened about their capacity to achieve positive (or expected) outcomes. Just because a policy is evidence-based, that does not mean that desired outcomes can be attained. In some cases, outcomes can be different to those expected. The Young People's Development Programme (YPDP) (based on another US programme) attracted excited press attention after it emerged that young women on the programme had *higher* rates of teenage pregnancy than those in the control group (Wiggins *et al.*, 2009). Practitioners are rarely able to address structural/macro-level influences on behaviour, such as deprivation, and one of the downsides of greater research literacy is that practitioners may come to realise that the evidence about 'what works' is either scant, or shows no effects (and might even have the opposite effect, as the example of the YPDP shows). This realisation can undermine practitioner confidence in their role.

Third, the work reported here is exploratory. It can provide pointers for practice only, and much work remains to be done on the best ways to help practitioners in their work with pregnant and parenting teenagers. The literature on effectiveness is often not practice-relevant and researchers working to establish effectiveness could incorporate greater detail about how findings can be used in everyday settings, not just *if* an intervention works, but *how* it works as well (Roberts *et al.*, 2006). Dissemination activities arising from scholarly work on effectiveness should reflect the importance of the researcher–practitioner partnership.

Note

[1] Search terms for interrogation of databases and other resources included 'teenage', 'pregnancy', 'mothers' and 'practitioners'. The major inclusion criteria were that items had to report an intervention (or components of an intervention), or its evaluation, be focused on prevention of teenage (under 20) pregnancy or on the needs of pregnant teenagers or those already parenting (mothers were the primary focus, but research on young fathers was not excluded). Guides to good practice (based on identifiable practice-relevant research or practitioner experience) were included, as were other items focusing on practical aspects of working with teenagers or on issues of service access and/or use (and which drew on research and/ or practitioner experience). General commentaries or 'think pieces', reports on the epidemiology of teenage pregnancy/fertility, studies reporting research on the experience of being a teenage parent (that did not explore service use in a significant way) and items reporting solely clinical aspects of teenage pregnancy and/or fertility were excluded, as were brief news, information and editorial items. Items were included if they focused on the situation in the UK nations and were published in English from 1999 (the start of the TPS) on. Items without abstracts were excluded. Fuller details of the search strategy are available from the author.

References

Allen, I., Bourke Dowling, S. and Rolfe, H. (1998) *Teenage Mothers: Decisions and Outcomes*, London: Policy Studies Institute.

Arai, L. (2009) *Teenage Pregnancy: The Making and Unmaking of a Problem*, Bristol: The Policy Press.

Bethea, J., Hippisley-Cox, J., Coupland, C. and Pringle, M. (2007) 'General practitioners' attitudes towards the provision of services to young people aged under 16: a cross-sectional survey', *Quality in Primary Care*, vol 15, no 1, pp 11-19.

Bonell, C., Fletcher, A. and McCambridge, J. (2007) 'Improving school ethos may reduce substance misuse and teenage pregnancy', *BMJ*, vol 334, pp 614-16.

Clarke, L. and Thomson, K. (2001) 'Teenage mums', in A. Park *et al.* (eds) *British Social Attitudes: The 18th BSA Report: Public Policy, Social Ties*, London: Sage Publications.

Cochrane, A.L. (1971) *Effectiveness and Efficiency: Random Reflections of Health Services* (2nd edn), London: Nuffield Provincial Hospitals Trust.

Coleman, L. (2002) 'New opportunities for reducing the risk from teenage pregnancy – what is the evidence base for tackling risk behaviours in combination?', *Health, Risk & Society*, vol 4, no 1, pp 77-93.

Cunnington, A.J. (2001) 'What's so bad about teenage pregnancy?', *Journal of Family Planning & Reproductive Health Care*, vol 27, no 1, pp 36-41.

Daily Telegraph (2006) 'Pregnant at 11 and "happy to be a mum"', 14 May.

DCSF (Department for Children, Schools and Families) (2009) 'More cash for contraception', Press release (www.dcsf.gov.uk/pns/DisplayPN.cgi?pn_id=2009_0041).

de Jonge, A. (2001) 'Support for teenage mothers: a qualitative study into the views of women about the support they received as teenage mothers', *Journal of Advanced Nursing*, vol 36, no 1, pp 49-57.

Derbyshire, E. (2007) 'Nutrition in pregnant teenagers: how can nurses help?', *British Journal of Nursing*, vol 16, no 3, pp 144-5.

Dewan, N., Wood, L., Maxwell, S., Cooper, C. and Brabin, B. (2002) 'Breast-feeding knowledge and attitudes of teenage mothers in Liverpool', *Journal of Human Nutrition & Dietetics*, vol 15, no 1, pp 33-7.

DfES (Department for Education and Skills) (2005) *Enabling Young People to Access Contraceptive and Sexual Health Advice: Guidance for Youth Support Workers*, London: The Stationery Office.

DfES (2007) *Improving Access to Sexual Health Services for Young People in Further Education Settings*, London: The Stationery Office.

DHSSPS (Department of Health, Social Services and Public Safety) (2000) *Myths and Reality. Report of the Working Group on Teenage Pregnancy and Parenthood*, Belfast: DHSSPS.

DiCenso, A., Guyatt, G., Willan, A. and Griffith, L. (2002) 'Interventions to reduce unintended pregnancies among adolescents: systematic review of randomised controlled trials', *BMJ*, vol 324, no 7351, pp 1426-30.

Dykes, F., Moran, V.H., Burt, S. and Edwards, J. (2003) 'Adolescent mothers and breastfeeding: experiences and support needs – an exploratory study', *Journal of Human Lactation*, vol 19, no 4, pp 391-401.

Fletcher, A., Harden, A., Brunton, G., Oakley, A. and Bonell, C. (2008) 'Interventions addressing the social determinants of teenage pregnancy', *Health Education*, vol 108, no 1, pp 29-39.

Furey, A. (2004) 'Are support and parenting programmes of value for teenage parents? Who should provide them and what are the main goals?', *Public Health*, vol 118, no 4, pp 262-7.

Liabo, K. (2005) 'What works for children and what works in research implementation? Experiences from a research and development project in the United Kingdom', *Social Policy Journal of New Zealand*, vol 24, pp 34-54.

Macdonald, G., Bennett, C., Dennis, J., Coren, E., Patterson, J., Astin, M. *et al*. (2007) 'Home-based support for disadvantaged teenage mothers', *Cochrane Database of Systematic Reviews* (Online).

MacLure, M. (2005) '"Clarity bordering on stupidity": where's the quality in systematic review?', *Journal of Education Policy*, vol 20, no 4, pp 393-416.

Marks, D.F. (2002) 'Perspectives on evidence-based practice', Presented at the Second Meeting of the Public Health Evidence Steering Group, 18 October.

Meldrum, J. and Pringle, A. (2006) 'Sex, lives and videotape', *The Journal of the Royal Society for the Promotion of Health*, vol 126, no 4, pp 172-7.

Nutley, S., Walter, I. and Davies, H.T.O. (2003) 'From knowing to doing. A framework for understanding the evidence-into-practice agenda', *Evaluation*, vol 9, no 2, pp 125-48.

ONS (Office for National Statistics) (2005) *Conception Statistics, 2005*, London: The Stationery Office.

ONS (2006) *Population Trends 126*, London: The Stationery Office.

Petticrew, M. (2003) 'Why certain systematic reviews reach uncertain conclusions', *BMJ*, vol 326, pp 756-8.

Phoenix, A. (1991) *Young Mothers?*, Cambridge: Polity Press.

Roberts, H., Arai, L., Roen, K. and Popay, J. (2006) 'What evidence do we have on implementation?', in A. Killoran, C. Swann and M.P. Kelly (eds) *Public Health Evidence: Tackling Health Inequalities*, Oxford: Oxford University Press, pp 299-308.

Sackett, D.L., Rosenberg, D.M., Gray, J.A., Haynes, R.B. and Richardson, W.S. (1996) 'Evidence-based medicine: what it is and what it isn't', *BMJ*, vol 312, no 7023, pp 71-2.

Shaw, M. and Woolhead, G. (2006) 'Supporting young mothers into education, employment and training: assessing progress towards the target', *Health & Social Care in the Community*, vol 14, no 2, pp 177-84.

Stevens, M. and Liabo, K. (2005) 'Review of the research priorities of social care practitioners working with children', *Child & Family Social Work*, vol 12, no 4, pp 295-305.

Swann, C., Bowe, K., McCormick, G. and Kosmin, M. (2003) *Teenage Pregnancy and Parenthood: A Review of Reviews. Evidence Briefing*, London: Health Development Agency.

Sykes, S. and O'Sullivan, K. (2006) 'A "mystery shopper" project to evaluate sexual health and contraceptive services for young people in Croydon', *Journal of Family Planning and Reproductive Health Care*, vol 32, no 1, pp 25-6.

Tripp, J. and Viner, R. (2005) 'Sexual health, contraception, and teenage pregnancy', *BMJ*, vol 330, pp 590-3.

Walter, I., Nutley, S., Percy-Smith, J., McNeish, D. and Frost, S. (2004) *Improving the Use of Research in Social Care Practice*, London: Social Care Institute for Excellence.

Walter, I., Nutley, S. and Davies, H.T.O. (2005) 'What works to promote EBP? A cross-sector review', *Evidence and Policy*, vol 1, no 3, pp 335-64.

Whitley, R. and Kirmayer, L.J. (2008) 'Perceived stigmatisation of young mothers: an exploratory study of psychological and social experience', *Social Science & Medicine*, vol 66, pp 339-48.

UNICEF (2001) *A League Table of Teenage Births in Rich Nations*, Innocenti Report Card No 3, Florence: Innocenti Research Centre.

Wiggins, M., Bonell, C., Sawtell, M., Austerberry, H., Burchett, H., Allen, E. and Strange, V. (2009) 'Health outcomes of youth development programme in England: prospective matched comparison study', *BMJ*, vol 339, b2534.

Three

'Walking on egg shells': multiculturalism, gender and domestic violence

Heidi Safia Mirza

Introduction

> Multiculturalism does not cause domestic violence, but it does facilitate its continuation through its creed of respect for cultural differences, its emphasis on non-interference in minority lifestyles and its insistence on community consultation (with male self-defined community leaders). This has resulted in women being invisibilised, their needs ignored and their voices silenced. (Beckett and Macey, 2001: 311)

Professionals working with children and young people in multicultural Britain must address the issue of gendered risk that ethnicised girls and young women can face within their own communities and families. But in a climate of increasing personal responsibility for risk, how do socially responsible professionals relate to girls and young women at risk of abuse, violence, even murder, in the context of the discourse of multiculturalism in Britain? This chapter seeks to address this question by looking at some of the tensions and confusions associated with the hard and sensitive issues of gendered human rights violations. Throughout the chapter I use the term 'ethnicised women' in order to emphasise the power relations and the process of *being* or *becoming* an objectified othered or racialised person (Bhavnani *et al.*, 2005). 'Ethnicised women' encompasses women of all faiths from majority global cultures who are now deemed minorities living in Britain.

Young women growing up in minority ethnic communities and subject to specific forms of cultural domestic violence, such as honour killing, forced marriage and female genital mutilation, are caught up in the contradictions of the cultural relativism of British multiculturalism on the one hand, and the private/public divide which characterises our approach to domestic violence on the other. Liberal multiculturalism is popularly conceived as celebrating diversity and tolerating cultural and religious values (Bhavnani *et al.*, 2005). However, this notion of mutual tolerance is fragile. Multiculturalism negotiates this fragility by maintaining a laissez-faire approach to gendered cultural difference. Consequently, professionals may find themselves 'walking on egg shells', that is, not wanting to offend the community's sensibilities, afraid of accusations of racism, or feeling a lack of cultural expertise and knowledge. Within this 'collision of discourses', ethnicised young women are both visible and pathologised as victims, in light of negative media attention and the discourse of Islamophobia. At the same time, they are largely absent in the normative (white) discourse on domestic violence (Carby, 1982; Mama, 1989; Williams Crenshaw, 1994). Within the discourse of multiculturalism, young women from minority ethnic communities are at risk of not being fully protected by the state as equal citizens. Ethnicised young women can 'slip through the cracks' of this malaise, and suffer a lack of protection, or inaction, from individuals and organisations charged with their well-being.

In the name of 'honour': cultural context of domestic violence

We may be incredulous when reading sensationalised press reports of fathers and other close relatives, including women, who inflict violence and brutality on their own children in the name of honour or *izzat*. But many young women facing familial domestic violence, forced marriage or honour killings are being cared for within our schools and by health, youth and care services. As socially responsible professionals we need to ask, how do we understand and act on this gendered risk?

Following a police review of 22 domestic homicides in Britain in 2005, 18 cases were reclassified as 'murder in the name of so-called honour' (Meetoo and Mirza, 2007). There may be as many as 17,000 female victims of honour-based crimes in Britain (Brady, 2008). Many are young women under the age of 18. Young women in their late teens and early twenties become victims of these crimes as their emerging sexuality comes under regulation and control by the family and wider community. A young woman's sexual purity and 'honour' define the status and regard with which a family is held in the community. The same may be said of forced marriage. A forced marriage, unlike an arranged marriage, is when a young person is coerced, under either physical or emotional duress, into a marriage against his or her will, and in the name of family honour (FCO, 2000). The Forced Marriage Unit (FMU) deals with approximately 300 cases annually of marriage conducted without freely given consent (FCO, 2006).

While extreme violence against women for breaking an honour code constitutes an abuse of human rights, there have been many attempts to justify it on religious or cultural grounds. Heshu Yones, a young Kurdish woman, was just 16 when she was brutally beaten and murdered by her father in 2004. He slashed her throat when he discovered that she was exchanging love letters with a boy in class in her London school. His 'cultural defence', supported by dozens of men from the Kurdish community, was that she had become too westernised and brought death on herself (Nickerson, 2006). Hannana Siddiqui, of Southall Black Sisters, argues that use of the term 'honour' in such a context is a misnomer. 'The crimes themselves are dishonourable: they are merely justified by the perpetrator, and wider community, in the name of honour' (RWA, 2003: 6). In this sense, honour crimes are acts of domestic violence where 'honour' is invoked to justify male violence. Only in relation to religious and ethnic communities is the concept of honour misappropriated in this way, thereby preventing women from escaping domestic violence (Phillips, 2003).

The concept of honour perpetuates violence against women in two ways. Perpetrators use honour as an excuse or mitigating factor in acts of violence against women. As Siddiqui argues, '[t]he state thinks that honour crimes are about cultural beliefs that they should not criticise. Implicitly this means the state accepts honour as a mitigating factor and condones crimes perpetuated in the name of it' (RWA, 2003: 6). For victims, however, the concept works differently. The opposite of honour is shame, and this emotive combination is a powerful means of social control for women. It isolates women still further, as the shame they suffer when affected by domestic violence prevents them from seeking outside help. Women fear punishment for bringing shame on the family's or community's honour, as a result of which they may suffer anything from social ostracism to violence or, in some cases, murder. As Jasvinder Sanghera, founder of Karma Nirvana (an Asian women's project providing confidential emotional and physical support for victims of domestic violence), explains: 'every woman who comes to us has a problem with shame. It is a form of social control which oppresses Asian women and suppresses their ability to speak' (Sanghera, 2006).

'Gender trap': multiculturalism, sexism, racism and domestic violence

It could be argued that extreme forms of honour-based domestic violence involve only a small number of young women of Asian, African, South American, Mediterranean and Middle Eastern origin, but the persistence of such crimes raises many issues about cultural sensitivity and the gendered nature of multiculturalism in the UK. Multiculturalism is a much-disputed term. In Britain it means respecting diversity and valuing cultural difference in the context of core shared values in society (Hall, 2000; Runnymede Trust, 2000; Blair, 2006; Parekh, 2006). It is often used loosely in political discourse to affirm the distinctness, uniqueness and individual validity of different cultures, groups or communities, and recognising the importance of acknowledging and accommodating them. However, this notion of mutual tolerance is fragile. More importantly, it is gender indifferent.

Gender differences within multiculturalism, now and in the past, have yet to be recognised (Okin, 1999; Phillips, 2007; Mirza, 2009). In *The Parekh Report: Commission on the Future of Multi-ethnic Britain*, women are mentioned in three of the 314 pages (Runnymede Trust, 2000). Similarly, community cohesion reports fail to look specifically at gendered social action (Bhavnani *et al.*, 2005). A gender-blind multiculturalism has consequences for ethnicised young women, who remain largely invisible, locked in the private sphere of the home, where gender-oppressive cultural and religious practices are played out. To understand the invisibility of gender and violence in multiculturalism we need to look at the way ethnicity has been reified and fixed among minority ethnic groups. This process of reification – whereby ethnic group identity becomes defensive, and cultural and religious practices are constructed within imagined but rigid boundaries – is called 'ethnic fundamentalism' (Yuval-Davis, 1997). Migration, whether forced or planned, often leads to the breakdown of traditional certainties and structures, thereby heightening anxieties of loss and belonging. For migrant women, who are seen as upholding traditional values, patriarchal practices can be amplified when estranged from their homelands. Under threat, certain aspects of culture may be preserved, ossified or romanticised – or 'pickled in aspic'. When this happens, as in the context of the discourse on Islamophobia, we witness a resurgence and persistence of fixed and regressive notions of ethnicity and nationalism as a primary basis for the elaboration of traditional beliefs (Elliot, 2002).

Focusing on culturally specific forms of domestic violence is often seen as controversial ground. By highlighting domestic violence issues in specific cultural and religious ethnic communities in the UK, are we at risk of stereotyping these communities as backward and barbaric? Does this place undue emphasis on the ethnicised woman, racialising her by distinguishing these forms of domestic violence as special cultural phenomena? These questions are key to understanding the tensions between recognising gender oppression and preserving multicultural difference.

The debate has centred on gendered sexualised practices in particular cultures, such as female genital mutilation, forced marriages and honour killings where the sanctity of (male) community rights are privileged over the bodily rights of individual (female) victims. However, black and Asian feminists must raise difficult issues of sexism and domestic violence within the black and Asian communities. Opposing the racist assertion that black and Asian men are more barbaric, Gupta (2003) argues that we must take a global perspective and see honour killing and forced marriage as part of a wider patriarchal phenomenon of violence. Women are beaten and murdered across the globe for similar reasons. Domestic violence cuts across 'race', class, religion and age; such violence is not particular to one culture or religious group or community. Patriarchal structures use violence extensively to subjugate women in relation to class, 'race' and ethnicity. Therefore, domestic violence is not an issue of racial or ethnic differences; it is a question of economic, political and social development, and of levels of democracy and the devolution of power within communities. Low-violence cultures tend to have female power and autonomy outside the home, as well as strong sanctions against interpersonal violence, a definition of masculinity that is not linked to male dominance or honour, and equality in relation to decision making and resources within the family (Gill, 2003). These progressive qualities are largely absent from societies in which female sexual purity is linked to familial and community dignity and social status, and where males are custodians of honour.

Islamophobia and the racialisation of risk: gender stereotypes in 'new times'

In the case of violence against ethnicised young women, particularly Muslim women, a question arises: why are their risks being highlighted now? Post 9/11, risks associated with gender-related violence are high on the public and political agenda. Mary Douglas (1992) suggests that particular risks are selected at particular times, and constructed and legitimated for public attention. Risks are chosen for their usefulness to the social system, and constructed through particular forms of social organisation and their interaction in the wider political culture. Describing the climate of supposed global threat to security from Islamic extremism, Fekete (2004) argues that we are living in a time of fear not only of 'outsiders', but of Muslims within the UK.

Since 9/11 and the 7/7 bombings, there has been overwhelming media preoccupation with Muslim women. The heightened focus on honour-based crimes must be seen within this climate of Islamophobia. While the focus on honour-based crimes has opened up the issue of individual human rights for ethnicised women, it has also exacerbated Islamophobia and fear of the 'other'. A pathological pattern of visibility characterises the popular representation of the 'ethnicised woman'. This pattern is underpinned, on the one hand, by a Eurocentric universalism, which reduces the complexity and individuality of these women's lives to a single objectified category – in this case, the ubiquitous, stereotypical 'Muslim woman'. On the other hand, the women are also characterised by a particular form of cultural relativism that highlights specific barbaric cultural practices. Press reports of honour-based crimes are often sensationalist (Majid and Hanif, 2003) and put the gaze on the racialised 'other'. The women are constructed as victims, either romantic heroines yearning for the 'West' against the wishes of cruel and inhuman fathers and families, or they are victims succumbing to backward and traditional 'Eastern' cultures (Puwar, 2003).

Culture is widely employed in the discourse on multiculturalism to deny the human agency of minority or non-western groups, who (unlike their western counterparts) are seen to be 'driven' by cultural traditions and practices that compel them to behave in particular ways (Phillips, 2007). Thus, while South Asian women are seen to suffer 'death by culture', white British or North American women (with their societies characterised by freedom, democracy and mobility) are deemed to be immune from culture, even when they become victims of culturally specific forms of patriarchal violence such as gun crime or domestic violence.

If they have agency, Asian and African women are often depicted as manipulative, scrounging refugees and asylum seekers, or as overbearing black female matriarchs who marginalise and emasculate their men folk. If they are victims, they are portrayed as disempowered

and sexually exploited mail–order brides, or as having been sold
into sexual slavery and trafficking. Clearly, the social and economic
realities of sexual exploitation and oppression need to be addressed.
However, my point here is the difficulty of escaping the racialised
and gendered stereotypes that mainstream society has of ethnicised
women. Stereotypes are powerful forms of knowledge, which
construct possibile identities through representation and so shape
the lived experience of ethnicised women. Black and post-colonial
feminists have taken issue with the cultural superiority of simplistic,
sensationalised cultural constructions of Muslim women in the media,
constructions that negate minority ethnic female identity and agency,
and depoliticise their (embodied) struggles for self-determination
(Mirza, 2009).

A clear example of this was provided by the heated debate triggered
by Labour Minister Jack Straw's admission in late 2006 that, after 25
years in office he felt uncomfortable with Muslim women wearing
the face veil (*niqab*) in his constituency surgery in Blackburn (Bunting,
2006). As media hysteria grew over several weeks, stories of 'the
Muslim woman' appeared regularly on newspaper front pages. Her
body became a battlefield in the symbolic war against Islam, the
barbaric 'other', and the Muslim enemy 'within'. Her complex dress
was given symbolic meaning greater than its religious and social status
(Dwyer, 1999). Her private reasons for wearing the *niqab* became
public property, a 'weapon' used by many different competing interests,
from male politicians to white feminists, to argue their cases for and
against assimilation, multiculturalism and human rights. In what
Chandra Talpade Mohanty has called the 'latent ethnocentrism' of the
West, Muslim women are presented as voiceless, stereotyped, racialised
victims rather than active agents working to determine and engage
their rights as individuals (Mohanty, 2003). Articulate Muslim women
were hardly heard in the cacophony of competing interests for her
agenda (Fawcett Society, 2006); those who showed self-determination
were vilified, as in the case of the Muslim teacher who refused to
remove her *niqab* (BBC, 2006).

Honour-based crimes are real in *effect* – women *are* brutally
murdered. However, honour-based crimes are also constructed as
ethnicised phenomena within the racialised multicultural discourse,
and as such they are an *affect*, or emotive manifestation, of this
discourse. In this way, media reports have a real consequence: they
place women at risk by sensationalising these crimes and treating them
as voyeuristic spectacles. Their outraged cries – 'how dreadful!' – are

soon followed by multicultural paralysis and inaction – 'it's nothing to do with us! It's part of their culture'.

Negotiating risk: gender difference in multicultural settings

How can professionals working with young people approach the issue of domestic violence and gendered human rights violations in multicultural contexts? With the government's comprehensive *Every Child Matters* agenda, schools, criminal justice, health and social services are key actors in safeguarding children and identifying a young person at risk (DCSF, 2009b). Professionals are seen as part of the 'new class intellectuals', with privileged access to young people, and they are therefore instrumental in monitoring who is 'at risk' (Kelly, 2007). The emphasis on risk has consequences for how sensitive social problems, such as domestic violence, are dealt with.

Radford and Tsutsumi (2004) argue that feminist activism against domestic violence has taken place within a policy context of crime control, whereby risk assessment and risk management are an increasingly important part of how agencies, such as the police and probation, handle their workloads, meet their targets and manage resources. The tendency in crime reduction agencies is to focus on the 'dangerousness' of individuals and their violence in terms of who presents the most risk to a woman. Such approaches to risk management can be seen as a new form of social control through actuarialism and rationing of resources (Young, 2002). In this climate of accountability and risk assessment, individuals and organisations are charged with getting risk right, and they are often required to defend decisions from litigation and assessment. However, while feminists have seen the risk discourse as an opportunity to open up a dialogue with key agencies (thereby uncovering violence and getting it taken seriously by the police and courts), it has also meant rationing strategies limited to women deemed to be 'most at risk' (Radford and Tsutsumi, 2004). Consequently, protection is denied to the majority of women, and the broader issue of gendered violence and human rights is subsumed.

In social policy generally, the individual is more accountable, as social problems are reconstructed as individual choices and responsibilities (Kemshall, 2002). When risk is used in relation to particular ethnic groups, it is to identify the ethnic groups at most risk from, say, cultural habits and diets, for which the individual is responsible (Nazroo, 2003). The danger of this individualisation, and

the racialisation of ethnic groups, is that social inequalities remain
hidden and collective responses de-legitimated. So, while risks have
become a considerable force for mobilisation, they often obscure local
inequalities of social class, 'race' and gender, and their manifestations
(Adam and van Loon, 2000; Elliot, 2002).

The tendency to individualisation and accountability in the
discourse on risk, along with a laissez-faire multicultural approach
to violent gendered cultural practices within the domestic sphere,
can easily lead to non-interventionism or what I call 'multicultural
paralysis' in cases of domestic violence. From primary research with
healthcare physicians, Puri (2005) cites cases where GPs breached
confidentiality by telling the family about a woman's injuries, were
unable to handle a patient's 'cultural baggage', or even allowed a
patient's husband to be present during a physical examination.

This was particularly apparent in the recent case of Banaz Mahmod,
a 20-year-old Kurdish woman, who was sexually brutalised and
murdered by her father and uncle because her boyfriend was not a
strict Muslim from their community. She was strangled with a shoelace
and her body stuffed in a suitcase. The police had not responded to
her repeated cries for help. She was described by one police officer,
in a gendered and racist stereotypical way, as 'melodramatic and
manipulative' (McVeigh, 2007).

Yasmin, a 19-year-old Asian woman, had a similar experience. At 15,
her parents told her she was going abroad to get married. 'My stepfather, he beat me up so badly because he always used to punch me.
Once he punched me in the jaw and I couldn't open it for two weeks.'
Describing what happened when she told her teacher, Yasmin said:
'My teacher just laughed it off. She didn't believe it was happening
to me. The teacher – the school – should have at least said something,
done something. Or social services could've at least visited me to see if
I was OK ... but no-one bothered' (Choudhury, 2007).

It may be difficult to tackle the issue of domestic violence when
young women wish to protect their families' honour and divert
attention away from the abuse. For example, 'S', a 14-year-old British
girl of Bangladeshi origin, was a bright pupil with a good school
record (FCO, 2005a). By 16, she was withdrawn, and began to truant.
When marks on her wrists and back raised concerns among teachers,
'S' explained them, convincingly, as the result of 'intergenerational
tensions'. She disappeared after her GCSEs, was drugged and sent to
Bangladesh to be forcibly married. Her teacher called the FMU. 'S'
was made a ward of the High Court but did not complain as she did
not want to bring shame on her parents. No action was taken. On

her return to the UK, 'S' ran away from home and sought shelter in a refuge, as she had been raped by her husband. Despite intervening on behalf of 'S', the agencies and services tasked with her protection nonetheless failed to protect her.

While an overly sensitive multicultural approach can lead to negative action or inaction, it can also replicate structures of oppression within communities. The voluntary group Karma Nirvana has experienced problems when disseminating information through schools, as schools are concerned about damaging their relationships with parents (Sanghera, 2006). As BBC research shows, schools are central to the debate on domestic violence, as they are able to see when female pupils are absent, and should report suspected cases of forced marriage to the appropriate authorities (Choudhury, 2007). However, while the FMU and DCSF provide schools with guidelines on forced marriage (FCO, 2005b; DCSF, 2009a), the majority of councils have no record of numbers of cases, and no guidance on dealing with them.

Black and minority ethnic women's groups have been crucial in raising awareness and tackling domestic violence, sexuality and cultural and religious conservatism within specific communities. They have helped place minority ethnic women's issues on the agenda, and various services have been developed as a result. In evidence to the Working Party on Forced Marriage, Southall Black Sisters highlighted the failure of service providers to address the needs of women and girls at risk of forced marriages and honour killings (CIMEL/Interights, 2001). Service providers may cite cultural grounds for this failure, the assumption being that minority communities are self-policing and that services do not need to intervene on behalf of women (Burman *et al.*, 2004). Many community leaders consulted by the Working Group on Forced Marriages denied that a problem existed. Many were hostile to women who refused forced marriages, and to women's organisations that worked with victims. Some even argued that concern about forced marriage was a form of racism constituting an attack on the community and its cultural and religious heritage (Siddiqui, 2003).

Despite the work of women's groups, male community leaders remain influential within certain communities. Ali Jan Haider, a Muslim social worker, has described how male family members and community elders threatened him and his family after he helped a 21-year-old woman and her five children to escape domestic violence by placing them in a refuge. The woman had come to the UK, aged 16, from the rural Mirpur district of Pakistan, and was subjected for several years to persistent physical and mental abuse by her husband and in-laws. As Haider explained:

... the community interference began in earnest. I had
a phone call from a local Asian Councillor asking me
if I could explain why I had taken mum and children
away and broken up this respectable family. I then had
phone calls and visits from countless community elders
including a local religious leader. He did not waste
any time castigating my actions and telling me what
I had done was sinful. He told me how I should be
personally held responsible for the family's loss of face,
and the distress I had caused them. (Haider, 2003: 4)

In outlining an Islamic perspective to domestic violence, Haider
explains the complex interrelationship of the Muslim religion
and Pakistani culture on the one hand, and the practice of social
services and his white and non-Muslim colleagues on the other.
Such complexity often leads to institutional paralysis or community
resistance, and prevents Muslim women from seeking help when they
need it most.

Conclusion

I began by asking how, as socially responsible professionals, we can
understand and act on the gendered risk faced by many ethnicised
young women in their own communities and in the name of 'honour'.
Clearly, there are many tensions that underpin an analysis of gendered
human rights violations in a multicultural context. A key issue is that
ethnicised young women are caught up in a 'collision of discourses'.
These women are *invisible* within the discourse of multiculturalism,
and so they are at risk of not receiving the full protection of the state
agencies to which all citizens are entitled. They fall between the cracks
of the multicultural discourse, as 'race' and ethnicity are prioritised, and
gender differences and inequalities rendered invisible. Their invisibility
is compounded by their absence from the normative mainstream
(white) discourse on domestic violence.

   At the same time, many of these women are rendered highly *visible*
by the media discourse on Islamophobia, which represents Muslim
women as pathologised victims of their families, religion and culture.
While we need to be vigilant about the post-9/11 Islamophobic
media discourse, and its preoccupation and purpose with highlighting
Muslim barbarism against women, we must accept that domestic
violence is a reality in our ethnicised communities. Violence against
women must never be seen as a cultural matter, but always as a human

rights issue (Salim, 2003). At the 1995 United Nations World Congress on Women, the Beijing Platform for Action declared that culture, tradition and religion could not be used by the state to avoid its obligation to protect women (Kelly, 2005).

Often, when we are immersed in the cultural context of respecting and accommodating cultural difference, we do not see the bigger picture of universal violence against women and the accompanying human rights violations. In relation to racism, multiculturalism means learning to 'walk on egg shells' and to respect cultural differences, often without question, for fear of offending communities and ethnic groups. Consequently, ethnicised young women can go unprotected. To develop a truly multicultural, multi-agency policy framework under *Every Child Matters*, our education, health, criminal justice and social services need to be resolute in their approach to cultural forms of domestic violence.

When dealing with ethnicised community groups and state agencies, public sector professionals should be ever vigilant about whose perspectives are being heard, and whose voices marginalised, and by whom. This is not an easy task. It is a frontline position, and there are issues of personal safety to be considered on all sides. But only by challenging the multicultural status quo can we move towards a more just and equitable response to the global issue of domestic violence that festers within all our communities, black, white and Asian.

References

Adam, B. and van Loon, J. (2000) 'Repositioning risk: the challenge for social theory', in B. Adam, U. Beck and J. van Loon (eds) *The Risk Society and Beyond: Critical Issues for Social Theory*, London: Sage Publications, pp 1-33.

BBC (2006) 'Veil teacher should be sacked', 15 October (http://news.bbc.co.uk).

Beckett, C. and Macey, M. (2001) 'Race, gender and sexuality: the oppression of multiculturalism', *Women's Studies International Forum*, vol 24, no 3/4, pp 309-19.

Bhavnani, R., Mirza, H.S. and Meetoo, V. (2005) *Tackling the Roots of Racism: Lessons for Success*, Bristol: The Policy Press.

Blair, T. (2006) Full text of Blair's multiculturalism speech, *The Daily Telegraph*, 9 December.

Bunting, M. (2006) 'Straw's storm of prejudice', *The Guardian Unlimited Weekly*, 13 October.

Burman, E., Smailes, S.L. and Chantler, K. (2004) 'Culture as a barrier to service provision and delivery: domestic violence services for minoritized women', *Critical Social Policy*, vol 24, no 3, pp 332–57.

Brady, B. (2008) 'A question of honour: police say 17,000 women are victims every year', *The Independent*, Sunday, 10 February.

Carby, H. (1982) 'White women listen! Black feminism and the boundaries of sisterhood', in Centre for Contemporary Cultural Studies, *The Empire Strikes Back: Race and Racism in 70s Britain*, London: Hutchinson.

Choudhury, B. (2007) 'Battle to stamp out forced marriage', 26 January (http://news.bbc.co.uk).

CIMEL (Centre for Islamic and Middle Eastern Law)/Interights (2001) *Roundtable on Strategies to Address 'Crimes of Honour': Summary Report*, Women Living Under Muslim Laws Occasional Paper No 12, November, London: CIMEL/Interights.

DCSF (Department for Children, Schools and Families) (2009a) *Spectrum* (http://publications.teachernet.gov.uk/).

DCSF (2009b) *Every Child Matters* (www.dcsf.gov.uk/everychildmatters/about/aims/).

Douglas, M. (1992) *Risk and Blame: Essays in Cultural Theory*, London: Routledge.

Dwyer, C. (1999) 'Veiled meanings: young British Muslim women and the negotiation of difference', *Gender, Place and Culture*, vol 6, no 1, pp 5–26.

Elliot, A. (2002) 'Beck's sociology of risk: a critical assessment', *Sociology*, vol 36, no 2, pp 293–315.

Fawcett Society (2006) 'The veil, feminism and Muslim women: a debate', 14 December (www.fawcettsociety.org.uk/index.asp?PageID=378).

FCO (Foreign and Commonwealth Office) (2000) *A Choice by Right: Working Group on Forced Marriage*, London: FCO (www.fco.gov.uk).

FCO (2005a) *Forced Marriage: A Wrong Not a Right*, London: FCO (www.fco.gov.uk).

FCO (2005b) *Dealing with Cases of Forced Marriage: Guidance for Education Professionals* (1st edn), January, London: FCO (www.fco.gov.uk).

FCO (2006) *Forced Marriage: A Wrong Not a Right – Consultation Report*, London: The Stationery Office.

Fekete, L. (2004) 'Anti-Muslim racism and the European security state', *Race and Class*, vol 46, no 1, pp 3–29.

Gill, A. (2003) 'A question of honour', *Community Care*, 27 March.

Gupta, R. (2003) 'Some recurring themes: Southall Black Sisters 1979–2003 – and still going strong', in R. Gupta (ed) *From Homemakers to Jailbreakers: Southall Black Sisters*, London: Zed Books, pp 1-27.

Haider, A.J. (2003) 'Domestic violence: an Islamic perspective', Paper delivered at the 'Tackling Domestic Violence in the Asian Community' Conference, Cardiff, September.

Hall, S. (2000) 'The multicultural question', in B. Hesse (ed) *Un/settled Multiculturalisms: Diasporas, Entanglements, 'Transruptions'*, London: Zed Books, pp 209-41.

Kelly, L. (2005) 'Inside outsiders: mainstreaming violence against women into human rights discourse and practice', *International Feminist Journal of Politics*, December, vol 7, no 4, pp 471-95.

Kelly, P. (2007) 'Governing individualised risk biographies: new class intellectuals and the problem of youth at risk', *British Journal of Sociology of Education*, vol 28, no 1, January, pp 39-53.

Kemshall, H. (2002) *Risk, Social Policy and Welfare*, Buckingham: Open University Press.

Majid, R. and Hanif, S. (2003) *Language, Power and Honour: Using Murder to Demonise Muslims*, October, Wembley: Islamic Human Rights Commission (www.ihrc.org).

McVeigh, K. (2007) 'Special units to crack down on honour killings', *The Guardian*, 16 June.

Mama, A. (1989) 'Violence against black women: gender, race, and state responses', *Feminist Review*, no 32, summer, pp 30-48.

Meetoo, V. and Mirza, H.S. (2007) 'There is nothing honourable about honour killings: gender, violence and the limits of multiculturalism', *Women's Studies International Forum*, vol 30, no 3, pp 187-200.

Mirza, H.S. (2009) *Race, Gender and Educational Desire: Why Black Women Succeed and Fail*, London: Routledge.

Mohanty, C.T. (2003) *Feminism Without Borders: Decolonising Theory, Practicing Solidarity*, Durham, NC and London: Duke University Press.

Nazroo, J. (2003) 'Patterns and explanations for ethnic inequalities in health', in D. Mason (ed) *Explaining Ethnic Differences: Changing Patterns of Disadvantage in Britain*, Bristol: The Policy Press.

Nickerson, C. (2006) 'For Muslim women, a deadly defiance: "honor killings" on rise in Europe', *The Boston Globe*, 16 January.

Okin, S.M. (1999) 'Is multiculturalism bad for women?', in J. Cohen, M. Howard and M.C. Nussbaum (eds) *Is Multiculturalism Bad for Women? Susan Moller Okin with Respondents*, Princeton, NJ: Princeton University Press.

Parekh, B. (2006) *Rethinking Multiculturalism: Cultural Diversity and Political Theory*, Basingstoke: Palgrave Macmillan.

Phillips, A. (2003) 'When culture means gender: issues of cultural defence in English courts', *The Modern Law Review*, vol 66, no 4, July, pp 510-31.

Phillips, A. (2007) *Multiculturalism Without Culture*, Princeton, NJ: Princeton University Press.

Puri, S. (2005) 'Rhetoric v. reality: the effect of "multiculturalism" on doctors' responses to battered South Asian women in the United States and Britain', *Patterns of Prejudice*, vol 39, no 4, pp 416-30.

Puwar, N. (2003) 'Melodramatic postures and constructions', in N. Puwar and P. Raghuram (eds) *South Asian Women in the Diaspora*, Oxford: Berg, pp 21-41.

Radford, L. and Tsutsumi, K. (2004) 'Globalization and violence against women: inequalities in risks, responsibilities and blame in the UK and Japan', *Women's Studies International Forum*, vol 27, pp 1-12.

Runnymede Trust (2000) *The Parekh Report: Commission on the Future of Multi-ethnic Britain*, London: Profile Books.

RWA (Refugee Women's Association) (2003) *Refugee Women's News*, June and July, issue 23.

Salim, S. (2003) 'It's about women's rights and women's rights are human rights', Interview with Sawsan Salim, Coordinator of Kurdistan Refugee Women's Organisation (KRWO), received at 'Stop Violence Against Women Honour Killing' Conference, 28 October 2005, London.

Sanghera, J. (2006) 'Honour abuse: the victims' story', Karma Nirvana, Amnesty International 'Honour Killings' Conference, London.

Siddiqui, H. (2003) 'It was written in her kismet: forced marriage', in R. Gupta (ed) *From Homebreakers to Jailbreakers*, London: Zed Books, pp 67-108.

Williams Crenshaw, K. (1994) 'Mapping the margins: intersectionality, identity politics, and violence against women of color', in M. Albertson Fineman and R. Mykitiuk (eds) *The Public Nature of Private Violence*, New York, NY: Routledge, pp 93-118.

Young, J. (2002) 'Crime and social exclusion', in M. Maguire, R. Morgan and R. Reiner (eds) *The Oxford Handbook of Criminology* (3rd edn), Oxford: Oxford University Press, pp 457-90.

Yuval-Davis, N. (1997) *Gender and Nation*, London: Sage Publications.

Four

Children's perspectives informing professional welfare practice: a comparative view

Maria Eriksson and Keith Pringle

Introduction

In recent years there has been a rapidly developing interest in terms of research, policy and a range of practice arenas (James and James, 2001; Miller, 2003) concerning the agency of children within a power relational and societal perspective. Miller (2003) emphasises that children's effective participation in decision making not only offers important benefits for children themselves but also for parents, the groups in which children operate and for society as a whole, and that the main barrier to such participation is the unrealistically low expectation of many adults about children's potential. The *United Nations Convention on the Rights of the Child* (UNCRC) has underpinned this focus and the Committee which monitors implementation of the Convention internationally has regularly recorded lack of progress on Article 12, the section of the Convention where dialogue with children is particularly emphasised. For instance, in 2008 the Committee took the British government to serious task for its failings in this respect.

The aim of this chapter is to critically explore the degree to which children are accorded agency by welfare practitioners and are approached as capable social actors in contrast to the ageism to which they have historically been subject, not least in welfare research, policy and practice. In the limited space available to us here we necessarily focus on one specific 'case' in order to begin the exploration of the broader situation. That 'case' is children exposed to men's violence against women in the family. The choice of this topic derives from several imperatives. On the one hand, there has been relatively little previous scholarly focus on the participation of this particular group of children either in the UK or internationally. At the same time, we can draw on a recently completed, large qualitative Swedish research project which focused on children's participation in family law proceedings (Eriksson and Näsman, 2008).

Moreover, we wish to initiate the process of exploring how far particular welfare contexts may impact on children's participation by building in a comparative perspective to our analysis. The movements to enable children's participation have developed at different rates and in different ways across countries within Europe (Eriksson *et al.*, 2005). Once again, in the space available, we have narrowed that comparative focus to two welfare contexts: Sweden and England. This choice was also dictated by various factors. In terms of Esping-Andersen's welfare paradigms, these welfare systems are often regarded as closest in a European context to the two most contrasting of his three original welfare 'regimes': the Scandinavian/Social Democratic and the neoliberal respectively (Esping-Andersen, 1990). Moreover, it is especially interesting to compare these two social welfare systems partly because they are embedded in societies with very similar levels of per capita GDP and because several decades ago they shared a rather similar welfare profile (Pringle, 1998). However, their welfare trajectories over the past 40 years have been very different, hence the fact that their current status as welfare systems is now so often contrasted – largely positively in the case of Sweden, largely negatively in relation to the UK. Within that contrast, child welfare is often cited as a major dimension of difference. In repeated international surveys comparing children's well-being, Sweden is often cited as one of the most benevolent and 'child-friendly', while the UK is generally accorded an ignominious position (Bradshaw and Richardson, 2009) – and with good reason along dimensions such as degrees of alleviation of child poverty. So, it is particularly apposite to juxtapose these two countries when exploring issues of children's participation in welfare practices.

In this chapter, first we focus on the general issue of the place of 'children's voices' in welfare practice before moving on to explore more detailed themes emerging from the recent Swedish study of children's participation in 'visitation and contact' welfare assessments in cases where there has been violence in families. Those themes are then viewed within the broader contextualisation of existing comparisons of child welfare research, policy and practice in Sweden and the UK. This wider perspective finally leads into a concluding discussion about the necessity – as well as the degree of potential – for children's participation in welfare policy and practice if we are truly interested

in the promotion of childhood well-being among some of the most
marginalised young people in our societies.

Child welfare and children's participation

As noted, participation by children (Article 12) is a fundamental
right in the UNCRC, which has been ratified now by 193 countries
including all members of the UN except Somalia and the US.
However, previous research – mainly in Europe and the Anglophone
countries – shows that in many cases such an approach is not put
into practice in welfare settings (for example, James and James, 2001;
Eriksson and Näsman, 2008). In particular this research suggests
children's competence regarding participation and the value of their
opinions in decision-making processes often seem to be questioned.
Such questioning of children's participation in individual cases
indicates a double-ness as regards the perspective on children. On
the one hand, they are constructed as subjects; on the other hand,
as objects. The ambiguity concerning children has sometimes been
framed as the tension between a welfare principle, 'that assumes
children to be inadequately socialized dependants in need of care,
protection and control', and a rights-oriented perspective on children
that constructs them 'as creative social and moral agents with the
capacity to act, to interact and to influence the scope of their
childhoods' (Neale, 2002: 456).

Participation as the foundation for welfare

The way of talking about the ambiguity in the perspective on children
outlined above implies that there is a contradiction between 'welfare'
and 'participation'. However, as Eriksson and Näsman (2008) have
argued, participation may be viewed not as an antithesis to welfare,
but rather as a fundamental condition for, and aspect of, welfare.
For example, contemporary Swedish welfare research is based on
a definition of welfare as the resources to which the individual has
access in order for the individual to control her or his own life. In
the Swedish context, welfare is thus largely associated with the active
subject, rather than a passive object. Moreover, political resources and
participation in decision-making processes have been included among
welfare indicators in Sweden. In such a discourse *welfare is not an
antithesis to agency, but includes agency.* This is especially the case when
the children in question are vulnerable, victimised and/or the object of
interventions by welfare agencies (Eriksson and Näsman, 2008).

This argument can be substantiated through our case in point: children exposed to men's violence against women in their family. As with many groups of children who experience childhood adversity, it has been argued that children exposed to violence need to share their experiences with others, including other children with a similar background. For instance, Leira (2002) argued that in many contexts there are cultural taboos against talking about violence that occurs in the private sphere of the family. Therefore, children who experience such violence are subjected to traumas that are taboo. The consequence of the taboo is that children's opportunities to interpret and make sense of what they have been through become limited. Leira argues that when this is the case they will be carriers of catastrophic secrets, feelings of helplessness, loneliness, shame and a notion of themselves as 'the problem'. In order to be able to work through what they have seen, heard and felt and to find strategies to deal with their life situation, children need to be able to get their experiences recognised and affirmed, or *validated*, as Leira terms it (2002).

Taking Leira's claim as the point of departure, we suggest that a lack of opportunity for validation of experiences of violence directly contributes to already vulnerable children's (continued) victimisation (Eriksson and Näsman, 2008). In addition, lack of information, consultation and participation in decision making puts children in a position where they have very little control over what will happen to them. In many cases, this kind of dependency and lack of control has shaped the everyday life at home for children exposed to violence. They may have been living in a situation that for them is unpredictable, incomprehensible and beyond their control. For this group of children the possibility to get information, overview, control – to be participants in the process – is even more important than for children without difficult experiences, such as of violence at home. Here, the care principle and the rights principle merge: it becomes apparent that agency is not an antithesis to welfare, but the basis for welfare (Eriksson and Näsman, 2008). In summary, while children's participation is often mainly associated with an actor and rights perspective, we argue that participation can also be defined as something central for children in relation to welfare and their need of care. It can create possibilities for validation of children's difficult experiences and following from that, support to children's recovery after violence and abuse.

Children's participation and welfare practice

The conceptualisation of participation as the foundation for welfare does of course put pressure on welfare practitioners to make sure that the children they encounter are *informed* properly about the welfare processes going on in the children's lives, that children are *consulted* and get opportunities to *take part in decision making* (see Hart, 1992). That such demands can be somewhat of a challenge for practitioners can be illustrated by a study in Sweden on children as social actors in family law proceedings. The study draws, among other data, on a set of semi-structured individual interviews with children (a) whose father was violent to their mother and (b) who had experienced a family law investigation process that involved talking with specialised social workers. Since 1996, professionals in Sweden carrying out investigations of the child's situation in this context, usually social workers specialising in family law (comparable in England to the Children and Family Court Advisory Support Service, CAFCASS), are obliged to document the child's views and present them to the court, unless it is outright inappropriate to talk to them. In the interviews children describe and interpret their own encounters with the social workers and their participation in the investigation process. Information has been gathered from 17 children, 10 boys and 7 girls, 8 to 17 years old (Eriksson and Näsman, 2008). The analysis of the material focused on, among other things, the social workers' approaches to children, as they come across in the children's narratives. The concept of approach refers to the child's description and interpretation of the social worker's perspective on the child, the space for action given to the child and to what extent the child is focused on by the social worker. From the approach follows the position ascribed to the child, the degree of participation given to the child and the different dimensions of participation: that the child gets *information*; that the child is also *consulted*; that the child is allowed to take part in the *decision making*; and that there is space for the child's own *initiative* (Eriksson and Näsman, 2008).

Two clear patterns in the material emerge regarding the investigation process. Some of the interviewed children come across as *protected children*, given that the social workers seem to create only limited opportunities for children's participation. Children who convey this picture of social workers' approaches also describe the social workers as sensitive and empathic when talking to them. However, these children come across as objects for adult care, and not as parties to the case: they have had very limited opportunities to influence how the encounters have been carried out (time and place, for example); they have had very little information about the aim of the encounters; and they have had very little feedback concerning the continuation and outcomes of the investigation. The other clear pattern emerging from the material is descriptions of a protective approach from the social workers when it comes to participation in the investigation process, combined with an adult-oriented approach in encounters between the social workers and the child. The adult orientation which children describe relates to both (a) the question of whose perspective, needs and feelings are at the centre of attention in these encounters, and (b) the nature of the encounters themselves. Some of the child interviewees convey a picture of them being expected to sit still and talk, to be focused on the topic of conversation, not to be side-tracked too much or play (take the initiative themselves), to appreciate a glass of water offered, and so on. In other words, they have been approached *as if* they were adults. On the other hand, since they have had limited opportunities to actually influence where, when and how the talks are carried out, or the process, this child position implies only partially being treated as an adult. Instead, the child is approached as a *disqualified adult*.

Therefore, in relation to the investigation process, the overall tendency is that children do *not* tend to describe the kind of approach envisioned by Swedish policy makers in regulation and guidance: that is, that children should be approached in a child-oriented way at the same time as they are granted a high degree of participation, that they should be positioned as a *participating child*.

When it comes to the topic of violence, the picture becomes even more problematic. The research project was particularly concerned with the extent to which issues such as vulnerability, fear and protection had been on the agenda in the children's encounters with the social workers. To what extent had children's own thoughts and feelings associated with the violence been discussed? How much information were the children given about the violence and about the social workers' knowledge concerning it? To what extent was the violence against the mother – or the child – mentioned at all?

In their narratives, some of the children describe themselves as protected from further experiences of violence. The protected situation may be due to the fact that the child does not see the father at all, and in other cases contact with the father is not associated with violence. At the same time, the children say that they have not talked to the family law social workers about the violence. A notion that children should not be 'involved in parents' conflicts' can sometimes be found among social workers. Instead, children are presumed to benefit from protection from what is happening 'between the parents' (Eriksson *et al.*, 2005). Against the backdrop of such notions it seems that social workers may feel it is important to protect children from 'problems' in the parents' relationship, not least when children are perceived as already vulnerable due to the legal dispute between the parents. This child position is thus the position of a *protected victim*.

Other children describe actions and ways of encountering them that make their own experience of violence invisible, in spite of the fact that they still find themselves in a difficult situation. When the child's experiences of and feelings associated with the violence remain invisible or are invalidated, when the violence – including its consequences – is not made a topic of conversation in the dialogue between child and social worker and the child simultaneously finds her- or himself in a vulnerable situation, then we suggest that the child is forced into the position of *invisible victim*.

In addition, some of the children describe a situation where their continued victimisation was in fact communicated to adults around them but they were left without protection. When, on the one hand, social workers make the violence visible by asking and talking about it, but on the other hand, the way of handling the child's life situation makes her or him vulnerable to further abuse, then we interpret the child as positioned as an *unprotected victim*.

In line with Leira's perspective mentioned earlier, we suggest the validation of children's experiences of violence *as violence*, and as something unacceptable, requires another kind of approach than the ones we have outlined above. First of all, the child's feelings and thoughts associated with the violence must be talked about. Secondly, the child's situation must be handled so that she or he is protected. The data from this Swedish study include only one example where the child clearly describes such an approach. In summary, the social workers involved in these cases seem to have had great difficulties in approaching vulnerable children as *both* victims *and* actors: to both validate children's experiences of violence and at the same time offer them participation in the investigation process.

Different welfare systems, different opportunities for participation?

To what extent, then, is this somewhat disturbing picture outlined above context-specific and particular to Sweden? This question now leads us into the realm of comparative welfare analysis. Over the past 10 to 15 years there has been considerable critique of Esping-Andersen's well-known comparative welfare typologies (1990) when applied to broader considerations of welfare than Esping-Andersen had himself envisaged. Yet these critiques – all of which tend to focus, one way or another, on issues associated with work in the home and/or in the labour market – have required only limited adaptations to the original Esping-Andersen model. For instance, the feminist critique which focused on women's work positions at home and/or in the labour market disaggregated the Nordic model to a degree but still left it intact as one of the most progressive in Europe, relatively speaking (Sainsbury, 1999).

More recently, a deeper critique of Esping-Andersen's typologies has been developed by commentators (including the authors) who have focused on the extent to which various welfare systems – and the societies contextualising them – respond (or do not respond) to forms of disadvantage which are associated with 'bodily integrity' (Eriksson *et al.*, 2005; Hearn and Pringle, 2006) or 'bodily citizenship' (Pringle, 2009) rather than work. By using the concept of bodily citizenship we mean that the degree to which a person may be regarded as a stakeholder in society partly depends on the extent to which their bodily integrity is respected. The central conclusion derived from this focus on comparative welfare responses to issues of bodily citizenship is that the pattern of those responses, in terms of research, policy and welfare practice, seems to be in many respects the *reverse* of the pattern derived from a more 'mainstream' focus on issues associated with work. For in some (but not all) respects, the Nordic welfare systems appear to be less responsive to violations of bodily integrity than they are to issues of work in the home and/or labour market (Balkmar *et al.*, 2009), even though there is clear evidence that issues such as men's violence to women (Eriksson *et al.*, 2005) and racism (Pringle, 2009) are major social problems in the Nordic societies. At the same time, English research, policy and practice seem to be more responsive to social problems associated with bodily citizenship – in many but not all respects – than their Nordic counterparts, even though the former are clearly far less responsive than the latter when addressing issues of work in the home and/or the labour market (Hearn and Pringle, 2006). To some extent we have also extended this analytical frame to the area of child welfare, especially in relation to the topic of child sexual abuse (Hearn and Pringle, 2006).

Participation in different welfare regimes

The question that arises here is to what extent the issue of children's participation in welfare practice, as explored in the Swedish study above, fits into this previous analysis based on violations of bodily integrity. In many ways it seems to fit rather well given that the study indicates a potentially large gap between, on the one hand, the rhetoric of commonality around children's agency, care and protection within Swedish regulation/guidance and, on the other hand, actual welfare practice where there was considerable separation of children's participation from protection. This is not the outcome one would hope for or expect from a welfare system deemed to be one of the most comprehensively child-friendly in the world. Of course, we need to exercise extreme caution in how far we interpret the situation. The Swedish study reported here is only one qualitative research project. In addition, it relates to one very specific aspect of welfare practice with children in Sweden. We need far more – and broader – research to create a clearer picture on these matters in the Swedish context. Nevertheless, it is suggestive, especially in the context of explorations around Swedish welfare responses to other aspects of bodily citizenship.

In seeking to explore this question, we must first fully acknowledge that we lack the focused research necessary to make anything like a definitive judgement. However, there are several interesting indications that at least suggest the possibility of greater responsiveness to children's participation within some aspects of the UK welfare context than in the Swedish one. In the space available, we now highlight three of these indications. The first of these can be located in the qualifying education provided for social workers in the UK and Swedish contexts. Perhaps most striking is the surprising fact that until recently almost no social work qualifying courses in Sweden offered any systematic tuition on how social work students could communicate with children (Eriksson *et al.*, 2005). The assumption was – and often still is on many programmes – that if there are 'problems with' children, these can or should be explored via parents and not the children themselves. Even now, such training is not extensive in Sweden. The absence of this education has effectively silenced children's 'voices' in terms of their encounters with social workers. By contrast, although such education is not as extensive in British social work qualifying programmes as it perhaps once was (or as some of us would now wish), nevertheless it is present for many social work students hoping to work with children in the UK. And this is often still not true in Sweden despite the fact that there have been a number of calls for improvement by various Swedish governmental and quasi-governmental bodies. Such a specific but highly important difference may betray a surprisingly greater degree of ageism relating to children in some vital aspects of Swedish social work education compared with its British counterparts (Eriksson *et al.*, 2005). More centrally, it calls into question how far Swedish social workers working with children are capable of recognising or facilitating children's participation compared with their British professional peers.

The second pointer towards greater potential recognition of children's participation in the UK welfare context than the Swedish one is located in the realm of service user groups and policy formation. Speaking more generally, a significant difference between the welfare profiles of the UK and the Nordic countries as a whole is the much greater space occupied by campaigning and politically challenging service user organisations in the former compared to the latter. This applies most strikingly in terms of the disability movement. However, it is also true of child welfare in terms of parents advocating for abused children and adult survivors of childhood adversity (Pringle, 1998). It is also true in terms of children as service users themselves. There is not the space to undertake a full review here of the situations in the two countries. However, in the Swedish context you can but look in vain for broad campaigning, politically engaged children's and youth organisations comparable to Democracy for Young People (www.democracyforyoungpeople.co.uk/4604.html) and the Youth Parliament (www.ukyouthparliament.org.uk/). Similarly, you will not find in Sweden anything similar to Children are Unbeatable, a children's and young persons' organisation aimed at ending corporal punishment in the UK (www.childrenareunbeatable.org.uk/index. html). And lest we should forget, although all forms of physical abuse including corporal punishment have been banned in Sweden since 1979, physical abuse and neglect of children do still occur at significant levels even if they are lower than those in the UK. Indeed, the most recent research indicates that some forms of physical abuse are on the increase in Sweden (Pringle, 2009). Nor are there local or national organisations – with young people at their core – aimed at the care system such as Your Voice (www.voiceyp.org/ngen_public/default. asp?id=7).

This is not to say that there are no organisations in Sweden on behalf of children and young people. However, they tend to place far more emphasis on adults being responsible for protecting the interests of children, with children and young people generally occupying a considerably more distanced, consultative role than is common in the UK. This can be seen clearly for instance in the operation and approach of the children's ombudsman and the Swedish National Board for Youth Affairs (Ungdomsstyrelsen, see www. ungdomsstyrelsen.se/english_main/0,2693,,00.html). This state of affairs is, of course, reminiscent of the positions accorded by social workers to children in the Swedish study summarised earlier in this chapter. We do not wish to make this connection too strongly based on very limited data, but the potential connection should surely be explored in future research. And the contrast with the UK landscape in terms of children's and young people's campaigning groups is certainly relatively clear.

The third and final 'circumstantial' piece of evidence that we wish to adduce in order to make the preliminary case for a potentially more responsive environment in the UK as a whole regarding children's participation is located in the area of welfare practice and is related directly to our 'case' – children exposed to men's violence against women in their family. In the Scottish Government's *National Domestic Abuse Delivery Plan for Children and Young People* from 2008 each of the 13 priority areas has been defined and developed in partnership with children and young people from across Scotland who have themselves experienced violence (Scottish Government, 2008). It is emphasised that children's perspectives and their participation has been central both to the development of the plan itself, and to various research projects and consultation processes underpinning it (see, for instance, Houghton, 2008). Although parallel examples of this particular group of children's participation in the development of welfare services can be found elsewhere in the Anglophone world (for example, New Zealand; see Kenkel and Couling, 2006), no comparable example can be found in Sweden.

To summarise, the three examples discussed above, taken together with the potential implications of the Swedish study summarised earlier, suggest that there are grounds for further serious exploration of the possibility that the UK welfare context in some respects offers more scope for children's participation in the realms of welfare practice and policy than the Swedish context, despite the reputation of Swedish society more broadly for child-friendliness.

Conclusion

In this chapter we have sought to make a case for the importance of children's individual and collective participation and agency in welfare systems as a central pre-condition of their well-being. Moreover, this applies equally – and perhaps even more so – for children who have been subject to major traumas in their lives. Furthermore, we have suggested that the scope for development of such agency and participation may currently be broader in the UK welfare systems than in the Swedish one. We realise that this is a surprising suggestion in view of the usual positions occupied by those contrasting contexts in mainstream international welfare comparisons. However, we have also argued that it looks less surprising when placed inside the frame of wider debates about comparative welfare responses to issues other than poverty alleviation and work, for example violations of bodily integrity. Nevertheless, we need to remind both readers and ourselves that these comparative suggestions are only tentative, based as they are on fragments of evidence. We need far more systematic exploration of them in the future not only to establish whether there is broader validity but also to clarify the processes involved if that greater validity seems more convincing. What already appears beyond doubt to us is that – regardless of the comparative situation – the participation and agency of children must be a core objective of any welfare system if it truly seeks to ensure their care, protection and well-being.

References

Balkmar, D., Iovanni, L. and Pringle, K. (2009) 'A re-consideration of two "welfare paradises": research and policy responses to men's violence in Denmark and Sweden', *Men and Masculinities*, vol 12, no 2, pp 155-74.

Bradshaw, J. and Richardson, D. (2009) 'An index of child wellbeing in Europe', *Child Indicators Research*, vol 2, no 3, pp 319-51.

Eriksson, M. and Näsman, E. (2008) 'Participation in family law proceedings for children whose father is violent to their mother', *Childhood*, vol 15, no 2, pp 259-75.

Eriksson, M., Hester, M., Keskinen, S. and Pringle, K. (eds) (2005) *Tackling Men's Violence in Families – Nordic Issues and Dilemmas*, Bristol: The Policy Press.

Esping-Andersen, G. (1990) *The Three Worlds of Welfare Capitalism*, Cambridge: Polity Press.

Hart, R. (1992) *Children's Participation: From Tokenism to Citizenship*, Innocenti Report No 41, Florence: UNICEF International Child Development Centre.

Hearn, J. and Pringle, K. with members of Critical Research on Men in Europe (2006) *European Perspectives on Men and Masculinities*, Basingstoke: Palgrave.

Houghton, C. (2008) *Making a Difference: Young People Speak to Scottish Ministers About Their Priorities for the National Domestic Abuse Delivery Plan for Children and Young People*, Edinburgh: Scottish Government.

James, A.L. and James, A. (2001) 'Tightening the net: children, community and control', *British Journal of Sociology*, vol 52, pp 211-28.

Kenkel, D. and Couling, M. (2006) 'Child advocacy: a dialogue of inclusion', *Community Development Journal*, vol 41, no 4, pp 481-91.

Leira, H.K. (2002) 'From tabooed trauma to affirmation and recognition I & II', in M. Eriksson, A. Nenola and M.M. Nilsen (eds) *Gender and Violence in the Nordic Countries*, Copenhagen: Nordic Council of Ministers, *TemaNord*, vol 545, pp 285-305.

Miller, J. (2003) *Never Too Young: How Young Children Can Take Responsibility and Make Decisions*, London: Save the Children.

Neale, B. (2002) 'Dialogues with children. Children, divorce and citizenship', *Childhood*, vol 9, no 4, pp 445-75.

Pringle, K. (1998) *Children and Social Welfare in Europe*, Milton Keynes: Open University Press.

Pringle, K. (2009) 'Swedish welfare responses to ethnicity: the case of children and their families', *European Journal of Social Work*, First published on: 21 December 2009 (iFirst).

Sainsbury, D. (ed) (1999) *Gender and Welfare State Regimes*, Oxford: Oxford University Press.

Scottish Government (2008) *National Domestic Abuse Delivery Plan for Children and Young People*, Edinburgh: Scottish Government.

Five

The impact of devolution on policies for children in Scotland

Jane Aldgate

Introduction

This chapter outlines and comments on the impact of devolution on policies for children's services in Scotland. It looks at some of the main policy areas for children, particularly the principles and practice of the umbrella multi-agency policy *Getting it right for every child* (Scottish Government, 2008a). It also considers briefly the key areas that affect children's well-being, such as health, education, early years, youth justice, child protection and anti-poverty strategies, all of which feed into *Getting it right for every child*.

Devolution: some definitions and responsibilities

In 1999, the Scottish Parliament was re-established after 300 years. Prior to 1999, Scotland had been able to pass its own laws in relation to health, education and social work through the Westminster Government; now the Scottish Parliament clarified the areas of responsibility that were solely the domain of the Scottish Government. Legislation related directly to the welfare of children is now fully the responsibility of the Scottish Parliament.

The Westminster Government retains responsibility for defence, security, immigration and Income Support, including child benefits and any carers' allowances for children or parents. There have been tensions in relation to some of these 'reserved' policies, as they are called, which have inevitably influenced the implementation of the Scottish Government's anti-poverty strategy. For example, grandparents might have benefited from separate government policies. The Scottish Government has been able to introduce allowances for kinship carers of children who are looked after by the local authority, but has not been able to assist in cases where there is no order on the child.

Legal and policy context prior to devolution

Contemporary responses to children's welfare can be traced back
to the Kilbrandon Report of 1964 (Kilbrandon, 1964). In 1961, an
expert committee, chaired by Lord Kilbrandon, was set up to review
compulsory measures for children. As Morgan-Klein (2008) suggests,
Kilbrandon's recommendations were based on:

> ... [a]n understanding that there were no meaningful
> differences between children about whom there are child
> protection concerns and children who have committed
> offences. Both types of cases indicated possible problems
> with the care the child was receiving, and could only
> be resolved by addressing the child's needs and with the
> involvement of his or her family. (Morgan-Klein, 2008: 15)

As we will see, this holistic and inclusive approach to children remains
the hallmark of Scottish policies for vulnerable children, exemplified
by *Getting it right for every child* (Scottish Government, 2008a).

In 1968, Scotland introduced the children's hearings system, which
was unique within the UK (Murray and Hill, 1991). The children's
hearings replaced juvenile courts. The system separates the establishing
of grounds for compulsory action by the courts from decisions about
actions to be taken. Decision making has a distinctly welfare approach
in the children's hearings system. Children in need of care and
protection, and those who have committed most offences, are dealt
with through a hearing, and decisions made by lay panels consisting
of members of the public. An official (the reporter) decides if there are
sufficient grounds for a child or young person to be brought before
a hearing. Children can be referred by their families, by professionals
and, in rare cases, by themselves. The hearings system covers child
protection, juvenile justice and children looked after by the local
authority. Children and parents have the opportunity to discuss, in a
round-table forum, the issues leading to the child's referral.

Since 1968, each local authority has had a director of social work
services or a chief social work officer. Social workers have a key role
in the children's hearings. They prepare reports for the hearings,
they make recommendations about help to be put in place, and they
are responsible for the coordination and monitoring of services the
panel deems necessary to support the child. In the early days, panels
were mostly concerned with children who committed offences, but
during the 1970s and early 1980s hearings were increasingly used for

care and protection cases (Stafford and Vincent, 2008). The hearings system was altered in 2004, following a review and audit of child protection (Scottish Executive, 2002a). Overall, the welfare system has been retained, with some proposed modifications in operational arrangements (Scottish Government, 2009a).

1995 Children (Scotland) Act

The 1995 Children (Scotland) Act remains the primary legislation for children's welfare. The Act stresses paramountcy of a child's welfare in court cases, and the rights of children to be consulted about decisions affecting their lives, thus allowing Scotland to enact the *United Nations Convention on the Rights of the Child* (UNCRC) (1989). The Act seeks to create balance by avoiding compulsory measures where possible and adopting a 'no order' principle. It also advocates that intervention should be proportionate: the 'minimum intervention' principle.

Scotland adopted a wide definition of children who are looked after by the local authority, introducing the provision for supervision orders with residence at home or elsewhere as a measured response to children in need who warrant compulsory action, reserving the use of care orders for the most serious cases. It also gave social workers a mandated role to work with children and families and be accountable both to them and the children's hearings. Sadly, implementation has proved inconsistent, and there are wide-ranging definitions of children in need across the 32 Scottish local authorities. Additionally, there has been a tendency to use compulsory measures to obtain resources to help families. The principle of minimum intervention has sometimes been interpreted as 'minimal' intervention (Aldgate and McIntosh, 2006), with families not receiving help unless they can be seen to qualify as child protection cases (Vincent and Morgan-Klein, 2008). Altering this narrow interpretation of the law, and making sure children get the help they need, has been an important policy driver since devolution.

The 1995 Children (Scotland) Act was accompanied by three volumes of guidance and regulations. In 1998 specific guidance on child protection was published (Scottish Office, 1998). National care standards for children's residential care were introduced through the 2001 Regulation of Care Act.

Getting it right for every child

Increasingly since devolution, in Scotland the overarching aims for children have been driven by three perspectives: rights, social justice and children's well-being. Stewart (2004) believes there is an increased coherence in policies for children in Scotland, reflecting the growing confidence of the devolved government. There are clear aspirations for all children as they reach adulthood (well-becoming). To achieve well-becoming, everyone has a duty to help promote children's well-being throughout childhood. All children should be safe, healthy, achieving, nurtured, active, respected, responsible and included (Scottish Government, 2008a). The *Getting it right for every child* programme is the common policy underpinning systems, culture and practice in all agencies. Support for children begins in the universal services but is equally relevant for targeted services for children at risk or those with complex needs (Scottish Government, 2008a).

Integrated, long-term approach to children's policies

There are several distinctive features of the Scottish policies for children and young people, policies that encompass all major areas, from the universal services of health and education to targeted services such as social work and youth justice.

Effective policies for children require an integrated organisational and practice approach from all services concerned with children and their families and communities. Children and families should have a full say in the help they receive. Each service needs to recognise its own particular knowledge and skills while taking account of a child's ecology and considering how service input may affect the whole child. Preventive and long-term strategies are just as important as tackling immediate problems (Scottish Executive, 2001; Scottish Government, 2008a, 2008b).

Some policy changes, such as the 2001 Regulation of Care Act, the 2004 Additional Support for Learning Act and the 2004 Antisocial Behaviour Act have been introduced by legislation. Other policies have been implemented by persuasion and partnership, an approach with strengths and weaknesses. For example, the policy document *The Same as You* (Scottish Executive, 2000a), which was designed to address deficits in services for people with learning disabilities, including children, has been only partially implemented (Dumbleton, 2006). Similarly, there has been criticism (Scottish Executive, 2002a) of the disproportionate amount of time spent on child protection investigations, and arguments have been made for strengthening integrated family support services to protect children in the short and long term, practices now being addressed through *Getting it right for every child* (Scottish Government, 2008a) and the strategy for the Early Years, known as *Early Years Strategy* (2008b).

Scotland's approach has emphasised the contribution and expertise of the Scottish people, be they children, families or professionals. Therefore, while there is a drive towards agencies working effectively together, using shared tools and a common language, respect for all disciplines and their professional knowledge and expertise is retained. For example, a review of social work (Scottish Executive, 2006a) recommended the distinct skills of social workers be valued and strengthened, and bureaucracy streamlined, so social workers spend more time with services users.

For Scotland's children (2001)

Getting it right for every child had its origins in *For Scotland's children* (Scottish Executive, 2001). This significant and comprehensive policy document set out a vision for improving circumstances for all children in Scotland. It was honest in recounting the shortcomings of Scotland's services for children, and recognised that a lack of service coordination had failed children and left the most vulnerable 'born to fail' (Vincent and Morgan-Klein, 2008: 50). It gave an enhanced role to the universal services of health and education, whereby every child should have a 'named professional' to facilitate access to services at an early stage. Locally, services were urged to create joint children's services plans and introduce organisational mechanisms for working together. These changes are part of the implementation of *Getting it right for every child*. There is evidence of progress towards integrated services. Highland, for example, embraced the integrated services policy wholeheartedly, and set about reorganising children's services to create an integrated approach while preserving the skills and expertise of each service. The changes were cascaded down from management to those working daily with children and families (MacNeil and Stradling, 2007).

Poverty: an enduring challenge for children's services

Combating poverty has been a major challenge for the Scottish Government before and since devolution. In 1999, a Scottish Parliament research note revealed that '34% of Scottish children, 41% of those aged under five, live in poverty' (Scottish Parliament, 1999: 2).

Children growing up in poverty are likely to experience fewer positive life chances than other children, and poverty often leads to social exclusion (Scott, 2006).

The devolved government faced the problem that many key policies involving tax and benefits systems were reserved to the Westminster Government. Consequently, in 1999 the Scottish Executive chose to concentrate its strategies on long-term solutions to poverty (Scottish Executive, 1999), so reflecting the principles of the Kilbrandon Report.

Evidently Scotland has made some progress in tackling poverty. One report (Palmer *et al.*, 2004) suggests that in 2004 there were twice as many indicators of improvement as there were signs of deterioration, a trend that was unchanged in 2006-07 (Palmer *et al.*, 2008). Yet problems remain, and the Scottish Government estimates that 210,000 children were in poverty in 2006 (Scottish Government, 2008c). The policy framework entitled *Achieving Our Potential* (Scottish Government, 2008c) overtly promotes an integrated approach between government departments, and between central and local government. Tackling poverty now links with policies on employment (of parents), early intervention, health inequalities and education (including health and well-being), as well as housing, tackling substance misuse and regenerating disadvantaged communities. Research highlighted the difficulties faced by kinship carers of looked-after children (Aldgate and McIntosh, 2006), who are entitled now to allowances equivalent to those paid for foster children (Scottish Government, 2008c).

Children's health policies

The policy emphasis on early intervention and prevention can be found in health policies for children. In 2004, the Scottish Executive launched its primary health programme, *Health for all children 4*, with extensive guidance for its implementation. This became known as *Hall 4 Guidance* (Scottish Executive, 2005).

The recommendations in *Hall 4* reflect a move away from a wholly medical model of screening for disorders, towards health promotion, primary prevention and active intervention for children and families at risk. Integrated support and seamless services are among the key aims, together with promoting an holistic model of family care whereby adult services recognise the impact on children of adult physical or mental ill health. The policy stresses the integrated role of health and other services such as education and social work. It anticipates multi-agency assessment using a shared assessment framework with a common language, now an integral part of *Getting it right for every*

child. *Hall 4* proposes three levels of support for children, according
to their vulnerability: core, additional, and intensive. The thrust of the
policy is to allow primary healthcare professionals to target children
with serious and complex needs who might need intensive support
(Scottish Executive, 2005).

Implementation of *Hall 4* has been criticised by public health
nurses. While an emphasis on universal preventive public health has
been retained in some places (for example, in the Highland area),
in others, routine surveillance has been pared down to a minimum,
meaning children may not receive routine health checks between
four months and pre-school age, unless their parents ask for checks
to be done (oral evidence from public health nurses, Paisley, April
2009). At the time of writing in 2009, the Scottish Government has
pledged to review the arrangements.

By targeting the most vulnerable families, *Hall 4* was meant to
help improve the health chances of children, but the scale of social
inequality in the health of children and families continues to exercise
policy makers. In 2008, the Scottish Government set up a Ministerial
Task Force, *Equally Well* (Scottish Government, 2008d), to look at
inequalities in health and to decide what might be done to address
them. The group recognised the complexity of assessing causes of
health inequalities, and recommended an ecological, whole-child
approach in keeping with *Getting it right for ever child*.

Education policies

Since devolution, Scotland has developed distinctive policies for
children's education, which reflect national objectives for building
human capital. The value base in education policy emphasises the
four values inscribed on the mace of the Scottish Parliament: wisdom,
justice, compassion and integrity (Scottish Executive, 2006b). In 2007,
the Organisation for Economic Co-operation and Development
(OECD) reported that 'Scotland has one of the most equitable
systems in the OECD' (2007: 14). However, the OECD identified
discrepancies in the educational achievement of children living in
affluent areas and those in poorer circumstances, so highlighting
how poverty and disadvantage continue to frustrate the Scottish
Government's aim of social inclusion and social justice for all children
(OECD, 2007).

Education policies are supported by standards and a professional
development framework for teachers. The *National Priorities for Education*
(Scottish Executive, 2000b) aspire to move Scottish education to a child-

centred approach, including creativity and emotional literacy alongside maintaining standards of attainment (Clark, 2006). *A Curriculum for Excellence* was launched in 2004 and subsequently underpinned (see, for example, Scottish Executive, 2006b). The curriculum retains and builds on the traditional broad approach to education while emphasising health and well-being. In 2004, the Additional Support for Learning Act was passed. Support for learning is interpreted broadly. The policy targets 'any barrier to learning' and gives 'far greater legal rights to children and young people' with additional support needs (Clark, 2006: 314). Health and social work agencies have a duty to coordinate and deliver additional support.

Learning and achievements are supported by the *Assessment is for Learning* programme (see Robertson and Dakers, 2004), which aims to support teachers using assessment to raise pupils' achievement. It is based on the idea that pupils improve most when they understand their learning.

Although the devolved aims, philosophy, aspirations and assessment system seem laudable, and while the Scottish Highers qualification has been endorsed as being of a high standard by UCAS (Scottish Government, 2008e), a note of caution is sounded in a report by Her Majesty's Inspectorate for Education (HMIE, 2009), which found room for improvement in the uneven quality of the learning experience in secondary education.

The *Early Years Strategy*

The *Early Years Strategy* is a flagship post-devolution children's policy aimed at providing 'the best start for all our children' (Scottish Government, 2008b: 4). Its prominence has been strengthened since 2007 with the creation of a Ministry for Children and Early Years. The strategy takes a whole-child approach to children's well-being, bringing together health, education, social work services and the voluntary sector. It is a long-term policy based on partnership between local and national government and all services for children. It pays attention to children's diet and activity as well as to their nurture. Given continuing concern about child poverty, free school meal pilots are being introduced. The implementation of the *Early Years Strategy* is facilitated by the *Getting it right for every child* programme (see below). Children's services can be offered to support families and help them build skills and social networks as part of the early years' agenda. A good example of the child-centred aspiration of this policy is the introduction by some local authorities of a buddy system for young children entering Primary 1.

Child protection policies

In 2001, Scotland set up a major audit and review of child protection services following the death of three-year-old Kennedy McFarlane. Professionals were criticised for poor joint working and failure to recognise the seriousness of the situation. The government review, by a broad panel of 'experts', was wide ranging. It was published by the Scottish Executive in 2002 as *It's everyone's job to make sure I'm alright* (Scottish Executive, 2002a), a distinctly Scottish title emphasising that child protection is not solely the domain of social work.

In a measured response, the Scottish Government introduced a complex three-year Child Protection Reform Programme, the implementation of which has had an impact on child protection practice (Daniel *et al.*, 2007), especially by creating a renewed sense of shared responsibility among professionals. The main components of the reform programme include a charter for children (Scottish Executive, 2004a) and a Framework for Standards (Scottish Executive, 2004b), which established multi-agency inspection and writing guidance for child protection committees. The reform also introduced Key Capabilities in Child Care and Protection (Scottish Institute for Excellence in Social Work Education *et al.*, 2006) to improve awareness of and training in child care and protection for social workers at all levels, and other measures to widen professional training in other disciplines (Daniel *et al.*, 2007)

Review of children's hearings

The Child Protection Audit and Review (Scottish Executive, 2002b) recommended a review of referrals to the children's hearings system. Beginning in 2004, the Scottish Executive drew attention to the poor outcomes for some children, especially persistent offenders and those looked after by the local authority. The review coincided with the introduction of Anti-social Behaviour Orders (ASBOs) for young people under 16, which some see as breaking the welfare approach to all children with additional needs (McPhail, 2006). In a 2008 review of the workings of ASBOs, the Scottish Government was at pains to stress that equal emphasis had been put on early intervention and intensive supportive measures. Following the review, children's hearings have been retained, but the system will be updated and strengthened by future legislation (Scottish Government, 2009b).

Developing and implementing *Getting it right for every child*

Getting it right for every child draws together the Scottish Government's focus on children's rights, the emphasis on social justice and the push towards early intervention. It gives all practitioners across Scotland a common set of values and principles that apply in any circumstance. Its overarching aim is to provide children and families with help that is timely (early intervention) and proportionate (only as much assessment and help as is needed), and which puts children and families at the centre (by seeking their views and accommodating their circumstances). It begins in the universal services of health and education, and applies to targeted services.

Although the programme began as part of the review of children's hearings and the child protection reform programme, the Scottish Government now sees it as the overarching vehicle through which all government policies for children are translated into practice. Different government departments express the *Getting it right* ethos in slogans such as *Getting it right for every child in kinship care and foster care* (Scottish Government, 2007). Each policy is intended to come under the *Getting it right for every child* umbrella (see, for example, Scottish Government, 2009b).

Between 2006 and 2009, *Getting it right for every child* was refined in its aims, identity and, most importantly, its strategy for implementation.

The Scottish system adopts a whole-child approach, and *Getting it right for every child* is heavily influenced by Scotland's evidence-informed policy for children (Scottish Government, 2008a). These elements have helped to shape the 10 core components, which can be applied in any setting and any circumstance. They provide the benchmark approach that practitioners are to apply in their areas of work:

1. A focus on improving outcomes for children, young people and their families based on a shared understanding of well-being.

2. A common approach to gaining consent and sharing information where appropriate.

3.   An integral role for children, young people and families in assessment, planning and intervention.

4.   A co-ordinated and unified approach to identifying concerns, assessing needs, and agreeing actions and outcomes, based on the well-being indicators.

5.   Streamlined planning, assessment and decision-making processes that lead to the right help at the right time.

6.   Consistent high standards of cooperation, joint working and communication where more than one agency needs to be involved, locally and across Scotland.

7.   A lead professional to co-ordinate and monitor multi-agency activity where necessary.

8.   Maximising the skilled workforce within universal services to address needs and risks at the earliest possible time.

9.   A competent and confident workforce across all services for children, young people and their families.

10.   The capacity to share demographic, assessment and planning information electronically within and across agency boundaries through the national eCare programme, where appropriate.

(Scottish Government, 2008a: 14)

The Scottish Government has concentrated on changing practice and culture while urging local agencies to streamline systems, but it has left alone the organisational structures of the local authority that provide governance for implementing *Getting it right for every child*.

Getting it right for every child has developed a practice model that all practitioners can use, either on a single agency or multi-agency basis, to assess, plan, take action and review a child's progress (Scottish Government 2008a). The practice model is based around the eight areas of well-being in the national vision for children. Any practitioner, child or family can use these well-being indicators to identify concerns, to help formulate a Child's Plan, either in a single agency or on a multi-agency basis, and to measure outcomes after a review of progress has taken place. There are five questions every practitioner should ask when concern arises:

1.   What is getting in the way of this child's well-being?

2.   Do I have all the information I need to help this child or young person?

3.   What can I do now to help this child or young person?

4.   What can my agency do to help this child or young person?

5.   What additional help, if any, may be needed from others?

(Scottish Government, 2008a: 24)

There are no fixed templates for professionals to use, and no timescales are set for completion of assessment, such is the emphasis placed on recognising and valuing the skills and judgement of professionals. Agencies are urged to streamline meetings and bureaucracy, and to ensure a plan exists for every child that needs one.

Where needs are straightforward, a plan can be put in place using the well-being indicators, and it is expected that agencies will cooperate on the basis of trust, without elaborate referral systems. If agencies need further information, practitioners can use the child-centred assessment triangle (the *My World Triangle*), which places the child at the centre of thinking and activity. There is a *Resilience Matrix* to help practitioners analyse the information they gather (see Scottish Government, 2008a).

Highland Council has aligned assessment and planning for all children, and integrated the *Getting it right* model with child protection procedures. Children in need of care and protection, looked-after children, children who have offended and others who need compulsory measures, all are assessed and have one plan. Where legislation demands certain actions be taken, as where a child may need an educational support plan, this will be incorporated into an overarching plan. Where two or more agencies are working together, a lead professional is appointed, usually from the agency most appropriate to the child's needs. Significantly, Highland Council has introduced the recommendation in *For Scotland's Children* (Scottish Executive, 2001), that every child should have a named professional (now called a named person) in health or education, to provide a contact point for early intervention.

Computer systems are being developed nationally to help share information, albeit on a need-to-know basis as each agency keeps its own child records. Scotland has chosen systems that are as simple as possible.

At the time of writing, the Highland Pathfinder is beginning to show significant improvements in culture, systems and practice. There are fewer meetings, fewer referrals to the reporter, fewer children on the child protection register, but more plans for individual children. Children and families report feeling more equal and more included (Consultation exercise in Inverness, Spring 2009). Three other local authorities have become learning partners, and are keen to follow suit. Others are moving towards change, and it seems that the policy directive of partnership and persuasion is beginning to gain momentum. The Scottish Government's timescale for full implementation is 2011.

Single outcome agreements

The relationship between national and local government has shaped the implementation of services. Since devolution, many changes have been introduced through guidance and discussion, rather than by imposition.

The relationship between local and national government in Scotland has always been marked by diversity in the way each of the 32 local authorities organises its services. In 2007, the Nationalist Government introduced a Concordat and a system of single outcome agreements between the Scottish Government and local authorities (Scottish Government and COSLA, 2007). This is a radical departure from previous policies, and is unique within the UK. It brings an outcomes-based approach to the organisation and delivery of local council services, including education and social work, as well as any voluntary sector services commissioned by the local authority. It affects all council services relating to children, including services to support families, services for looked-after children and youth justice services. The aim is threefold: to devolve to local authorities decisions on spending annual settlements as they best see fit to meet local needs; to cut down on documentation and bureaucracy; and to support these arrangements by streamlined external scrutiny. The agreements are linked into 15 national outcomes, and local authorities have to provide a single agreement showing how their activities will meet the Scottish Government's targets.

The significance of these arrangements for children's services is that, in theory, they should allow local services to be matched with targeted needs. However, questions can be asked about the viability of the new arrangements. Will the voluntary sector be able to access support, or will it be vulnerable to cuts in a time of recession? Will child protection continue to be prioritised above early intervention and prevention? Will the goal of enhanced roles for health and educational professionals be at risk?

These are early days for the concordat, and at the time of writing there are no indications that it is working. Perhaps the fears are groundless, and local authorities will develop a child-centred approach that ensures each child gets the necessary support and services in the way that is most helpful. Perhaps *Getting it right for every child* will live up to its name.

References

Aldgate, J. and McIntosh, M. (2006) *Looking After the Family: a study of children looked after in kinship care in Scotland*, Edinburgh: Social Work Inspection Agency.

Clark, C. (2006) 'Scottish education in the 21st century: a story of tradition, myth and progress', in G. Mooney, T. Sweeney and A. Law (eds) *Social Care, Health and Welfare in Contemporary Scotland*, Paisley: Kynoch and Blaney, pp 297-330.

Daniel, B., Vincent, S. and Ogilvie-Whyte, S. (2007) *A Process Review of the Child Protection Reform Programme*, Edinburgh: Scottish Executive.

Dumbleton, S. (2006) 'Learning disability in 21st century Scotland', in G. Mooney, T. Sweeney, and A. Law (eds) (2006) *Social Care, Health and Welfare in Contemporary Scotland*, Paisley: Kynoch and Blaney, pp 215-38.

HMIE (Her Majesty's Inspectorate for Education) (2009) *Improving Scottish Education*, Livingstone: HMIE.

Kilbrandon, Lord (Chair) (1964) *The Kilbrandon Report, Children and Young Persons, Scotland; Report by the Committee Appointed by the Secretary of State for Scotland*, Edinburgh: Her Majesty's Stationery Office.

MacNeil, M. and Stradling, R. (2007) *Delivering Integrated Services for Children in Highland: An Overview of Challenges, Developments and Outcomes*, Inverness: University of the Highlands and Islands, Millennium Institute.

McPhail, M. (2006) 'Children and young people: social work and Scotland', in G. Mooney, T. Sweeney, and A. Law (eds) (2006) *Social Care, Health and Welfare in Contemporary Scotland*, Paisley: Kynoch and Blaney, pp 169-194.

Morgan-Klein, N. (2008) 'The Social Work (Scotland) Act 1968 to the Children (Scotland) Act 1995', in A. Stafford and S. Vincent, *Safeguarding and Protecting Children and Young People*, Edinburgh: Dunedin Press, pp 17-33.

Murray, K. and Hill, M. (1991) 'The recent history of Scottish child welfare', *Children and Society*, vol 5, no 3, pp 266-81.

OECD (Organisation for Economic Co-operation and Development) (2007) *Quality and Equity of Schooling in Scotland*, Paris: OECD.

Palmer, G., Macinnes, T. and Kenning, P. (2004) *Monitoring Poverty and Social Exclusion in Scotland 2004*, York: Joseph Rowntree Foundation.

Palmer, G., MacInnes, T. and Kenning, P. (2008) *Monitoring Poverty and Social Exclusion in Scotland 2008*, York: Joseph Rowntree Foundation.

Robertson, P. and Dakers, J. (2004) *AifL Development Programme – Personal Learning Programme: 2002-2004 Evaluation Report*, Edinburgh: Scottish Executive, Scottish Qualifications Authority, Teaching and Learning Scotland.

Scott, G. (2006) 'Poverty and disadvantage in contemporary Scotland: examining the policy responses', in G. Mooney, T. Sweeney and A. Law (eds) *Social Care, Health and Welfare in Contemporary Scotland*, Paisley: Kynoch and Blaney, pp 99-122.

Scottish Executive (1999) 'Ministers pledge to tackle causes of poverty', News release 1094/99, 27 May, Edinburgh: Scottish Executive.

Scottish Executive (2000a) *The same as you: a review of services for people with learning disabilities*, Edinburgh: Scottish Executive.

Scottish Executive (2000b) *National Priorities for Education*, Edinburgh: Scottish Executive.

Scottish Executive (2001) *For Scotland's children*, Edinburgh: Scottish Executive.

Scottish Executive (2002a) *'It's everyone's job to make sure I'm alright', Report of the Child Protection Audit and Review*, Edinburgh: Scottish Executive.

Scottish Executive (2002b) *Growing Support: A Review of Services for Vulnerable Families with Very Young Children*, Edinburgh: Scottish Executive.

Scottish Executive (2004a) *Protecting Children and Young People: The Charter*, Edinburgh: Scottish Executive.

Scottish Executive (2004b) *Protecting Children and Young People: Framework for Standards*, Edinburgh: Scottish Executive.

Scottish Executive (2005) *Health for All Children 4: Guidance on Implementation in Scotland 2005*, Edinburgh: Scottish Executive.

Scottish Executive (2006a) *Changing Lives: Report of the 21st Century Social Work Review*, Edinburgh: Scottish Executive.

Scottish Executive (2006b) *A Curriculum for Excellence, Building the Curriculum 1, The Content of Curriculum Areas*, Edinburgh: Scottish Executive.

Scottish Government (2007) *Getting it right for every child in kinship and foster care – A National Strategy*, Edinburgh: Scottish Government.

Scottish Government and Convention of Scottish Local Authorities (COSLA) (2007) *Concordat between the Scottish Government and Local Government* (www.scotland.gov.uk/Resource/Doc/923/0054147.pdf).

Scottish Government (2008a) *A Guide to Getting it Right for Every Child*, 22 September, Edinburgh: Scottish Government.

Scottish Government (2008b) *Strategy for the Early Years – Consultation*, Edinburgh: Scottish Government.

Scottish Government (2008c) *Achieving our Potential: A Framework to tackle poverty and income inequality in Scotland*, 24 November, Edinburgh: Scottish Government.

Scottish Government (2008d) *Equally Well – Report of the Ministerial Task Force on Health Inequalities*, 19 June, Edinburgh: Scottish Government.

Scottish Government (2008e) 'Review of Scottish qualifications', News release, 17 December, Edinburgh: Scottish Government.

Scottish Government (2009a) 'Strengthening Scotland's forensic regime', News release (www.scotland.gov.uk/News/Releases/2009/02/24124302).

Scottish Government (2009b) *Promoting Positive Outcomes: Working Together to Prevent Antisocial Behaviour in Scotland – Volumes 1 and 2*, Edinburgh: Scottish Government (www.scotland.gov.uk/2009/03/18112243/8).

Scottish Institute for Excellence in Social Work Education, Scottish Social Services Council and Scottish Executive (2006) *Key Capabilities in Child Care and Protection*, Edinburgh: Scottish Executive.

Scottish Office (1998) *Protecting Children: A Shared Responsibility*, Edinburgh: Her Majesty's Stationery Office.

Scottish Parliament (1999) *Poverty in Scotland*, Research Note, 99/7 4 June, Edinburgh: Scottish Parliament Information Centre.

Stafford, A. and Vincent, S. (2008) *Safeguarding and Protecting Children and Young People*, Edinburgh: Dunedin Press.

Stewart, J. (2004) *Taking Stock: Scottish Social Welfare after Devolution*, Bristol: The Policy Press.

UN (United Nations) (1989) *UN Convention on the Rights of the Child*, Geneva: UN.

Vincent, S. and Morgan-Klein, N. (2008) 'From 2000: a period of significant reform', in A. Stafford and S. Vincent, *Safeguarding and Protecting Children and Young People*, Edinburgh: Dunedin Press, pp 49-73.

Six

Green Well Fair: thinking differently about welfare and public service delivery

Jane Franklin

Introduction

In this chapter I outline a new approach to welfare policy and practice. This approach, known as 'Green Well Fair' (GWF) is based on the premise that the New Labour third way framework is inappropriate for dealing with three current major national and international issues: economic instability, social inequality and climate change. Like the third way, GWF is social democratic, based on principles of sustainable social justice and equality. Unlike the third way, it is developed in critique of the current economic system, holding that not only do capitalist economies produce and maintain social inequality, but they are also a major cause of rising levels of greenhouse gases and climate change (nef, 2008; Jackson, 2009). The GWF approach predicts that the combined effects of economic instability and climate change are likely to undermine the financial and organisational capacity of welfare states to deliver public services. This, in turn, is likely to produce more inequality: if the economy is less able to support a welfare state, the balance of responsibility for producing services will inevitably shift to society, where many people are already disadvantaged and struggling with limited resources (Coote and Franklin, 2009). What kind of welfare settlement can support this shift while reducing inequalities?

From the GWF perspective, the means to sustainable social justice is through the dynamic between structural economic transition, individual agency and social change. In the short term, and in the process of transition, society would need to adapt to low carbon living and a follow-on reduction in economic resources to pay for public services. This chapter explores how the GWF settlement emerges in contrast to previous settlements and in critical engagement with the current third way paradigm. The chapter ends with a discussion of 'co-production', a policy mechanism that is intended to harness the resources or agency of individuals in shaping their own lives and the world around them.

Welfare settlements since 1945

Welfare settlements are shaped by the competing social, political and economic values and interests of their time. They reflect, but also 'create ... arrangements of social divisions and differences, identities and inequalities, relationships and resources' (Clarke, 2004: 147). The post-Second World War welfare settlement reflected a balance between liberal and social democratic politics, and economic and social interests. While capitalist economies delivered growth and prosperity, the social democratic analysis at the time was that they also produced social inequalities. The purpose of this settlement was to facilitate the relationship between economy and society, to redistribute wealth and opportunity, by mitigating social inequalities produced by industrial production. This settlement provided the framework for universal, cradle-to-grave social security, and radical reform of health and education systems. Designed to tackle social class inequality, the reforms of the welfare state nevertheless assumed a gendered division of labour, and an economic model which relied on full male employment, a family wage and women's commitment to home and family. This paternalistic arrangement was reflected in welfare practice, where professional knowledge and judgement were largely unchallenged, and individuals trusted and relied on expert advice and care.

Variations of this social democratic settlement were adopted by Conservative and Labour governments, until 1979, when the Thatcher government took a neoliberal approach to economics, sidelining any commitment to social and economic equality. In this view, the 'dependency culture' of the welfare state, and the power of trades unions pointed to the failure of social democracy. Individuals and families should be free to look after themselves with a residual welfare state for those who could not. This challenged the power of professional knowledge, and people came to be seen as consumers, with voice, responsibility and a right to choose. A new economic individualism seeped into public consciousness, and although it was challenged by a rise in social unrest and political dissent, it legitimised cuts in welfare spending so that policy and practice came to be judged by their economic efficiency rather than their contribution to social justice.

The third way

Since 1997 the New Labour welfare settlement, or 'third way', has shaped policy and practice in Britain. Distancing itself from the old left and the new right, it is based on a pragmatic adaptation of both, and an attempt to reconcile oppositional interests in all layers of society (Blair, 1998; Giddens, 1998). Neither the direct involvement of the old social democratic state, nor the minimal state of the neoliberal model, the third way underpins a 'social investment state', and a partnership of mutual responsibility between the state and civil society (Giddens, 1998: 79). In this model of social democracy, social relationships rather than the social effects of capitalism become a key factor in explaining levels of inequality, economic prosperity and political participation (Gamarnikow and Green, 1999). New Labour policies have tended to focus on individual and social behaviour, with social justice standing for a fair distribution of opportunities. Individuals are encouraged to make good choices and take up opportunities offered by the state and the market. They are called on to take more responsibility for their health and well-being in partnership with professionals and welfare institutions (Powell, 2002).

The promotion of individual well-being has been a powerful tool for the third way approach (Sointu, 2005). For some writers, well-being is about happiness (Layard, 2006), life satisfaction and the means to enhance positive attitudes (Dolan et al., 2006). Others focus on the connections between well-being, social justice and the 'good' or sustainable society (Gough, 2004; nef, 2004; Coote and Franklin, 2009). The subjective well-being approach has been influential in New Labour policy making. It looks beyond external, objective measures of social well-being like inequality and income distribution to focus on what is 'working well' for individuals from their point of view. It looks to individual assets and individual resources, seeing people as agents rather than as problems to be solved. It carries the assumption that individual change is the answer to social problems, and in turn, supports an approach that targets pockets of disadvantage and 'vulnerability' rather than improving the well-being of everyone as a means to narrowing inequalities (Wilkinson and Pickett, 2009).

Thus, New Labour's approach has offered a way of separating social problems from their economic causes. It looks to social exclusion rather than class or social divisions to explain inequalities. Policies to reduce inequalities are therefore focused on society rather than economy. Third way politics assumes a coincidence of interests and a partnership between economy and society. While it has had some benefit to society, focusing resources on social exclusion and vulnerable groups, this partnership works primarily and strategically in economic and financial interests, maintaining social and economic relationships of power (Franklin, 2007).

Green Well Fair

The GWF settlement is based on the dynamic interplay between economy, society and environment, drawing on theories of climate change and sustainable development. It recognises that there are conflicting, as well as shared, interests between economy and society. While individuals have a degree of freedom or autonomy in shaping their lives, they do so in the context of economically and culturally driven structures of class, gender and ethnicity which affect their life chances. Thus, policies designed to target social or individual behaviour without attending to these structures, as in the third way, can have no long-term or sustainable impact on inequalities. At the same time, the option of generating economic growth as a means of supporting extensive welfare provision is off the agenda due to climate change. Thus, the key question for the GWF settlement is how to promote social justice when economic resources are contingent on growth that is increasingly unsustainable (Jackson, 2009).

This question and the proposed answer are systemic and long term, based on the idea of sustainable development, as defined in the UK government's strategy, *Securing the Future* (Defra, 2005). Sustainable development depends on five principles that are interdependent and mutually reinforcing: living within environmental limits; ensuring a strong, healthy and just society; promoting a sustainable economy; good governance; and sound science. Together, it is argued, these principles provide an integrated, systemic framework for policy making, with a long-term perspective and a focus on intergenerational equity (Lafferty and Langhelle, 2009).

In this context, social justice is understood as the fair and equal distribution of resources between individuals, social groups and nations, to be sustained across future generations (Craig *et al.*, 2008). Recent studies suggest that less equal societies are more divided and less at ease with themselves, less likely to nurture shared values and social solidarity, while a more equal and solidaristic society is likely to be more robust and adaptable to change (Wilkinson and Pickett, 2009). For this reason, the third way approach that might focus on the impacts of climate change on low-income groups and search for ways to diminish their negative effects are likely to be of limited value. It is argued that through an understanding of the social, economic and cultural context of change, policy interventions have the potential to help people in all social groups reduce their carbon footprint, and ensure that the transition to low-carbon living helps to narrow rather than intensify social inequalities (Evans and Jackson, 2008).

However, in the short term, before inequalities have had a chance to narrow, more strain will be placed on the social or 'core' economy as financial resources dwindle (Coote and Franklin, 2009). The idea of the core economy is as central to GWF as a low-growth economic system. It is defined in critical relation to previous settlements:

> It works from the premise that people are not merely repositories of need or recipients of services. They are more than a workforce that must be nurtured for a productive economy. They are not merely consumers who must go on shopping to keep the global market growing. Nor are they just welfare customers choosing from a market of services. They cannot be reduced to 'communities' responsible for their own problems, where 'social capital' must be accumulated to combat dysfunction, decline and disorder. (Coote and Franklin, 2009: 10)

The core economy

The social, human or 'core economy' refers loosely to social resources, to reciprocal everyday things people do as they care for each other, bring up their children, look after elderly friends and relatives and sustain different kinds of friendships (Coote and Franklin, 2009). It also refers to wider social networks and activities in civil society. In short, it stands for intimate and informal practices, and the physical, cultural, material and emotional resources that sustain human life. Crucially, since these resources are also shaped by structure, culture and agency (Franklin, 2007), the core economy is also the site where inequalities and social conflicts are played out and maintained.

Thus, to promote social justice in the short and long term, as advocated by GWF, policy making needs first to recognise and value individual and social resources; and second, to change the ways that the unequal distribution of resources, work and time reproduce social and economic divisions and inequalities. Most of the care work that sustains the core economy, for example, also supports and sustains a gendered division of labour (Bryson, 2008). Care work is largely carried out by women working without wages, a pattern that generates lasting inequalities in formal work, income and power between women and men. These inequalities are then compounded by class, ethnicity and other divisions; and by an unequal distribution of time. While everyone has the same amount of time, some people have a lot more control over how they use it than others (Bryson, 2007). Again, many women have low-paid jobs as well as caring responsibilities, so they are poor in both time and income (Bryson, 2008). With an approach like the third way, which relies on paid work and in-work benefits as the major route out of poverty for lone parents, women have to juggle paid work and looking after their children (Sevenhuijsen, 2002). Recent research has shown, yet again, that this dual role does not improve the lives of women and their children, since around half of lone parents do not earn enough to stay out of poverty, no matter how long or hard they work (Burchardt, 2008).

So, if the core economy is to underpin and help create a more equal society, social resources, power and responsibilities, or more concretely, care, work and time will need to be fairly distributed across the social spectrum (Bryson, 2007, 2008). This in turn relies on a dynamic model of individual agency and well-being, in structural and material context. As Richard Wilkinson argues, while individual and social action can 'partially offset the effects of material deprivation ... so often it is the material disadvantages and divisions themselves which undermine supportive community and family life' (Wilkinson, 2006: 2). Relative deprivation, he suggests, can undermine sources of resilience, and it is always the most vulnerable who suffer the consequences (Wilkinson, 2006). To put these ideas into practice, the GWF approach supports the idea of 'co-production' (Ryan-Collins et al., 2008; Stephens et al., 2008).

Co-production

Co-production is a policy mechanism that shifts the balance of power, responsibility and resources from professionals to individuals, by involving people in the design and delivery of their own services. It recognises that 'people are not merely repositories of need or recipients of services' (Coote and Franklin, 2009: 10). They bring their experiences and resources, and more potential than the current system allows, to shape and change their lives and the world around them. Thus, the rationale behind the co-production model is not so much to consult or to encourage participation, but to focus on the individual as part of the process and solution (Stephens et al., 2008). To reflect the focus of this book, I present two case studies of services co-produced with children and young people, to illustrate how the model works in practice. The first is a project that involves students in secondary and primary education, and the second is a young people's timebanking project.

Learning to Lead

Learning to Lead (www.learningtolead.org.uk) is a training and consultancy organisation born out of a concern for the lack of opportunity for student involvement in school life, where pupils experience education that is 'done to them' rather than 'with them'. Over the past five years they have created a *model of a school community council* where students can 'self-elect' to be a part of a supportive framework of student-led teams. In these teams, they develop their ideas and are responsible for turning these ideas into action.

The Learning to Lead project began in the Blue School, a large comprehensive school in Somerset, and as a result of its success it is being piloted in 10 other secondary schools across the UK. With the support of the Healthy Schools programme it has also developed a whole-school approach for primary schools, where, in 'community classrooms', children 'self-elect' to take increasing responsibility for their school life. Children and young people are supported as they form teams around their own interests, skills experiences and motivations. The team training begins by exploring different roles within the team, helping to develop existing skills and ideas and build up new life skills. Students gravitate towards a team that reflects their experience or they have a desire to change. The work of the team often begins with members reflecting on their past experiences and then developing solutions and planning for change. For example two students in the Africa Link team were twins who had an African background and had lost both parents. The team provided a safe place for life stories to be shared and valued.

For some the record of their work in the Learning to Lead programme has helped them to get a job or access further education or vocational training. One participant, with dyslexia, who found his academic work a real challenge, was accepted for a business studies course at the University of Bristol due to his ability to talk about the work that he had done through the Finance Support team. Through the programme he developed excellent skills in understanding spreadsheets and working with figures. Another young participant from the 'toilet team' was involved in redesigning the toilet block. He went on to become a director of the Learning to Lead Community Interest Company and is now pursuing a degree in architecture. The young people's work is recognised through certificates that they can keep in their record of achievement and an end of term event where they can share their work and celebrate their collective achievements.

At the heart of the design of the Learning to Lead programme is the understanding that the young people are involved in all decision-making processes within the school. In the Blue School the participants formed an elected year representative's team. It works as an intermediary team on behalf of the other teams, with weekly meetings to discuss any issues raised. This 'voice' team has no more power than the other teams but is seen to have a specific role within the school in the same way as the toilet team, garden team, quiet team or the other teams have. The staff found that, as active participants in the school, students who would not previously have spoken in public are able to speak with confidence and to contribute meaningfully to discussions. Learning to Lead believes that young people have a more powerful voice when they can speak from their own experience of finding solutions to their own identified needs.

Learning to Lead redefines the relationships between professionals and students, since the young people become contributors rather than passive recipients of education. More equal relationships with the community teacher and other key staff are possible, in which the young people are able to share their school and broader life experiences. For example, the site manager is involved in discussion with pupils about the public spaces; the cleaners are involved in discussion about the toilets. Learning to Lead begins to connect all the different parts of the school community and enables the students to understand and appreciate what goes on behind the scenes.

Source: Adapted from Stephens (2009)

Glyncoch Youth Timebanking Project

Glyncoch is a housing estate on the outskirts of Pontypridd in the South Wales Valleys; it has approximately 3,000 residents, many of whom face a range of socioeconomic challenges including high unemployment, high levels of child poverty and low educational attainment. The Glyncoch Youth Timebanking Project is a Welsh Assembly Government initiative, which began in 2005. It works on the principle that for every hour a participant gives to the youth group and the wider community they earn one time credit. If a young person gives five hours to help run a youth environmental day they would earn five time credits. These can be used to go on youth trips and activities and to join in community events. As these are accessed through time credits rather than being given away free, the young people value them more, attendance is higher and behaviour is better. They understand that even though they do not have money they still have something of value that the youth group and the wider community needs. They are no longer defined as being in need of free trips, but are given the opportunity to feel valued and needed.

The project encourages and works with the skills and talents of the young people involved and their understanding of what their community needs. This has led to a number of initiatives including environmental projects, peer learning projects (for example, sexual health sessions), an arson DVD, running youth sessions for the younger youth and supporting other community groups in Glyncoch.

The Timebanking Project also supports young people to develop new skills. It runs 'learn something new nights', where young people use their time credits to learn street dancing, DJ-ing, guitar, cooking, jewellery making and hair and beauty. Older people also come along to teach their skills, like knitting for example, and in return the young people show them how to text with their mobile phones.

The project supports young people's involvement in all aspects of design, delivery and evaluation of projects. For example, with the support of a youth performance organisation, a number of young people who were talented singers put on two concerts for the community. They were involved in designing the concerts, designing and producing publicity materials and selling tickets. Both concerts were attended by over 200 people, and the young people earned time credits for the time spent putting on the concert.

The young people have a say in the way things are run, how money is spent and how the programme is developed. Through their involvement in the project, they come to feel valued and believe that change is possible, going to the theatre for the first time, for example, or overcoming a fear while gorge walking or meeting young people from another community. They are also supported more formally with their school work, job applications, CVs and interview skills. As a result of increased confidence, support from workers in the application process and new opportunities the first ever young people from Glyncoch will be going to university.

Source: Adapted from Stephens (2009); see also www.timebankingwales.org.uk

Case studies like these highlight the benefits and also the limitations of the model (Stephens *et al.*, 2008). For example, it has been found that since co-production challenges the assumptions of current institutional and professional practice, it has been most successful in projects independent of government funding, like those outlined above, and where there is administrative distance from welfare institutions (Boyle *et al.*, 2006). Similarly, the success of state-funded co-produced services, as found in Sure Start children's centres, tends to depend on the extent to which welfare institutions and third sector organisations and practices which surround it reflect its goals and support its processes (Pemberton and Mason, 2009). Interventions seem to work best when they do not challenge existing public service administrative systems and assumptions directly (Boyle *et al.*, 2006).

Research also suggests that the success of co-produced services rests on the quality of the interdependent relationships between professionals and people, sometimes referred to as co-practitioners, and on the negotiation of difference, power and inequality (Bovaird, 2007; Pemberton and Mason, 2009). Co-production blurs and equalises the distinction between people and professionals so that people get to act in both roles (Boyle *et al.*, 2006). In practice, this will depend on how this more equal relationship is negotiated between people with different values, resources, knowledge and experience. The responsibility for shaping these relationships lies initially with professionals who are called up to shift from being 'fixers who focus on problems to enablers who focus on abilities' (Stephens *et al.*, 2008: 13). They have to 'be prepared to trust the decisions and behaviours of service users, and the communities in which they live, rather than dictate them' (Bovaird, 2007: 17).

These findings point to a potential problem with the co-production model from the perspective of the GWF settlement. If it is practised with a welfare framework that focuses on individual capacity and social cohesion, its impact on social inequalities is likely to be limited. In an evaluation of co-production in Sure Start children's centres, it was found that inequalities of gender, class and ethnicity tended to shape the experience of co-production. Some parents felt more comfortable than others in talking about themselves and the services they needed. Some were uneasy about developing more equal relationships with professionals (Pemberton and Mason, 2009). Researchers found a tendency for more women than men to be involved in the co-production of Sure Start children's centres. Fathers would be more likely to participate if competitive sports were organised, or if times of activities were changed to suit working hours. Similarly, middle-class women were more likely to be involved in the administration of Sure Start activities, some of whom went on to become paid workers (Pemberton and Mason, 2009). Thus, if co-production is practised in conditions of social and economic inequality, it is more likely that social divisions will be reproduced, and the short-term targeting of disadvantaged and vulnerable groups will continue (Pemberton and Mason, 2009).

Conclusion

This chapter has explored ideas and practices developed for an alternative welfare settlement to the current third way approach. The GWF settlement is based on a systemic analysis of the links between economic instability, climate change and social inequalities. It is informed by an understanding of social justice in which inequalities are produced in the dynamic between individual agency and the wider systemic context. It is also informed by a politics that recognises that public services at their current level are unsustainable in the context of an economy in recession and the acceleration of climate change. The aim is to develop ideas and policies to underpin the transition to a low-growth economy, low-carbon living and sustainable social justice (nef, 2008; Coote and Franklin, 2009). It is different from previous settlements, since it aims to tackle structural inequalities without the benefit of economic growth. Instead, it brings the social or core economy to the centre of policy making, and is premised on the idea that individual agency and social resources could be mobilised through co-production, and that these resources could shape and be shaped by structural economic change (Coote and Franklin, 2009; Jackson, 2009).

A critical factor in the development of the GWF settlement is that its attention towards the core economy and co-production is resonant of the third way, in as much as it focuses on changing individual lives as a means to social and economic change. However, for the GWF settlement, individual agency and social change must take place in relation to the restructuring of the economy or the impact on social inequality will be minimal. One way of distinguishing GWF from the third way in this regard, is to use, as I have done in this chapter, a different conceptual narrative. Where the third way uses a communitarian language of 'community', 'individual behaviour' and 'social capital' to reflect its concern with local community and individualised change (Everingham, 2003; Franklin, 2007), GWF adopts a social/cultural analysis and a language of individual and social resources, agency, social change or transition and structure (Evans and Jackson, 2008; Uzzell, 2008; Räthzel, 2009).

The GWF settlement is designed to pursue a long and short-term strategy for change. It embodies a long-term commitment to sustainable social justice, achieved through the structural transformation of economic and social systems. It also recognises that in the short term, policy mechanisms like co-production are likely to have local effect, as illustrated in the two case studies above, but will be hampered by the unequal distribution of income and material resources. Thus, co-production could be seen to chime with the third way framework, leading to a practice that may enhance individual or local well-being, while perpetuating existing gender, class and other social divisions. However, if the co-production approach is premised on a more dynamic understanding of social justice which captures the interplay between individual agency and wider social change, it may have the potential to generate processes which enhance individual critical autonomy, competence and creativity in concert with policies which make sustainable social justice the leading rationale of policy making.

References

Blair, T. (1998) *The Third Way: New Politics for the New Century*, Fabian Pamphlet 588, London: Fabian Society.

Bovaird, T. (2007) 'Beyond engagement and participation – user and community coproduction of services', *Public Administration Review*, vol 67, no 5, pp 846-60.

Boyle, D., Clark, S. and Burns, S. (2006) *Hidden Work: Co-production by People Outside Paid Employment*, York: Joseph Rowntree Foundation.

Bryson, V. (2007) 'The politics of time', *Soundings*.

Bryson, V. (2008) 'Poverty, work and care', invited article for *Soundings online debate*, June.

Burchardt, T. (2008) *Time and Income Poverty*, CASEreport 57, London: Centre for Analysis of Social Exclusion, London School of Economics and Political Science.

Clarke, J. (2004) *Changing Welfare, Changing State: New Directions in Social Policy*, London: Sage Publications.

Coote, A. and Franklin, J. (2009) *Green Well Fair: Three Economies for Social Justice*, London: new economics foundation.

Craig, G., Burchardt, T. and Gordon, D. (eds) (2008) *Social Justice and Public Policy: Seeking Fairness in Diverse Societies*, Bristol: The Policy Press.

Defra (Department for Environment, Food and Rural Affairs) (2005) *Securing the Future: Delivering UK Sustainable Development Strategy*, Cm 6467, London: The Stationery Office.

Dolan, P., Peasgood, T. and White, M. (2006) *Review of Research on the Influences on Personal Well-being and Application to Policy Making*, Final report for Defra, August.

Evans, D. and Jackson, T. (2008) *Sustainable Consumption: Perspectives from Social and Cultural Theory*, RESOLVE Working Paper Series 05-08, Guildford: University of Surrey, September.

Everingham, C. (2003) *Social Justice and the Politics of Community*, Aldershot: Ashgate.

Franklin, J. (2007) *Social Capital: Between Harmony and Dissonance*, Families and Social Capital ESRC Research Group Working Paper No 22, London: South Bank University.

Gamarnikow, E. and Green, A. (1999) 'The third way and social capital: education action zones and a new agenda for education, parents and community?', *International Studies in Sociology of Education*, vol 8, no 1, pp 3-22.

Giddens, A. (1998) *The Third Way: The Renewal of Social Democracy*, Cambridge: Polity Press.

Gough, I. (2004) 'Human well-being and social structures: relating the universal and the local', *Global Social Policy*, vol 4, pp 289-310.

Jackson, T. (2009) *Prosperity Without Growth*, London: Sustainable Development Commission (www.sd-commission.org.uk/).

Lafferty, W.M. and Langhelle, O. (eds) (2009) *Towards Sustainable Development: The Goals of Development – and the Conditions for Sustainability*, Basingstoke: Macmillan.

Layard, R. (2006) *Happiness: Lessons From a New Science*, London: Penguin Books.

nef (new economics foundation) (2004) *A Well Being Manifesto for a Flourishing Society*, London: nef.

nef (2008) *Triple Crunch: Joined-up Solutions to Financial Chaos, Oil Decline and Climate Change to Transform the Economy*, London: nef.

Pemberton, S. and Mason, J. (2009) 'Co-production and Sure Start children's centres: reflecting upon users' perspectives and implications for service delivery, planning and evaluation', *Social Policy and Society*, vol 8, pp 13-24.

Powell, M. (ed) (2002) *Evaluating New Labour's Welfare Reforms*, Bristol: The Policy Press.

Räthzel, N. (2009) 'Critical psychology – an approach for changing environmental behaviour change policies', RESOLVE Conference Paper presented at 'Sustainable Lives? The Challenges of Low Carbon Living in a Changing Economic Environment', 19 June.

Ryan-Collins, J., Stephens, L. and Coote, A. (2008) *The New Wealth of Time: How Timebanking Helps People Build Better Public Services*, London: new economics foundation.

Sevenhuijsen, S. (2002) 'A third way? Morality, ethics and families: an approach through the ethic of care', in A. Carling *et al.* (2002) *Analysing Families: Morality and Rationality in Policy and Practice*, London: Routledge, pp 129-44.

Sointu, E. (2005) 'The rise of an ideal: tracing changing discourses of wellbeing', *The Sociological Review*, vol 53, no 2, pp 255-74.

Stephens, L. (2009) 'Co-production case study: Glycoch Youth Timebanking Project', unpublished, London: new economics foundation.

Stephens, L., Ryan-Collins, J. and Boyle, D. (2008) *Co-production: A Manifesto for Growing the Core Economy*, London: new economics foundation.

Uzzell, D. (2008) 'Challenging assumptions in the psychology of climate change', *Bulletin of the Australian Psychological Society*, vol 30, issue 4, pp 10-13.

Wilkinson, R. (2006) Foreword to *Capabilities and Resilience: Health assets in the life course*, London: UCL Department of Epidemiology and Public Health on behalf of the ESRC Priority Network on Capability and Resilience (2004–2007).

Wilkinson, R.G. and Pickett, K. (2009) *The Spirit Level: Why More Equal Societies Almost Always Do Better*, London: Allen Lane.

Part Two
Organisational context

Seven

A 'whole system' for the whole child? Integrated services, interprofessional working and the development of effective practice with children and their families

Barry Luckock

Introduction

On the face of it, the policy of integrating services makes obvious sense. If the circumstances that contribute to low aspirations, limited opportunities and poor outcomes for children are linked, so too should be the response. Remember the famous dual formulation: 'joined-up problems demand joined-up solutions' (Blair, 1997), and 'Nothing – no existing organization, no existing structures – should be allowed to stand in the way' (Milburn, 2003). And if the aim is to improve the well-being, resilience and achievement of every child while continuing to safeguard the welfare of the most vulnerable, integration is needed across service levels, as well as between service agencies and at each stage of intervention.

The organisational logic of 'progressive universalism' (Hobbs *et al.*, 2006) seems undeniable, that is, 'giving everyone a stake in the system while offering more help to those who need it most' (HM Treasury, 2002, para 5), and doing so by joining up universal, targeted and specialist services in a preventive strategy (DfES, 2003). So too does the decision to develop additional practice tools and procedures to enable improved communication of concern via a shared database, earlier identification of need using a common language and assessment framework, and timely access to coordinated professional help and support from services operating with shared values and goals. Indeed, the idea of a 'whole systems' approach (DfES, 2004), 'narrowing the gap' (LGA, 2007) in social opportunities and child outcomes, becomes even more compelling when it involves the active participation of children and parents. This approach should allow services and interventions to be 'personalised' to the needs of the individual child (DCSF, 2007, 2008a), and lead to power and responsibility being shared in an inclusive, integrated system that ensures an appropriate 'pathway' through the education and wider service system. Thus, the capacity and motivation of service providers and family members alike should be enhanced to ensure we achieve the opportunities and outcomes we want for children.

Yet things are not really turning out this way. Despite the apparent coherence of the policy link between the analysis of the problem and the development of the solution, policy makers are frustrated by evidence that change for children remains elusive in terms of organisational transformation (University of East Anglia, 2005, 2007; Audit Commission, 2008) and child outcomes (Ofsted, 2008). A note of impatience can also be detected in some sympathetic academic accounts of the myriad cultural and psychological barriers to joint working exposed by recent research on integrated working (Brown and White, 2006; Atkinson *et al.*, 2007; Robinson *et al.*, 2008; Edwards *et al.*, 2009). And political irritation is directed at local leadership and management over the slow and hesitant pace of implementation. This was seen first in 2006, when alarm about disappointing improvements in school standards prompted a 'priorities review' (Hughes, 2006) and renewed commitment to the *Every Child Matters* agenda in schools (Jeffery and Tabberer, 2006; Taylor, 2006). It resurfaced dramatically in 2008, with the deeply discomforting realisation that services were unable even to prevent children being murdered almost before professionals' very eyes (Laming, 2009).

Given events, the anger is understandable, as is the widespread concern over the condition of childhood and standards of family life in this country (Social Justice Policy Group, 2006; UNICEF, 2007; Layard and Dunn, 2008). But it may be that deeper anxieties are betrayed here, as 'the symbolic and expressive' appeal of service coordination (Weiss, 1981) falters in the face of evidence of problems on the ground. What if slow progress in delivering 'whole systems' reform is symptomatic of intrinsic fault lines in the policy itself?

In this chapter we critically explore whether the *Every Child Matters/Children's Plan* organisational reforms really do provide an opportunity for 'change for children'. The New Labour objective

of service integration, alongside its activist anti-poverty and work–
life balance policies for families, was unquestionably a serious and
sustained attempt to tackle deep-seated patterns of social inequality.
Whatever the helpful lessons to be learned, the frustration of policy
makers and their academic allies at the difficulty of 'breaking down
barriers' (Milburn, 2003) perhaps points to the core vision's underlying
problems. Our primary aim here is to explore these problems.

Integrated working in practice

Research evidence on the early experience and impact of the *Every
Child Matters/Children's Plan* model of 'whole systems working' remains
limited. We know a good deal about joint working in specific areas
of the new 'children's services', including young offenders (Audit
Commission, 2004), children with disabilities (Townsley *et al.*, 2004;
Boddy *et al.*, 2006), children under five (NESS, 2008) and child
protection (Wilson and James, 2007). There is also a literature on
interprofessional teamwork in and across different settings (see, for
example, Anning *et al.*, 2006), and a growing body of work on 'extended'
schools (Dyson *et al.*, 2002; Cummings *et al.*, 2007; Conlan, 2009).
In contrast, the main studies of the 'change for children' model are
restricted to pilot studies of specific methods and tools (Cleaver *et al.*,
2004; Brandon *et al.*, 2006) or self-report surveys of local management
experiences of whole programme roll-out (University of East Anglia,
2005, 2007; Robinson *et al.*, 2008). There are few independent studies
of the experience of children, parents and practitioners of the impact
of policy assumptions and organisational changes (Gilligan and Manby,
2008; Peckover *et al.*, 2008a, 2008b; White *et al.*, 2008; Edwards *et al.*,
2009; Pithouse *et al.*, 2009). Research has been impeded by difficulties in
programme implementation since 2005.[1]

Consequently, the following discussion of practice dilemmas, and their
implications for the integrity of the 'whole systems' vision, is grounded
in illustrative case examples from one large county in the south of
England.[2] The normal cautions should apply where evidence and
analysis are based on a case study method. Nonetheless, the examples are
illuminating in themselves and consistent with the emergent findings
(if not the analyses) of the other recent studies cited. Although they
cannot represent joint work at every stage of the service continuum
or child and family life course, they capture practice dynamics at these
boundaries and transition points, where the assumptions and claims of
'whole systems' integration are most challenged.

Case study 1

Zara Smith[3] is 10 years old. She lives with her mother, stepfather and younger half-brother and sister. The children's centre started the eCAF [electronic Common Assessment Framework] process by agreement with Mrs Smith, who depended on the centre's support with her younger children and had confided her desperation about Zara's aggressive and uncontrollable behaviour at home. Mrs Smith wanted to talk about the role of Zara's father (in prison) in explaining the behaviour. Mrs Smith had discussed her worries with a (voluntary agency) child and family support worker at Zara's school. The 'team-around-the-child' (TAC)[4] meeting involved Zara, her mother, the school support worker, Zara's headteacher, the children's centre worker, primary mental health worker (PMHW) and family centre workers from the integrated service team. Mrs Smith and Zara were asked what support they would like. They said they valued being able to talk about their anxieties, and would appreciate more structured activities for Zara and pastoral support at school. Mrs Smith was unsure about the proposal that she attend a Webster-Stratton parenting group, saying her partner would sabotage it. All agreed to continue the existing children's centre and school support arrangements, and use budget holder lead professional money to fund horse-riding lessons for Zara. The PMHW would be the designated lead professional and offer, together with a family centre worker, family-based work in the home to improve relationships. At the end of the research period, Mrs Smith had declined the parenting group under pressure from her partner, who also opposed the family sessions in the home. She insisted Zara be referred to the consultant at Child and Adolescent Mental Health Services (CAMHS) for a mental health assessment. Although the horse riding had started, Zara was using her mother 'as a punch-bag'. Zara raised renewed professional concerns by hinting that her mother was hitting her, prompting a review meeting to consider that a social work assessment be requested. Her partner's fury about this caused Mrs Smith to say she was considering 'pulling out' of involvement with the integrated service altogether.

Case study 2

Stevie Brown is 12 years old. He lives with his mother, father and two older brothers. His mother has a chronic history of alcohol abuse, and the parental relationship is volatile. School concerns about Stevie's non-attendance and possible cannabis use had been referred by a field social worker to the integrated service team. The eCAF started by the education welfare officer (EWO) was completed by team members and a TAC meeting held, attended by the three boys, their parents, a 'family resource team' social worker, the school nurse, the EWO and the head of year. The older boys and Mr Brown blamed the mother's renewed drinking for the current problems at school. Stevie's mother said his father had encouraged the drinking to maintain power and control in the home. A plan was agreed for the family resource team to lead work with the whole family, using a solution-focused model designed to prevent family breakdown and admission to care. A Youth Offending Team (YOT) worker would provide Stevie with social activities and opportunities, and a community family worker (CFW) would offer emotional and practical help in the home. At the end of the research period, the family had not been fully engaged in the plan. Stevie absented himself whenever workers called. Mr Brown said the family had been let down by the service's failure to deliver on promises. The problems at school and the drinking and arguments at home persisted, and the family resource team was considering a joint referral to the EWO for a prosecution of the parents, and to the social work team for a risk assessment. However, Mrs Smith said she valued the help of the CFW, who had introduced her to Addaction and boosted her confidence.

Practice dynamics and policy fault lines in the 'whole systems' model

The fault lines of the *Every Child Matters/Children's Plan* model of integrated and inclusive practice can be seen by comparing the practice dynamics in the case examples with the policy assumptions underpinning this approach. Problematic assumptions are exposed in all three key aspects of the 'programme logic' of integrated and inclusive working with Zara Smith, Stevie Brown and their families: the nature and extent of the problem to be tackled; the understanding of service systems and the distribution of professional roles, responsibilities and authority; and the expectation of the 'service provider' and 'service user' relationship.

Nature and extent of the problem to be tackled

Targeted investment in family-based services, to establish and maintain children on optimal developmental pathways, appears to be an effective and just way of using scarce social resources to enhance current well-being and future social mobility (HM Treasury/DfES, 2007). Longitudinal research supports the policy aspiration to use 'resilience' as a mechanism to mitigate adversity and risk from the start (Schoon, 2006). However, research findings and practice logic and experience cause us to remain cautious on two counts.

First, we need to be realistic about what can be achieved in the face of the entrenched structural dynamics of economic and social inequality and their destructive psycho-social impact (Hills *et al.*, 2009; Wilkinson and Pickett, 2009). Early childhood investment (a 'Sure Start') appears to have a pay-off in enhanced developmental progress and social opportunity for many children (NESS, 2008), while ensuring childhood is likely to be a time of fun and enjoyment, not worry and grief. However, success is often hard-won. Stevie's and Zara's circumstances and prospects do not suggest an easy resolution of entrenched family problems. Zara's mother had received several years of highly valued support from the children's centre, and all the children were doing well educationally. This did not mean that she and Zara would be resilient enough to manage the impact of the father's violence and imprisonment as Zara grew up and as family dynamics changed with the arrival of a new partner. Stevie's move to secondary school, combined with his mother's drinking, produced fresh concerns over a chronic family problem that had moved on and off the radar of specialist services over a period of years, a problem not readily susceptible to resolution.

Second, research evidence and simple logic urge us to take care in our assumptions about what it is we are trying to prevent when deciding to provide services at all stages. Faced with anxieties about resources and the need to normalise family upbringing, the tendency is to break the 'golden rule' of prevention, that is, 'never to think in terms of providing one type of service in order to prevent another' (Dartington Social Research Unit, 2004: 18). For example, Sure Start children's centre support for Mrs Smith should not be designed to prevent her children being made subjects of child protection plans, and the solution-focused work planned for the Brown family should not be aimed at preventing Stevie's admission to care. Protection plans and care placements are service outcomes, not child well-being objectives. The preventive goal must be child-centred, with the objective of reducing the escalation of problems and needs. Children must be diverted from harmful developmental pathways rather than from high-cost or high-'tariff' services. Decisions about interventions should be taken on a case-by-case basis and in response to individual need, not in accordance with general service-led principles of prevention.

There is sufficient evidence to remind us of the many circumstances in which formal protective interventions (Brandon and Thoburn, 2008) and admission to care (Forrester *et al.*, 2008) should be 'the best available option rather than a last resort' (House of Commons, 2009: 7). Attempts to pre-empt service use risk taking the focus off the primary task of resolving the underlying problems and needs, and they tend not to work as those services have to be used later when problems have worsened (Brandon and Thoburn, 2008). So there are no short cuts to prevention, either by changing the thresholds to re-designate cases from 'child protection' to 'family support' (Brandon *et al.*, 2008), or by shifting resources back down the line to divert children from specialist support (House of Commons, 2009). One example of the government's belated realisation of the extent of the challenge is the retraction of the idea trailed in *Care Matters* (compare DfES, 2006 and 2007b), namely inserting services at the 'edge of care' to reduce admissions and cap the number of children in care. It is also demonstrated in the recognition of the prevalence of the entrenched and chronic family problems faced by professionals in day-to-day practice (Cabinet Office, 2007, 2008).

Distribution of professional roles, responsibilities and authority

The idea of navigation is the central metaphor of 'whole systems' service integration (Audit Commission, 2002; Luckock and Hart, 2005; Luckock, 2007, 2008; Luckock *et al.*, 2008). A common set of 'unarguable' outcomes (Hobbs *et al.*, 2006: 62) must be identified, and organisational mechanisms and workforce changes put in place to enable efforts to be jointly targeted to achieve these outcomes. A 'shared meaning and purpose' enables professionals and agencies to 'assemble' themselves 'in a web of interdependence' (Pratt *et al.*, 2005: 2). A lead professional role is designated to coordinate services across boundaries, by linking 'core specialisms' to 'joint goals' (Hobbs *et al.*,

2006: 63). This provides the organisational context and driver for the child's journey, a developmental trajectory or pathway that maximises well-being and potential. Children can be kept on the 'right track' and 'the path to success' (DCFS, 2007: 12).

The image is powerful and the aspiration attractive, so why does it continue to be so difficult to achieve in practice? Studies of 'whole systems' working reveal problems in reconciling case-level experiences with systems-level principles (Bowles and Jones, 2005; Papworth and Crosland, 2005; Truss, 2008); others identify 'tensions and contradictions' (Edwards *et al.*, 2009: 106) in shifting the focus of the system from the part to the whole. Our case examples suggest that the problem is not limited to implementation. It seems that the holistic service aspiration – that the integration of services will flow from the integration of outcomes and expectations – misunderstands the nature of the service systems. In particular, it underestimates the problems of managing the distribution of authority represented by the different professional roles and deploying services through them.

If we accept that the overall outcomes intended for Zara and Stevie are 'unarguable' (Hobbs *et al.*, 2006), and that their achievement is a collective responsibility, it is logical to underpin that assumption with a new legal mandate[5] that requires agencies and practitioners to work holistically on behalf of the whole child. Yet it is implausible to expect the new 'whole' system to incorporate easily the distinctive agency duties, professional responsibilities and working arrangements that must be prioritised, as specific aspects of child well-being and progress arise over time. As the case examples demonstrate, it is not the separate services that need to be integrated in a whole new system around the child, but the separate service *systems*.

These systems are already more or less joined up in their own right at the case level by the deployment of professionals in lead roles with their own legal mandate and authority. For example, Stevie's safety from harm and his educational progress are primary concerns. Zara's schooling contributes to the resilience of her developmental trajectory, but there are questions about her safety at home and her mental health status and needs. When in Stevie's case the EWO joins the new TAC, she brings her knowledge and expertise in 'education' and 'welfare', and, more importantly, the responsibilities and authority derived from her school attendance enforcement role. This role is exercised in a different service system of court proceedings. If in each case the field social workers were to join the 'team', they too would connect it to a separate system (one dedicated to child protection and public care) through their roles and statutory status.

These authority systems – school attendance enforcement, child mental health and child protection – have not been dismantled as a result of the *Every Child Matters / Children's Plan* agenda. The CAF and TAC mechanisms of 'whole systems' integration temporarily re-configure the relationship between the separate systems, but they do not incorporate the systems in a new overriding 'whole' system. The mechanism may ensure that the collective professional eye remains focused on the achievement of all five *Every Child Matters* outcomes, but it does not set aside professional responsibility to decide on the outcomes to be prioritised, in which specific service system and by which lead professional role. This is why the EWO, the field social worker and the CAMHS consultant are expected to retain allegiance to their primary service system (and the professional status it confers). It also explains the widely reported dual problem of confirming the parameters and status of the lead professional role, and getting people to take it on (for example, Boddy *et al.*, 2006). In the case examples, the PMHW and the family resource centre social worker were designated the role and, with it, responsibility to lead and navigate, but neither could command the authority or resources necessary to ensure holistic working, such were the competing priorities of family members and professionals.

The 'whole systems' approach claims to facilitate interdependence through 'mechanisms to support professionals in working together more effectively and more efficiently across boundaries' (Hobbs *et al.*, 2006: 63). In practice, the mechanisms are super-imposed on existing service systems in the form of a parallel set of practices and administrative processes. In this service landscape, the Smith and Brown families' journeys are more like a series of expeditions, diversions and reversals; the route to the final destination seems uncertain and contested; and the lead role is taken up and dropped each time the pathway is marked out anew.

The crucial issue is not the familiar debate about cultural, historical and organisational barriers to interprofessional teamwork across institutional boundaries (see, for example, Anning *et al.*, 2006); still less is it a question of the benefits of the co-location of practitioners, as the evidence points in various directions (Atkinson *et al.*, 2007). What matters most of all is the nature of the contrasting statutory mandates that apply in each case, and the consequent deployment of professional roles and responsibilities. In the theoretical and research literature on professional and organisational learning, there has been much discussion about the 'distributed' nature of the work process (Edwards *et al.*, 2009). For some, this requires 'knowledge' to be brought together in the form of new 'communities of practice' (Wenger, 1998); for others, it suggests the more radical possibility of continuous or 'expansive learning' (Engeström, 2001). The expectation is for 'expertise' to be reshaped or 'co-configured' into new forms of joint action to address new objectives (Edwards *et al.*, 2009). However, both logic and the available evidence indicate that the greatest barrier to joint action is the distribution of statutory responsibility and authority, not the distribution of professional knowledge and expertise. In service systems, what matters most is the distribution of power, not expertise.

'Service provider' and 'service user' relationship

Of course, the impasse in the two case examples does not result simply from the difficulties of securing professional roles and responsibilities, and the relevant authority and resources, as if matching needs and services were a technical matter. Zara, Stevie and their parents are participants in the process of change. Commitment to an inclusive and integrated approach allows us to focus on the particularity and the individual's experience of the encounter with professionals and services.

However, this leaves open the question about the status in this 'dynamic interaction' of the respective parties and their authority in determining matters, especially where there are conflicting definitions of 'best interests' and contested assumptions about how professional engagement might contribute to achieving them. As the case examples show, these conflicts are hardly unusual where family circumstances are so persistently problematic, and where anxieties are raised by the recognition of the likely consequences if things do not change. Whether conflicts are exacerbated in practice, rather than contained and resolved, depends a good deal on the policy assumptions that shape the professional response. In the event, these assumptions are ambiguous and contradictory (Luckock and Hart, 2005; Luckock, 2008). The main problem lies in the extravagance of the policy's ambition to link enhanced professional effectiveness in individual cases to service modernisation overall, by redefining the status and responsibilities of children, parents and professionals.

At the heart of the policy lies a mixed message. The policy expects parents to be advocates for their children, and it requires both parties to act reasonably and responsibly as active participants in decision making about services. It does this because consumer voice and choice must complement organisational reform as drivers of service transformation (Le Grand, 2007), which, in turn, is necessary to ensure the success of the policy of investing in childhood for individual well-being, social mobility and national prosperity. However, policy expectations are turned on their head as services are required to enable or enforce the exercise of parental responsibility necessary to stimulate ambition in children and drive change in professional practice. In order to 'aim high' for children, the ultimate task is 'supporting parents to meet their responsibilities to raise their children' (HM Treasury/DfES, 2007: 1), or, rather more tortuously, to 'support families to exercise their rights to manage their own affairs while living up to the responsibilities they have (for example as parents)' (HM Government, 2007: 6).

This circular policy logic, putting parents and professionals alternately in charge of the child's progress through the service system, is defended as being a mutually reinforcing process of sharing responsibility for service improvement and child outcomes. In practice, at the level of the helping relationship, it contributes to the confusion and uncertainty in the distribution of responsibility for change seen in our case examples. We see this with Zara's mother, who is positioned as a consumer of services, exercising choice while acting responsibly by requesting additional support for her daughter. The lead professional role is one of facilitation and orchestration, as additional services are invited to join the TAC.

Yet it is clear that Mrs Smith cannot be treated simply as a customer to be satisfied by professionals acting as 'service providers'. There are three main reasons for saying this. First, the issue of matching needs to resources must be addressed. Zara's riding lessons cost several hundred pounds, and the discretionary fund that supports them is cash-limited. There are limits, too, on resources to support specialist health services for children with diagnosed 'disorders'. Professional judgements must be made about eligibility, even when the primary policy value is placed on consumer responsibility and choice.

Second, the choices and judgements of parents and professionals alike involve consideration of individual rights, especially those of children. Zara may not have consumer rights, but she does have human rights to protection, provision and participation in law and under convention (Fortin, 2009). Professional judgements about services must be informed by the underlying legal rights and entitlements of children (and parents), and by recipients' particular needs and level of eligibility. This explains the inclusion of Zara and her mother in the TAC meetings, which recognises and respects their rights to participate in decisions, and enables them to express preferences as service consumers. It also accounts for the initial professional judgement that Mrs Smith was struggling and would benefit from parenting classes, and that a child protection referral may be necessary. Mrs Smith may want to 'exercise her rights to manage her own affairs' as a parent and consumer by making an exit from services, but she may not be allowed to do so as Zara's right to safety and protection must come first.

Finally, we should question assumptions about the emotional dynamics of decision making by parents, children and professionals. The elegantly formulated policy vision and expectation seem far-removed from the uncertainty and ambivalence of family life and professional practice. For example, it is clear that Mrs Smith is in two minds about what best to do to be a good parent. Does she confide further in the children's centre and the school about what really goes on at home? Does she side with her partner, and close the door to the professionals he sees invading his family's privacy? Or does she continue to manage the tension through a covert strategy of engagement and retreat? While the questions remain unanswered, Zara's anger is unresolved and her behaviour worsens. In the Brown family case, parental conflict, and ambivalence about reasonable and responsible actions, is so entrenched that Stevie decides to vote with his feet.

In both cases, professional decisions involve tricky calculations about the right support to provide. Everyone may be trying to act rationally and do what seems right in the circumstances. Yet the circumstances are charged with anxiety because the stakes are so high. And while there is anxiety in the back seat, the journey is a very uncertain and unsettling experience.

Conclusion

The policy makers are right to be worried, and the academic commentators should reconsider the nature of barriers to integration. The 'whole system' model of reform is significantly flawed. It may even be dangerous. The death of Baby P is best seen as a warning about the vision, not the implementation. Policy and research now recognise the risk associated with attempts to blur the boundaries between specialist areas of expertise (DCSF, 2007, 2008a; Edwards et al., 2009), and there is general consensus about the need to strengthen expertise and to work more effectively across boundaries. Less well accepted are the risks associated with blurring the roles and service systems based on that expertise (Rushmer and Pallis, 2002). The distinction is vitally important, as early experience of the 'safeguarding' approach to child protection suggests (DCSF, 2008b; Butler, 2009). When everyone is responsible for safeguarding children, it may not be clear who is responsible for protecting a particular child at a particular time.

Yet the messages to be taken from early experience of attempted 'whole systems' reform are not unequivocally gloomy. Much encouragement can be taken from the new ways of working attempted with Zara and Stevie. All sorts of conceptual and organisational fault lines are exposed by their stories. The model of integration attempted in their local authorities has widened the boundaries across which developmental and service trajectories have to be negotiated and navigated. Nonetheless, by imposing new mechanisms and roles intended to bring professionals and parents together in a 'team around the child', new possibilities for working together creatively have been created.

The TAC was the key mechanism. Increasingly it is clear that information-processing mechanisms, such as ContactPoint, CAF and the integrated children's system (ICS), provide no guarantee of effective joint assessment and intervention. Practice is more than a technical process of problem identification and 'service delivery' (Peckover et al., 2008a, 2008b; White et al., 2008; Broadhurst et al., 2009). Moreover, when the problem is one of containing anxiety and managing emotion in the face of conflicting interests and objectives, and then negotiating agreements about appropriate and effective plans for change, what counts are the interpersonal dynamics of power and emotion, not the administrative processes and procedures. In this way, relationships become a means of integrating fragmented services (Edwards, 2005) and contradictory perspectives and experiences (Luckock, 2007, 2008).

Serious challenges of authorisation and capability remain, where lead roles and responsibilities are distributed in and beyond new service systems. Yet the establishment of TACs for children like Zara and Stevie provides a real opportunity for reconciling conflict and mobilising personal resources and social opportunities for change. Policy and research now need to address the problem of distributing authority more effectively in newly integrated service settings.

Notes

[1] Any evaluation of impact may be affected by lack of clarity about the 'theory of change' (Pawson and Tilley, 1997) embodied in the 'change for children' model, and the difference integration is expected to make.

[2] This local authority had decided to integrate the common assessment, decision-making and service delivery functions through a locality-based team model. This was intended to link a range of co-located childcare professionals with 'family groups' of local schools. The extent of the integration of field social workers responsible for initial assessment and investigation remained under discussion. Therefore, the authority was typical of several authorities active in leading the way in implementing change to 'whole systems' working in practice.

[3] All names have been anonymised to preserve confidentiality.

[4] The advised method for ensuring an inclusive and integrated assessment and action planning process.

[5] 2004 Children Act, Section 10.

References

Anning, A., Cottrell, D., Frost, N., Green, J. and Robinson, M. (2006) *Developing Multiprofessional Teamwork for Integrated Children's Services*, Maidenhead: Open University Press.

Atkinson, M., Jones, M. and Lamont, E. (2007) *Multi-agency Working and Its Implications for Practice, A Review of the Literature*, Reading: CfBT Education Trust.

Audit Commission (2002) *Integrated Services for Older People: Building a Whole System*, London: Audit Commission.

Audit Commission (2004) *Youth Justice 2004. A Review of the Reformed Youth Justice System*, London: Audit Commission.

Audit Commission (2008) *Are We There Yet? Improving Governance and Resource Management in Children's Trusts*, London: Audit Commission.

Blair, T. (1997) 'Bringing Britain together', Speech, South London, 8 December.

Boddy, J., Potts, P. and Staham, J. (2006) *Models of Good Practice in Joined-up Assessment: Working for Children With 'Significant and Complex Needs'*, London: Thomas Coram Research Unit, Institute of Education.

Bowles, N. and Jones, A. (2005) 'Whole systems working and acute inpatient psychiatry: an exploratory study', *Journal of Psychiatric and Mental Health Nursing*, vol 12, pp 283-9.

Brandon, M. and Thoburn, J. (2008) 'Safeguarding children in the UK: a longitudinal study of services to children suffering or likely to suffer significant harm', *Child and Family Social Work*, vol 13, no 4, pp 365-77.

Brandon, M., Howe, A., Dagley, V., Salter, C., Warren, C. and Black, J. (2006) *Evaluating the Common Assessment Framework and Lead Professional Guidance and Implementation in 2005-6*, DfES Research Report 740, London: Department for Education and Skills.

Brandon, M., Belderson, P., Warren, C., Gardner, R., Howe, D., Dodsworth, J. and Black, J. (2008) 'The preoccupation with thresholds in cases of child death or serious injury through abuse and neglect', *Child Abuse Review*, vol 17, no 5, pp 313-30.

Broadhurst, K., Wastell, D., White, S., Hall, C., Peckover, S., Thompson, K., Pithouse, A. and Davey, D. (2009) 'Performing "initial assessment": identifying the latent conditions for error at the front-door of local authority children's services', *British Journal of Social Work* [*British Journal of Social Work* Advance Access, published 18 January].

Brown, K. and White, K. (2006) *Exploring the Evidence Base for Integrated Children's Services*, Edinburgh: Scottish Executive Education Department.

Butler, P. (2009) 'Council services still fail to protect children despite reforms', *The Guardian*, 5 March.

Cabinet Office (2007) *Reaching Out: Think Family. Analysis and Themes from the Families at Risk Review*, London: Social Exclusion Taskforce.

Cabinet Office (2008) *Think Family: Improving the Life Chances of Families at Risk*, London: Social Exclusion Taskforce.

Cleaver, H., Barnes, J., Bliss, D. and Cleaver, D. (2004) *Developing Information Sharing and Assessment Systems*, DfES Research Report 597, London: Department for Education and Skills.

Conlan, G. (2009) *Extended Schools: Establishing a Baseline Methodology to Estimate the Impact of the Extended School Programme on Attainment*, DCSF Research Report 069, London: Department for Children, Schools and Families.

Cummings, C., Dyson, A., Muijs, D., Papps, I., Pearson, D., Raffo, C., Tiplady, L. and Todd, L. with Crowther, D. (2007) *Evaluation of the Full Service Extended Schools Initiative: Final Report*, DfES Research Report 852, London: Department for Education and Skills.

Dartington Social Research Unit (2004) *Refocusing Children's Services Towards Prevention: Lessons from the Literature*, DfES Research Report 510, London: Department for Education and Skills.

DCSF (Department for Children, Schools and Families) (2007) *The Children's Plan. Building Brighter Futures*, Nottingham: DCSF Publications.

DCSF (2008a) *The Children's Plan One Year On: A Progress Report*, Nottingham: DCSF Publications.

DCSF (2008b) *Staying Safe: Action Plan*, Nottingham: DCSF Publications.

DfES (Department for Education and Skills) (2003) *Every Child Matters*, London: The Stationery Office.

DfES (2004) *Every Child Matters: Change for Children*, London: The Stationery Office.

DfES (2006) *Care Matters: Transforming the Lives of Children and Young People in Care*, Cm 6932, London: The Stationery Office.

DfES (2007a) *Every Parent Matters*, Nottingham: DfES Publications.

DfES (2007b) *Care Matters: Time for Change*, Cm 3137, London: The Stationery Office.

Dyson, A., Millward, A. and Todd, L. (2002) *A Study of the Extended Schools Demonstration Projects*, DfES Research Report 381, London: Department for Education and Skills.

Edwards, A. (2005) 'Relational agency: learning to be a resourceful practitioner', *International Journal of Educational Research*, vol 43, no 3, pp 168–82.

Edwards, A., Daniels, H., Gallagher, T., Leadbetter, J. and Warmington, P. (2009) *Improving Inter-professional Collaborations. Multi-agency Working for Children's Well-being, Improving Learning Series*, London: Routledge.

Engeström, Y. (2001) 'Expansive learning at work: towards an activity theoretical reconceptualization', *Journal of Education and Work*, vol 14, no 1, pp 133–56.

Forrester, D., Copello, A., Waissbein, C. and Pokhrel, S. (2008) 'Evaluation of an intensive family preservation service for families affected by parental substance misuse', *Child Abuse Review*, vol 17, no 6, pp 410–26.

Fortin, J. (2009) *Children's Rights and the Developing Law* (3rd edn), Law in Context, London: Butterworths.

Gilligan, P. and Manby, M. (2008) 'The common assessment framework: does the reality match the rhetoric?', *Child and Family Social Work*, vol 13, no 2, pp 177–87.

Hills, J., Sefton, T. and Stewart, K. (eds) (2009) *Towards a More Equal Society? Poverty, Inequality and Policy Since 1997*, Bristol: The Policy Press.

HM Government (2007) *Building on Progress: Families, Policy Review*, London: Prime Minister's Strategy Unit, Cabinet Office.

HM Treasury (2002) *Pre-budget Statement*, available at www.hm-treasury.gov.uk/prebud_pbr02_speech.htm

HM Treasury/DfES (Department for Education and Skills) (2007) *Aiming High for Children: Supporting Families*, Norwich: Office of Public Sector Information.

Hobbs, T., Kaoukli, D. and Little, M. (2006) 'Meeting the challenges in implementing *Every Child Matters*: the view from the Director-General', *Journal of Children's Services*, vol 1, no 2, pp 61-9.

House of Commons (2009) *Looked-after Children. Third Report of Session 2008-09, Volume I, Report, together with formal minutes*, Children, Schools and Families Committee, available at www.publications. parliament.uk/pa/cm200809/cmselect/cmchilsch/111/11102.htm.

Hughes, B. (2006) *Supplementary Memorandum Submitted by the Rt Hon Beverley Hughes MP, Minister of State for Children, Young People and Families*, Department for Education and Skills Select Committee on Education and Skills Minutes of Evidence, available at www.publications.parliament.uk/pa/cm200607/cmselect/cmeduski/62/6112006.htm.

Jeffery, T. and Tabberer, R. (2006) *Every Child Matters and School Standards Letter to Director's of Children's Services*, 12 October, Published as Annex B, Select Committee on Education and Skills Minutes of Evidence, available at www.parliament.the-stationery-office.co.uk/pa/cm200607/cmselect/cmeduski/62/6112008.htm.

Laming, Lord (2009) *The Protection of Children in England: A Progress Report*, London: The Stationery Office.

Layard, R. and Dunn, J. (2008) *A Good Childhood: Searching for Values in a Competitive Age*, London: Penguin.

Le Grand, J. (2007) *The Other Invisible Hand: Delivering Public Services Through Choice and Competition*, Princeton, NJ: Princeton University Press.

LGA (Local Government Association) (2007) *Narrowing the Gap in Outcomes*, London: LGA.

Luckock, B. (2007) 'Safeguarding children and integrated children's services', in K. Wilson and A. James (eds) *The Child Protection Handbook: The Practitioner's Guide to Safeguarding Children* (3rd edn), London: Bailliere Tindall Elsevier.

Luckock, B. (2008) 'Adoption support and the reconciliation of ambivalence in family policy and children's services', *Journal of Law and Society Special Edition*, vol 35, no 1, pp 3-27.

Luckock, B. and Hart, A. (2005) 'Adoptive family life and adoption support: policy ambivalence and the development of effective services', *Child and Family Social Work*, vol 10, no 2, pp 125-37.

Luckock, B. with Stevens, P. and Young, J. (2008) 'Living through the experience: the social worker as the trusted ally and champion of young people in care', in B. Luckock and M. Lefevre (eds) *Direct Work. Social Work with Children and Young People in Care*, London: BAAF, Chapter 1.

Milburn, A. (2003) *Hansard*, 28 January, column 740.

NESS (National Evaluation of Sure Start) (2008) *The Impact of Sure Start Local Programmes on Three Year Olds and Their Families, The National Evaluation of Sure Start (NESS)*, London: Institute for the Study of Children, Families and Social Issues, Birkbeck, University of London.

Ofsted (2008) *Safeguarding Children, The Third Joint Chief Inspectors' Report on Arrangements to Safeguard Children*, London: Ofsted

Papworth, M. and Crosland, A. (2005) 'Health service use of whole system interventions', *The Journal of Management Development*, vol 24, pp 5/6.

Pawson, R. and Tilley, N. (1997) *Realistic Evaluation*, London: Sage Publications.

Peckover, S., Hall, C. and White, S. (2008b) 'From policy to practice: implementation and negotiation of technologies in everyday child welfare', *Children & Society* [Online Early Access doi:10.1111/j.1099-0860.2008.00143.x].

Peckover, S., White, S.J. and Hall, C. (2008a) 'Making and managing electronic children: e-assessment in child welfare', *Information, Communication and Society*, vol 11, no 3, pp 375-94.

Pithouse, A., Hall, C., Peckover, S. and White, S. (2009) 'A tale of two CAFs: the impact of the electronic common assessment framework', *British Journal of Social Work* [*British Journal of Social Work* Advance Access, published 25 February 2009].

Pratt, J., Gordon, P. and Plamping, D. (2005) *Working Whole Systems: Putting Theory into Practice in Organisations* (2nd edn), Oxford: Radcliffe.

Robinson, M., Atkinson, M. and Downing, D. (2008) *Supporting Theory Building in Integrated Services Research*, Slough: National Foundation for Educational Research.

Rushmer, R. and Pallis, G. (2002) 'Inter-professional working: the wisdom of integrated working and the disaster of blurred boundaries', *Public Money and Management*, vol 23, no 1, pp 59-66.

Schoon, I. (2006). *Risk and Resilience, Adaptations in Changing Times*, Cambridge: Cambridge University Press.

Social Justice Policy Group (2006) *Breakdown Britain. Interim Report on the State of the Nation*, London: Social Justice Policy Group, Centre for Social Justice.

Taylor, A. (2006) 'If we think we can relax on *Every Child Matters* we are deluded', Interview with John Coughlan, *Community Care*, 16 October.

Townsley, R., Abbott, D. and Watson, D. (2004) *Making a Difference?: Exploring the Impact of Multi-agency Working on Disabled Children with Complex Health Care Needs, Their Families and the Professionals Who Support Them*, Bristol: The Policy Press.

Truss, C. (2008) 'Peter's story: reconceptualising the UK SEN system', *European Journal of Special Needs Education*, vol 23, no 4, pp 365-77.

UNICEF (2007) *An Overview of Child Well-being in Rich Countries. A Comprehensive Assessment of the Lives and Well-being of Children and Adolescents in the Economically Advanced Nations*, Report Card 7, Florence: UNICEF Innocenti Research Centre.

University of East Anglia (2005) *Realising Children's Trust Arrangements: National Evaluation of Children's Trusts Phase 1 Report*, University of East Anglia in association with the National Children's Bureau, DfES Research Report 682, London: Department for Education and Skills.

University of East Anglia (2007) *Children's Trust Pathfinders: Innovative Partnerships for Improving the Well-being of Children and Young People: National Evaluation of Children's Trust Pathfinders Final Report*, University of East Anglia in association with the National Children's Bureau, DfES Research Report 839, London: Department for Education and Skills.

Weiss, J. (1981) 'Substance versus symbol in administrative reform', *Policy Analysis*, Winter, pp 20-45.

Wenger, E. (1998) *Communities of Practice: Learning, Meaning, and Identity*, Cambridge: Cambridge University Press.

White, S., Hall, C. and Peckover, S. (2008) 'The descriptive tyranny of the common assessment framework: technologies of categorization and professional practice in child welfare', *British Journal of Social Work* [*British Journal of Social Work* Advance Access, published online on 16 April 2008].

Wilkinson, R. and Pickett, K. (2009) *The Spirit Level: Why More Equal Societies Almost Always Do Better*, London: Allen Lane.

Wilson, K. and James, A. (eds) (2007) *The Child Protection Handbook: The Practitioners Guide to Safeguarding Children* (3rd edn), London: Bailliere Tindall Elsevier.

Eight

Safeguarding: the interagency dimension, risks and responsibilities

Michael Murphy and Eileen Oak

Introduction

This chapter examines the enduring challenge of achieving increased interagency collaboration in childcare, in the context of safeguarding vulnerable children and young people. The term 'interagency collaboration' refers to collaborative practice between practitioners of more than one agency. This type of collaboration is usually, but not always, interdisciplinary and multi-agency. As Shardlow *et al.* (2004) point out:

> Given that there are such a wide range of terms with similar or proximate meanings it is necessary to specify carefully how these are used. In such circumstances *inter-agency* implies that there are at least two distinct organisations working together to safeguard children. The word *inter-agency* is central and should be distinguished from other forms of work that may involve staff from different professional or occupational backgrounds who work together ... although inter-agency work in the context of safeguarding children will more usually involve several different agencies. (Shardlow *et al.*, 2004: 11)

Social policy context

Murphy (1996) demonstrates how various discourses on childhood led to the development of three action perspectives that influence social policy: the family welfare, child protection and children's rights perspectives. The family welfare perspective proposes that parents know best what is in their children's interests and the state should rarely intervene in family life (when the state does intervene it often makes significant mistakes). The child protection perspective views the differences of power within families as the context for child abuse and exploitation and therefore believes in more state intervention to ensure that parental power is not being abused. The children's rights perspective believes that children need families and they need protection, but most importantly, they need a say or a voice in what happens to them.

These three perspectives have heavily influenced the direction of social policy in the UK since the mid-19th century. They compete with each other for political ascendancy, create tensions and contradictions in policy implementation and predict the direction of social policy development.

Historical context

The child protection perspective first came to prominence in the middle of the Victorian era, through the campaigns of various children's charities and societies that sought to highlight the abuse and neglect of children and women in the private sphere of the family (Lewis, 1998). These amalgamated and became the NSPCC (National Society for the Prevention of Cruelty to Children) in 1884 and were instrumental in mobilising political support for the introduction of the 1889 Prevention of Cruelty to Children Act. However, by the middle of the 20th century, the family welfare perspective began to dominate social policy approaches, stimulated by the 'rescuing' zeal of many social workers prompted by the findings in the 1946 Curtis Report on conditions in children's residential care. The emphasis was on improving the public care system and hence the focus on problems inside the family was overlooked, further undermining the child protection perspective. However, the discovery of 'battered baby syndrome' in the US (Kempe and Kempe, 1978) and the rediscovery of child physical abuse as a social problem slowly increased the influence of the child protection perspective. This influence increased in the 1970s as the result of a plethora of child abuse fatalities and the high profile public inquiries into them. These public inquiries also heralded the birth of the modern child protection system.

In implementing this new system successive Conservative and Labour governments throughout the 1970s sought to institutionalise interagency collaboration and communication arrangements. This began in 1974 when the then Conservative government formalised the child protection system by combining the child protection case conference system with child protection registration under the 'umbrella' of the local area review committees. Thus, by forcing interprofessional meetings and communication in this way, the government presumed that such initiatives would automatically ensure greater interagency communication and collaboration. However, a shift in emphasis occurred in the 1980s following the dissemination of the Cleveland Inquiry (1988) summary that highlighted the dangers of excessive state intrusion in family life in order to protect children. The ensuing 1989 Children Act that was introduced in the wake of Cleveland sought to maintain a balance between the family welfare and child protection perspectives, while at the same time seeking to include the child's voice in the process.

The rationale behind this 'balance' was reinforced by the findings of a number of research studies (DHSS, 1985; Giller *et al.*, 1992; Denman and Thorpe, 1993) and various child abuse inquires (London Borough of Brent, 1985; Butler-Sloss, 1988). These and the 12 other research studies collectively known as *Child Protection: Messages from Research* (DH, 1995) were concerned mainly with the functioning of English and Welsh childcare systems. One common criticism identified by these research reports was that the child protection system was too cumbersome, sucking large numbers of children in need into the system, before excluding the majority without any service or assistance being offered. Consequently, *Messages from Research* (DH, 1995) gave impetus to a movement that became known as 're-focusing'. This movement attempted to transfer or to 're-focus' resources from child protection to children in need work, offering earlier preventative services instead of intruding to protect without offering services.

The re-focusing movement was still in its infancy when New Labour came to power in May 1997. Then the government concentrated its focus on its *Modernisation of Social Services Agenda* (DH, 1998) and tackling social exclusion. However, in 2003 it produced a green paper entitled *Every Child Matters* (DfES, 2003) that was developed into a full-blown social policy initiative. This sought to promote a shared commitment on the part of all public agencies to work collaboratively. The significance of *Every Child Matters* was that it extended the concept of safeguarding beyond simply the protection of children from abuse and neglect. The 2003 *Every Child Matters: Staying Safe Action Plan* emphasised the duty of all public agencies to keep children safe from accidents, crime and bullying and to promote their welfare in a healthy and safe environment. A crucial element in achieving this was interagency collaboration.

Interagency collaboration

Successive governments have been extolling the virtues of interagency collaboration since 1974 and to reinforce this a series of increasingly complex guidance (DHSS, 1986, 1988; DH, 1991a, 1999; HM Government, 2006) has been issued to all those working in the system. The whole ethos of integrated teams is to improve interagency collaboration with the objective of providing consistent and coordinated services to ensure the safety and well-being of children through securing the five outcomes of *Every Child Matters*.

Although the need for interagency collaboration has been accepted in principle for several decades, in practice serious case reviews (where children have been killed or seriously harmed) routinely cite the lack of interagency collaboration as a contributory factor in the failure to protect (DHSS, 1983; DH, 1991b; Reder and Duncan, 1999; Sinclair and Bullock, 2002; Brandon *et al.*, 2008; Rose and Barnes, 2008). Calder (2003) claims that systemic blockages to collaboration – including very different training, different perspectives on the family, professional roles, responsibilities, priorities and lines of authority between different practice groups – make interagency communication and collaboration more difficult to achieve. This theme is also explored by Murphy (2000), who suggests that as well as systemic blockages, practitioners are 'accultured' into their practice identities, giving them a way of perceiving the child's world and behaving in childcare practice that is intrinsically different from other practitioners.

Despite these challenges, the re-launch of Labour's childcare agenda in the form of *Every Child Matters* in 2003 proposed significant organisational restructuring that included a move to the integration of childcare teams. However, there are problems relating to the thresholds for intervention that were introduced under the auspices of *Every Child Matters* (DfES, 2003). There are seven thresholds, as follows:

1.   Universal: a child for whom universal services will be sufficient.

2.   Targeted services for vulnerable children.

3.   Children in need (as per the 1989 Children Act) requiring specialist provision.

4.   Section 47 inquiry: child in need of child protection inquiry or investigation to see if significant harm has occurred.

5.   Child in need of safeguarding/protective services, by an interagency group.

6.   Care proceedings: separation from birth family and placed in residential or foster care.

7.   Adoption: final separation from birth family and permanent placement with alternative family.

The main problem with these thresholds (which affects interagency collaboration) is the inconsistent manner in which they are applied by different agencies; for example, most of the integrated teams seem to centre their work with children in need (threshold 3) rather than with children in need of safeguarding (thresholds 4 and 5).

In England and Wales Reder and Duncan (2003) identify a host of barriers to interagency safeguarding which include poor recording, poor interagency coordination and information sharing (compounded by professional confusion regarding issues of confidentiality, consent and referral processes) and the failure of professionals to adopt a holistic picture because they fail to keep the wider safeguarding network in mind. These communication problems are exacerbated by professional mistrust of one another or the lack of respect for the other professional's expertise or perspective, or for other agencies in the safeguarding network, and differences in professional status and power.

These problems seem endemic to all four countries that constitute the UK. With regard to England and Wales this situation seems to be borne out by the findings of the two Laming reports (2003, 2009) and the three previous DH *Review of Safeguarding* reports of 2002, 2005 and 2008. The repeated concerns common to all these publications (which impact on effective interagency safeguarding policy and practice) relate to cultural and organisational barriers, a lack of professional consensus on what constitutes 'safeguarding', the different approaches adopted to children's welfare by the different agencies, the lack of adequate basic child protection training on abuse and neglect, and the recruitment and retention of trained child protection specialists. These reports specifically highlight these concerns with regard to education, health, Cafcass (Children and Family Court Advisory and Support Service), Connexions and Youth Offending Teams (YOTs) where staff are not adequately trained to identify children at risk of significant harm (DH, 2005, 2008). There are anxieties about the different approaches to children adopted by different welfare agencies. In young offender institutions concerns have been identified over the use of strip searches and restraining techniques that suggest an emphasis on containment and management of behaviour rather than on the welfare of the young person. In addition, the thresholds for intervention regarding a child or young person deemed at risk seem to be higher in youth offender institutions than for young people in foster placements or those living at home (DH, 2008).

Joint working and the development of strategic partnerships (to facilitate effective interagency collaboration) have been hampered by the lack of YOTs, Cafcass and Connexions' representation on the Local Safeguarding Children's Boards (LSCBs). These problems are compounded by assessment problems due to delays in dealing with referrals and the utilisation of different assessment frameworks by various agencies, such as the Asset and YOT assessment frameworks that have not been configured with either the DH (2000) *Framework for the Assessment of Children in Need and Their Families* or the DfES (2004) Common Assessment Framework (CAF) more commonly used in children's services (Calder, 2003; DH, 2008). In Scotland the response to the *Review of Safeguarding* reports' concerns has been to make training in risk compulsory for all social work staff working with children and adults.

These developments have possibly been prompted by similar problems evident with the Scottish child protection system. Daniel's (2004) study focused on the implementation of the interagency safeguarding system across 32 Scottish councils and included an audit of all key agencies in the safeguarding network working with 5,042 children with a smaller study of 118 child protection cases. The research identified common practice failings such as poor information sharing between agencies, poor interagency coordination and collaboration and poor quality assessments. In many of the child protection cases the researcher identified a tendency by GPs to see injuries as a 'one-off' and their failure to spot patterns of injuries or referrals. She also describes what she terms as 'poor quality assessments' characterised by a lack of rigour or not being extensive enough.

A similar feature was found in Devaney's (2004) research into child protection services in Northern Ireland. He analysed 53 child protection cases and found in 75% of them a lack of assessment or information on either parent's physical or emotional health. He identified the seriousness of this assessment omission by citing Sheppard's (2002) research which highlighted the large numbers of mothers of children deemed to be at risk who were suffering with undiagnosed depression, which had serious implications for their ability to work with child welfare practitioners.

Such weaknesses in assessment skills can have profound impact within the context of safeguarding. Research by Dale *et al.* (2002) identified the poor risk assessment skills of social workers. When the researchers analysed a group of serious cases they found that social workers had inappropriately classified concerning cases as 'child-in-need', which meant that no child protection risk assessment was undertaken. This issue is of particular concern given the repeated identification of the inappropriately high thresholds for intervention adopted by a number of social services departments (DH, 2005, 2008; Laming, 2009). This problem is exacerbated by the lack of interprofessional consensus on what constitutes 'safeguarding'.

Shardlow *et al.* (2004) conducted research on interagency collaboration in England and discovered that there was no agreement between agencies about what constituted good interagency practice and no common educational input, at a qualifying level, between the different practice groups. The researchers suggested eight interagency operational standards, and a series of common education and training standards to accompany them. These were to some extent reflected in the government's six common core elements of skills and knowledge for all who work with children in England and Wales (DCSF, 2005). However, there is no indication that these elements have been successfully included in the education and training of all childcare practitioners. Similar issues affect interagency practice in Ireland. Buckley's (2003) study of one interagency system suggested that unofficial, traditional ways of working which were largely hidden from other agencies often impeded interagency collaboration, and were very slow to change. This aspect is compounded by what many practitioners argue is increased regulation.

Regulation versus discretion

There is a dearth of research on the regulation of professional groups within the context of interagency collaboration and the capacity of various professionals to use their discretion, with the exception of Howe's (1986) work which concerns the regulation of interagency safeguarding groups and organisations. The early child protection procedures that were written in 1974 were short, simple and relatively straightforward, leaving maximum collective discretion with practitioners and managers in the safeguarding system. In a similar fashion the first *Working Together to Safeguard Children* (DHSS, 1988) was a short advisory document, within which quite wide parameters were set in which interagency groups were allowed significant amounts of discretion over their child protection processes. However, in response to the deaths of children in the 1980s and 1990s the then Conservative administration increased proceduralisation:

> There was a proliferation of what might be described
> as 'micro regulations' at a time when so much about
> regulation was anathema to New Right politicians in
> other forms of human endeavour. (Stevenson, 2000)

This process continued under New Labour particularly following the deaths of Victoria Climbié and Baby Peter (Laming, 2003, 2009).

Thus the interagency system has been increasingly proceduralised to avoid individual 'error'. In the process, individual discretion over decision making has also been eroded and the ability to make procedures 'fit' the needs of the individual child or family has also reduced.

The New Labour government has sought to address many of the barriers to effective safeguarding (including the problem of inappropriately high thresholds for child protection) in the form of social policy initiatives such as *Every Child Matters* (DfES, 2003) and the *Review of Safeguarding* (DH, 2005) that were both underpinned by the 2004 Children Act. However, there is some debate (Devaney, 2004; Reder and Duncan, 2004) as to whether this has been at the expense of professional autonomy and discretion. Laming's (2009) report once again focused on issues of retention and recruitment of child protection specialists and the quality of training and education for childcare social workers. This has been reinforced by the findings of the Social Work Task Force and its interim report (2009) which identified that many newly qualified social workers feel that their education and training had not equipped them for the demands of child protection work or direct work with children and their families.

In response to the recommendations in Laming's (2009) report, a series of measures are being introduced which include: the investment of £57.8 million in social work education and training and recruitment; a national marketing and recruitment campaign; a 'Return to Social Work' scheme (in an effort to attract experienced social workers back into the profession); and a graduate recruitment scheme to attract high-calibre graduates into social work as there is a belief that raising academic standards will improve the quality of practice. In addition, there are to be new inspections and statutory performance targets for safeguarding and child protection services as well as the introduction of an 'action plan for all local authorities', which outlines a greater accountability and leadership role for all directors of Children's Services and local councillors, and the establishment of a National Safeguarding Delivery Unit to provide an annual report to Parliament on all local authorities' safeguarding progress.

It is worth examining critically this social policy response in the context of Reder and Duncan's (2003) observations about the Laming inquiry of 2003 and all previous inquiries into serious case reviews. They argue that the legalistic approach of all such inquiries is a problem in itself because it leads to a simplistic understanding of the processes and nature of child protection work. This is because the approach is one in which the stories which seek to explain the circumstances of the case tend to be reconstructed in individual terms devoid of their context and relationship to the other people involved. Little attention is paid to the wider context in which the abuse occurred. Moreover, most of these inquiries conclude by making a host of recommendations without any explanation as to their rationale or underlying principles and hence they tend to be adopted by practitioners mechanistically. Thus, the opportunity is missed to provide learning opportunities or practice messages to promote critical reflexive practice. Consequently (commenting on the 2003 inquiry report into the death of Victoria Climbié), Reder and Duncan (2003) assert that Laming's recommendations would simply promote bureaucratic and organisational change without really addressing the practice failings that frontline staff need to address in order to improve their understanding of the complex nature of child protection work often characterised by parents' chaotic lifestyles, alcohol or substance misuse issues or domestic violence (Reder and Duncan, 2003). Similarly, Lord Laming's 2009 recommendations, which call for greater accountability and leadership by local councillors and directors of Children's Services, will not necessarily address the failures in assessment skills such as the lack of rigour in processing case information or addressing the complexity of problems in interagency communication.

The same point is made by Devaney (2004) when concluding his findings on child protection practice in Northern Ireland. He criticised the recommendations of Laming's (2003) report to introduce performance indicators for child protection work because this recommendation entailed an underlying assumption that:

> … performance indicator measures are a good 'proxy'
> measure of desired outcomes for children when this
> is often by no means clear. (Devaney, 2004: 27)

Devaney argued that these measures focused on targets such as the number of child protection registrations and de-registrations rather than how well safeguarding services addressed the emotional and psychological well-being of children who had experienced abuse and neglect. He asserted that these measures were too simplistic because they were designed only to monitor the operation of the child protection system rather than the impact of that system on the service users and its interventions in the lives of children deemed at risk. In the examination of 53 cases Devaney noted that within the interagency safeguarding network, social workers, health visitors and teachers were able to identify factors that caused them to have concerns regarding children's abuse and neglect, but then were not able to translate these abstract concerns into tangible characteristics that parents could understand or be clear as to what needed to change to eliminate such concerns. These were not issues of policy or procedures but problems of conceptualisation. Through conducting this research Devaney traced the characteristics and processes that led to both registration and de-registration in order to highlight the complexity of the child protection system that these measures could not capture.

He identified the flawed framework of analysis of government approaches to safeguarding. The current social policy problem-solving process is one in which complex problems are broken down into separate rational components that can be tackled systematically. However, he noted that Chapman (2002) identified the need to treat some public service networks as complicated, maladaptive systems, where problems did not simply build on one another in a linear fashion, but rather were compounded by interconnectedness. It is useful to see the interagency safeguarding system as such a complex and interconnected system.

Conclusion

A recurring barrier to effective interagency collaboration has been the lack of effective interagency communication. Reder and Duncan (2003) suggest that this is because many professionals fail to understand what they term the 'psychology of communication'. Psychological communication problems relate to how professionals think about a case, process the information available to them and interact with other professionals providing information. It is the ability to reflect on communication as a social process and to consider the important function of all the other professionals in the safeguarding network, to learn to impart information to them clearly and to attribute intended meaning from the messages received from them. Furthermore, it is the ability to recognise that all communication involves the transfer of information and the attribution of meaning to it. Reder and Duncan (2003) assert that the transfer of information has no impact (in terms of protecting children) unless communicators are capable of attributing meaning to the messages conveyed (that is, picking out what is salient and acting on it). For effective interagency communication both the messenger and receiver must take responsibility to ensure that both parties understand their communication and that the interpretation of meaning is the same as the conveyor of the message intended. Any covert information must be made overt and any misunderstandings checked out and clarified. Receivers of messages must be able to hypothesise the facts or concepts being sent to them. The dangers of miscommunication are identified in the Climbié case where the social worker interpreted the nurse's comment that "Victoria was fit for discharge" as meaning that hospital staff had no child protection concerns. However, all that the nurse meant by this comment was that Victoria was medically fit (Reder and Duncan, 2004: 86). Thus, it is important to adopt a theoretical perspective to understand the psychology of communication and in order to utilise the interagency communication network as fully as possible. To do this practitioners need to be more reflective and to conceptualise themselves as part of a wider safeguarding network by asking key questions such as 'who else requires this information to be processed?' or 'who else is involved in the case?'. These skills can also be enhanced by training and role-play exercises to help practitioners rehearse communication to develop these skills to a point where they become automatic (Reder and

Duncan, 2003). These skills constitute what Reder and Duncan refer
to as the 'communications mindset', crucial to effective interagency
collaboration. Without this they argue that no amount of social
policy changes in response to serious case reviews will be effective in
generating the good practice required to secure the safety and well-
being of children at risk or in need. As Reder and Duncan state:

> Communication involves a complex interplay between
> information-processing, interpersonal relating and
> inter-agency collaboration. The need to communicate
> purposefully and with meaning to relevant others
> must be borne in mind by all practitioners at all times.
> Effective communication is the responsibility of both
> the message initiator and the receiver and, as such, it is
> a mindset and skill that can be learned, rehearsed and
> refined. Only then will policies and technological aides
> have their optimal benefit. (Reder and Duncan, 2003: 8)

References

Brandon, M., Belderson, P., Warren, C., Howe, D., Gardner, R.,
Dodsworth, J. and Black, J. (2008) *Analysing Child Deaths and Serious
Injury Through Abuse and Neglect: What Can We Learn?*, London:
Department for Children, Schools and Families.

Buckley, H. (2003) *Child Protection Work: Beyond the Rhetoric*, London:
Jessica Kingsley Publishers.

Butler-Sloss, E. (1988) *Report of the Inquiry into Child Abuse in Cleveland
1987*, London: HMSO.

Calder, M. (2003) 'The assessment framework: a critique and re-
formulation', in M. Calder and S. Hackett, *Assessment in Child Care*,
Lyme Regis: Russell House, pp 3-60.

Chapman, J. (2002) *Systems Failure: Why Governments Must Learn to
Think Differently*, London: Demos.

Dale, P., Green, R. and Fellows, R. (2002) *What Really Happened: Child
Protection Case Management of Infants with Serious Injuries and Discrepant
Parental Explanations*, London: NSPCC.

Daniel, B. (2004) 'An overview of the Scottish multidisciplinary child
protection review', *Child and Family Social Work*, vol 9, no 3, pp 237-
46.

DCSF (Department for Children, Schools and Families) (2005)
Common Core of Children's Knowledge for the Children's Workforce,
London: The Stationery Office.

Denman, G. and Thorpe, D. (1993) *Family Participation and Patterns of Intervention in Child Protection in Gwent,* A Research Report for the Area Child Protection Committee, Gwent, Lancaster: Department of Applied Social Science, Lancaster University.

Devaney, J. (2004) 'Relating outcomes to objectives in child protection', *Child and Family Social Work,* vol 9, no 1, pp 27-38.

DfES (Department for Education and Skills) (2003) *Every Child Matters* (Green Paper), Cm 5860, London: The Stationery Office.

DfES (2004) *Common Assessment Framework* http://www.dcsf.gov.uk/consultations/downloadableocs/ACFA006.pdf (accessed 20/10/2009).

DH (Department of Health) (1991a) *Working Together Under the Children Act 1989,* London: HMSO.

DH (1991b) *Child Abuse: A Study of Inquiry Reports 1980-1989,* London: HMSO.

DH (1995) *Messages from Research,* London: HMSO.

DH (1998) *Modernising Social Services: Promoting Independence, Improving Protection, Raising Standards,* London: HMSO.

DH (1999) *Working Together to Safeguard Children,* London: The Stationery Office.

DH (2000) *Framework for the Assessment of Children in Need and Their Families,* London: HMSO.

DH (2002) *Review of Safeguarding,* London: The Stationery Office.

DH (2005) *Review of Safeguarding,* London: The Stationery Office.

DH (2008) *Review of Safeguarding,* London: The Stationery Office.

DHSS (Department of Health and Social Security) (1983) *Child Abuse – A Study of Inquiry Reports 1973-1981,* London: HMSO.

DHSS (1985) *Social Work Decisions in Child Care: Recent Research Findings and Their Implications,* London: HMSO.

DHSS (1986) *Child Abuse – Working Together: A Draft Guide to Arrangements for Interagency Cooperation for the Protection of Children,* London: HMSO.

DHSS (1988) *Working Together,* London: HMSO.

Giller, H., Gormley, C. and Williams, P. (1992) *The Effectiveness of Child Protection Procedures: An Evaluation of Child Protection Procedures in Four ACPC Areas,* Manchester: Social Information Systems.

HM Government (2006) *Working Together to Safeguard Children,* London: The Stationery Office.

Howe, D. (1986) *Social Workers and Their Practice in Welfare Bureaucracies,* Aldershot: Gower.

Kempe, R. and Kempe, C. (1978) *Child Abuse,* London: Fortuna.

Laming, H. (2003) *The Victoria Climbié Inquiry*, London: The Stationery Office.

Laming, Lord (2009) *The Protection of Children in England: A Progress Report*, London: Department for Children, Schools and Families.

Lewis, G. (1998) *Forming Nation, Framing Welfare*, London/Milton Keynes: Routledge/The Open University.

London Borough of Brent (1985) *A Child in Trust: The Report of the Panel of Inquiry into the Circumstances Surrounding the Death of Jasmine Beckford*, London: Borough of Brent.

Murphy, M. (1996) *The Child Protection Unit*, Aldershot: Ashgate.

Murphy, M. (2000) 'The interagency trainer', in M. Charles and E. Hendry (eds) *Training Together to Safeguard Children*, London: NSPCC, pp 56–68.

Reder, P. and Duncan, S. (1999) *Lost Innocents. A Follow-up Study of Fatal Child Abuse*, London: Routledge.

Reder, P. and Duncan, S. (2003) 'Understanding communication in child protection networks', *Child Abuse Review*, vol 12, issue 2, pp 82–100.

Reder, P. and Duncan, S. (2004) 'Making the most of the Victoria Climbié Inquiry Report', *Child Abuse Review*, vol 13, pp 95–114.

Rose, W. and Barnes, J. (2008) *Improving Safeguarding Practice: A Study of Serious Case Reviews 2001-2003*, London: Department for Children, Schools and Families.

Shardlow, S., Davis, C., Johnson, M., Long, T., Murphy, M. and Race, D. (2004) *Education and Training for Inter-agency Working: New Standards*, Salford: University of Salford.

Sheppard, M. (2002) 'Depressed mothers' experience of partnership in child and family care', *British Journal of Social Work*, vol 32, pp 93–112.

Sinclair, R. and Bullock, R. (2002) *Learning From Past Experience: A Review of Serious Case Reviews*, London: Department of Health.

Social Work Task Force (2009) *Facing Up to the Task: The Interim Report of the Social Work Task Force: July 2009*, London: DH Publications.

Stevenson, O. (2000) 'The mandate for inter-agency and inter-professional work and training', in M. Charles and E. Hendry (eds) *Training Together to Safeguard Children*, London: NSPCC, pp 5–13.

Nine

Multi-agency practice and professional identity

Anna Souhami

Introduction

Over the past 20 years multi-agency practice has transformed the youth justice system. Since the mid-1980s both practitioners and policy makers have espoused the importance of a 'joined-up' approach to preventing youth crime and partnership schemes have proliferated across a wide range of youth justice services (see, for example, Northampton Juvenile Liaison Bureau, 1985; Nacro, 1987; Audit Commission, 1996). The growing consensus about the benefits of multi-agency work in youth justice practice culminated in a radical restructuring of the English and Welsh youth justice system under the 1998 Crime and Disorder Act, when, for the first time, the entire delivery and management of youth justice services became a multi-agency responsibility.

The formation of Youth Offending Teams (YOTs) was at the heart of the new multi-agency system. These new, multi-agency units replaced the specialist teams of social workers known as 'juvenile justice teams' or 'youth justice teams' as providers of youth justice services. YOTs do not belong to any one agency but draw together practitioners from all the core agencies working with young offenders – social work, probation, police, education and health authorities, as well as staff from other relevant agencies or organisations. Staff are seconded to or employed by the YOT through the local authority. YOT management is also multi-agency – YOT managers can be appointed from any of the core partner agencies and YOTs are managed locally by multi-agency management boards and chief executives' departments. Nationally, YOTs are accountable to the Youth Justice Board (YJB), a non-departmental public body (NDPB) also established under the Crime and Disorder Act with responsibility for overseeing the youth justice system.

In this way, the youth justice system has become wholly restructured around multi-agency practice. However, this has brought into focus the difficulties it creates for practitioners both in youth justice and beyond. In particular, experiences in the youth justice system suggest that multi-agency work confronts practitioners with profound challenges to their sense of professional identity. Drawing on research in a developing YOT (Souhami, 2007), this chapter explores how problems of identity unfold in multi-agency practice. Why are questions of professional identity at issue in multi-agency practice? How do they become manifested in practitioners' working lives? And what challenges do they create for practitioners? First, however, the rationale for multi-agency practice in work with young offenders is explored. Why has it become central to contemporary youth justice?

Multi-agency practice and youth crime

The predominance of multi-agency practice in the youth justice system reflects important shifts in thinking about youth crime and its management. Multi-agency practice has developed alongside the move towards the 'new public management' in social policy (Hood, 1991), which prioritises managerialist goals of efficiency and effectiveness. Instead of being organised around traditional goals of reform or rehabilitation, the emergent 'corporatist' strategy was concerned with managing the offending population in the most efficient, economic way (for example, Pratt, 1989; Feeley and Simon, 1992). Similarly, youth justice services became re-focused towards identifying and pre-emptively targeting those young people thought to be most 'at risk' of offending. In line with this approach, it was recognised that it is more effective – and cheaper – to tackle offending behaviour at an early stage. Youth justice services therefore became increasingly reconfigured towards a particular understanding of crime prevention: pre-emptive intervention with young people who have not offended but are thought to be 'at risk' of doing so. Reflecting this, the 1998 Crime and Disorder Act established 'preventing offending by children and young persons' as the principal aim of the English and Welsh youth justice system.

At the same time, the growing interest in targeted criminal justice interventions reflected increasing optimism in the ability of the youth justice system to affect change in young people. The previous orthodoxy had been that criminal justice interventions were at best unable to prevent re-offending (Martinson, 1974), and at worst could establish delinquent identities and so do more harm than good (for example, Goldson, 2000). By contrast, an emerging 'what works' agenda suggested that, if targeted appropriately, some forms of intervention could be successful in reducing offending behaviour for some young people (Muncie, 2009).

In addition, offending behaviour has come to be understood as a complex phenomenon with multiple causes and effects. In other words, young people who offend often experience a range of connected problems, including family, schooling, health or social needs (for example, Farrington and West, 1990; Graham and Bowling, 1995). As a result, it has become accepted that offending behaviour cannot be effectively addressed by any single agency. Instead, effective approaches require input from a range of agencies to address the multifaceted nature of youth crime.

In this way, responses to youth offending are thought to require an economic and efficient approach, early identification and targeting of young people at risk of offending and the involvement of a range of agencies. In this context, multi-agency work can be seen to have a number of benefits.

Benefits of multi-agency work

First, by drawing together staff from the different agencies working with young offenders, partnerships can pool their funding, expertise, effort and information, allowing for a better coordinated use of resources. Further, multi-agency staff can act as 'brokers' for their home agencies (Burnett, 2005), thereby removing barriers to cooperation, facilitating referrals and providing easier access to information and services.

Second, as they are able to share expertise and information from the diverse services working with young people, multi-agency teams can identify the range of needs experienced by their service users and provide a holistic service to address them. Similarly, because they can share information across a range of 'risk factors', multi-agency teams are able to identify young people considered at risk of offending and attempt to divert them into 'more positive activities' (Youth Justice Board, 2004a: 4), a particularly important benefit in a policy climate that prioritises preventative intervention. Moreover, as staff work outside their traditional structures and practices, multi-agency practice fosters new ways of working and so encourages innovation and creativity (Burnett and Appleton, 2004; Souhami, 2007).

Finally, multi-agency work aims to produce a consistent and coherent approach among the diverse agencies that work with young people. Since agencies have different views about what they are trying to achieve (for example, Audit Commission, 1996; Labour Party, 1997), multi-agency work aims to bring various professional and interest groups into a collective whole and encourage the emergence of 'a common approach' to youth justice work (Home Office, 1997: para 8.9). In other words, multi-agency work is concerned not just with organisational change, but with cultural change too. It aims to consolidate differences in the purpose, values and principles of practice among diverse agencies and to promote a shared understanding. Of course, this is consistent with the emphasis on efficiency in contemporary youth justice: by 'designing out' conflict in the aims and values of different agencies (Pitts, 2000: 9), multi-agency work aims to remove barriers to cooperation and encourage the smooth and efficient running of the system (Audit Commission, 1996).

Professional identity and multi-agency practice

Questions of professional identity are of central importance to this understanding of the benefits of multi-agency work. It is assumed that staff bring to multi-agency work particular specialist skills, expertise and experience. Moreover, multi-agency staff bring a particular outlook or approach derived from their professional background. Through close relationships with colleagues from other agencies, multi-agency staff contribute to the development of a shared and mutually acceptable approach. However, experiences in the youth justice system indicate that multi-agency work in fact puts at issue both these elements of professional identity, and the nature of professional identity itself.

The following pages explore the challenges to practitioners' sense of occupational belonging posed by three features of multi-agency work: the nature of professional expertise in multi-agency practice; power relations between participating agencies; and conflicts in professional cultures.

Researching professional identity

In exploring these issues, this chapter draws on a detailed study of the development of a YOT in a Midlands town (Souhami, 2007). Questions of culture and identity are grounded in the lived experience of practitioners, emerging in interactions, actions and behaviours and the way these are understood, acted on and managed in practitioners' working lives (for example, Geertz, 1973; Schein, 1985; Schwartzman, 1993). In researching notions of professional identity, therefore, issues must be understood in the context in which they emerge. The research reported here therefore takes an ethnographic, case study approach. It draws on an intensive, 14-month period of observational fieldwork following the transition of one social services youth justice team into a multi-agency organisation, as practitioners attempted to develop new multi-agency roles and practice. At this time, important questions were raised about the nature and purpose of multi-agency work and its complexities and effects were brought into focus.

Professional expertise and professional identity

The rationale for multi-agency work assumes that drawing together staff from different professional backgrounds will inevitably result in the pooling of diverse professional skills and experience. However, experiences in the Midlands YOT suggest that this is in fact a highly complex and problematic process and one which puts at issue the nature of professional expertise.

Importing professional expertise

Staff joining a multi-agency team may find that their professional skills and experience are not always easily transposed to a multi-agency environment. Even when the transfer of specialist skills seems straightforward, the new context may demand critical changes in individual approaches to work. For example, guidance for the development of the roles of YOT members suggested that the responsibilities of probation officers should be very similar to their accustomed role, supervising community sentences, assessing and managing the risk of re-offending and providing support services for young people on bail (Home Office et al., 1998: para 83). However, probation staff in the Midlands YOT explained that while their new tasks appeared similar to their regular work with adult offenders, they found young people to be 'totally different clients' who required a fundamental change in the focus and scope of professional practice. As one probation officer explained, "probation is getting more and more to do with enforcement, specifically looking at offending behaviour and ways of changing that", yet working with children involves a different understanding of offending behaviour, which prioritises a wider range of issues in young people's lives. As he explained, "They [YOT workers] focus on other things. Offending behaviour is possibly not even on the list". How, then, could his professional expertise be applied in the multi-agency context?

Consequently, staff joining a multi-agency team may be confronted with the realisation that, as Gilling puts it, 'agencies effectively speak different languages: they have different cognitive frameworks, different assumptive worlds, and different discourses' (1994: 250). This can have a profound impact on practitioners' ability to put their skills into practice. As the probation officer put it, "I've come from a setting where it's very clear what your role is and what you should be doing ... but [here] I haven't got a clue".

Developing new expertise

In addition, multi-agency staff are likely to be required to take on new tasks and ways of thinking that blur professional boundaries and distance them from their established sense of professional expertise.

As staff are brought together to address shared problems and objectives, they are required to some extent to put aside their usual roles and to engage in shared ways of working and thinking (Crawford, 1997). In the case of YOTs, the development of 'generic' work is seen as a central strand of youth justice practice. According to official guidance, practitioners should 'expect to work flexibly'; 'in principle', any team member can undertake any function in the team (Home Office et al., 1998: para 80). Thus, in the Midlands YOT, multi-agency staff took responsibility for work that had been a core part of the former social work team, such as supervising offenders, writing pre-sentence reports (PSRs), attending court and taking part in assessments and reviews of young people's progress.

The chance to transcend usual agency roles can be an important attraction of multi-agency work. For example, an education officer said: "I was used to my old job, just thinking I was brilliant at it. It's good to take yourself out of that environment, it's better for me, definitely better for my development". The opportunity to become involved in shared tasks also appeared to be crucial for practitioners' feelings of inclusion within the team. For example, staff were initially unsure about how to involve police officers in the generic work of the Midlands YOT. As officers are prevented by law from acting as appropriate adults, was it appropriate for them to supervise casework or write court reports? Consequently, police staff described feeling marginalised, "snubbed" and "fobbed off".

Generalist or specialist expertise?

While it may be an important part of multi-agency practice, development of shared working practices raises a number of challenges for practitioners. First, it questions the nature of professional expertise in multi-agency practice. Are staff to be seen as specialists, bringing particular professional skills to the work of the team? Or are they generalists whose contribution is 'merged' into the practice of the partnership, with its common responsibilities?

The appropriate balance of specialist and generic aspects of practitioners' roles is a central (and much debated) question (see, for example, Holdaway et al., 2001; Burnett and Appleton, 2004; Burnett, 2005). Indeed, it has been argued that one advantage of multi-agency practice is that its inherent flexibility allows this balance to be determined according to individual skills and local needs (for example, Home Office et al., 1998). However, the pressures of multi-agency work may mean that an appropriate balance is difficult to determine or maintain. In particular, where teams experience high workloads, specialist staff can feel under pressure to take on tasks outside their areas of expertise (Youth Justice Board, 2004b). In the Midlands YOT, for example, education and health staff felt that they were being asked to spend less time on specialist interventions and more on generic 'social work' tasks such as casework or writing PSRs. This can have a powerful impact on job satisfaction. As the health officer put it, "it detracts from what I'm here for, doesn't it? If I'd wanted to be a social worker on the YOT, I would have trained as one, wouldn't I?"

Expertise or inexperience?

The development of generic practice calls into question the degree of expertise staff may be said to possess. For example, while specialist staff in a YOT may have extensive experience in their home agencies, it may not be obvious that they are equipped to be a case worker or write PSRs. In other words, given the shifts in focus and practice in a multi-agency context, how do professional experience and professional qualifications apply? For example, the emphasis on generic work in the Midlands YOT led staff from partner agencies to feel inexperienced and unprepared to undertake the work now required of them. An education officer said: "I've done no risk work, I've done no offence analysis work, but suddenly I'm looking at offence analysis and risk assessment. I don't think I should be doing that at all". As she explained, this made for an unhappy working life: "I feel totally out of my depth, and unsupported on a few of my cases, who've got real, social work needs ... I'm just sort of trying my best". Moreover, her lack of experience had serious implications for service users: "I've just done a PSR on my own ... I don't think it's right that I should be doing it ... it's a very grave thing ... it's somebody's justice, it's somebody's liberty".

Expertise and identity

The development of multi-agency practice may therefore have a profound impact on practitioners' sense of professional expertise. Moreover, it may lead staff to feel their skills are being eroded, and with them, their sense of professional identity. In the Midlands YOT, practitioners felt their professional expertise and experience had been made redundant and described feeling devalued and undermined. As the health officer put it, "I feel like the new girl ... if a session went badly you can feel like a piece of s★★★, is it me?" Moreover, by replacing their specialist input with what were seen as core social work tasks, practitioners felt they were becoming assimilated into another profession: as the health officer put it, they were "becoming social workers".

In this way, experiences in the Midlands YOT suggest that the regular use of professional skills and expertise is closely connected with a deep sense of professional identity. Simply laying claim to their profession's body of knowledge and skills – or the profession's 'functional territory' (Huntington, 1981) – is not enough to ensure practitioners' sense of occupational belonging. Instead, practitioners need to be able to put these into practice. Furthermore, by taking on tasks that are seen to 'belong' to another agency, practitioners may feel they are not only losing their professional identity but replacing it with that of a different profession. This can be a cause of acute resentment. As the education officer in the Midlands YOT explained, "I didn't want to be a social worker. Do you know what I mean? I could have gone and done the DipSW [social work qualification, Diploma in Social Work] just as easily as everybody else.... I didn't want to do it".

Power and professional identity

Experiences in the Midlands YOT reveal further insights into the dynamics of professional identity in multi-agency work; namely, that questions of expertise and identity are inextricable from power relations between participating agencies.

Power relations between agencies are often seen as a central issue in multi-agency work (for example, Sampson *et al.*, 1988; Pearson *et al.*, 1992; Crawford, 1994, 1997; Gilling, 1994; Crawford and Jones, 1995). Intrinsic, structural differences between agencies, such as their access to resources and status, result in important power differentials which can have a profound impact on the shape of multi-agency practice and the identities of those involved.

Defining professional expertise

One of the most important manifestations of power relations in multi-agency work is the extent to which agencies are able to influence the aims and activities of the partnership. The more powerful agencies set the agenda, dominate decision making and may even pull out of partnerships to suit their own interests (see, for example, Sampson *et al.*, 1991; Pearson *et al.*, 1992; Crawford and Jones, 1995). More particularly, power relations are manifested by agencies' relative power to define what a partnership does: its objectives, the nature of the problems to be addressed, or the courses of action considered legitimate (Crawford and Jones, 1995). As there is considerable elasticity in the definition of the aims and scope of multi-agency practice, there is significant scope for the exercise of power. Given the traditional dominance of the police service, for example, multi-agency work has been described as a 'police takeover', whereby the police co-opt other agencies into pursuing police goals (Sampson *et al.*, 1988). However, power differentials between agencies can fluctuate according to context. In the early stages of the development of YOTs, youth justice was dominated by social work, despite the low status traditionally held by that profession (see, for example, Thomas, 1986).

The experiences of staff in the Midlands YOT illustrate how questions of professional identity are connected to the individual agencies' power to define. Many of the challenges outlined above arose from the difficulty of using specialist skills in the multi-agency context, and the adoption of core 'social work' duties as shared, generic practice. In other words, multi-agency practitioners' contributions were understood solely in terms of how they support social casework, whether by staff supplying specialist support or becoming caseworkers themselves. However, this was not the only available definition of multi-agency roles. The official guidance (Home Office *et al.*, 1998) explicitly encourages a rather different conception of multi-agency roles. For example, it states that specialist input should be defined according to the talents of individual staff, and roles developed 'in the light of [practitioners'] personal skills and experience, not solely because of their professional background' (Home Office *et al.*, 1998: para 80). Thus, while the education officer expected that part of her work would involve assisting social workers, she had also anticipated providing different kinds of educational support: "there's a desperate need for prevention in schools across the city, and that's what I want to be doing … I thought that I'd be doing group work within schools … perhaps piloting a preventative project". This kind of preventative work would have supported the emphasis on early intervention following the 1998 Crime and Disorder Act, thereby forming an important part of the team's work. Moreover, it would have enabled the education officer to use her specialist skills in a way suited to the context, so helping maintain her sense of professional expertise and identity. However, the underlying power relationships in the team – and in particular the dominance of social workers' perspectives – excluded any other conception of multi-agency roles. As one social worker acknowledged, "I'm quite aware I'm talking from my perspective all the time, you see, about how they can help me do my job, not the other way round".

Professional cultures and professional identity

A further challenge to practitioners' sense of identity derives from a broader sense of occupational belonging. Multi-agency practice is based on the assumption that staff bring not only the skills of their home agencies but a professional culture as well. Agencies are assumed to have different aims, values and approaches. By drawing staff from diverse agencies into the same structures, multi-agency work is expected to create consistency in the aims and principles of practice. However, rather than straightforwardly bringing about a shared approach to practice, it is often argued that this element of professional identity instead creates capacity for conflict (for example, Sampson *et al.*, 1988; Pearson *et al.*, 1992; Crawford, 1994, 1997; Gilling, 1994; Crawford and Jones, 1995). Indeed, such conflict may be inevitable in multi-agency work: given their different traditions, cultures and working assumptions, staff are likely to have different conceptions of problems and appropriate solutions (Gilling, 1994; Crawford and Jones, 1995).

In particular, conflict is often anticipated between social workers and police staff who are considered to represent opposing interests within the criminal justice process, namely the traditional 'justice' approach of the criminal justice agencies, and the 'welfare' objectives of health and education authorities (see, for example, Thomas, 1986; Crawford,

1997). Indeed, the formation of multi-agency YOTs was meant to resolve this problematic relationship (Labour Party, 1997). Social workers in the Midlands YOT certainly thought the two agencies were incompatible. In contrast to the 'welfarist' approach of social work, the police were seen to have a punitive 'cop culture' geared towards 'criminalising', 'nicking' or 'setting up' young people. As one social worker said, "the police have always seen social workers as [being] in league with the service user. Social workers have always seen the police as bastards who are locking them up".

Such tensions may undermine multi-agency relationships. Given that practitioners from different agencies have "other agendas, different ways of thinking, different rules, different values" (as one social worker put it), how are effective working relationships to develop? In other words, through their conflicting cultures, the professional identities of multi-agency staff are seen to threaten the success of partnership work.

The experience of such conflict may be keenly felt by staff. But the conflict of agency cultures in fact conceals other, more complex questions about individual practitioners, their professional identity and the nature of their professional 'belonging'.

Unrepresentative representatives?

Multi-agency work reveals the complexity of practitioners' relationships with their parent agencies. As multi-agency work separates staff from their home agencies, it is more likely to appeal to those who feel some sense of detachment from their work and colleagues, particularly when the work of the multi-agency team is felt to conflict with important aspects of the organisational life of parent agencies.

For example, in the context of 'old-fashioned machismo' (Reiner, 2000: 97) in the police service, interagency work is often regarded pejoratively as 'pink and fluffy', or as 'social work' (Crawford and Jones, 1995; Foster *et al.*, 2005). Moreover, joining a YOT involves taking on work that was formerly 'owned' by social workers, work traditionally regarded as welfarist in approach and differently gendered. For these reasons, police staff who take up YOT positions are particularly likely to feel some sense of disconnection with the police service. Similarly, in the Midlands YOT, the two (male) police staff said they felt uncomfortable and out of place in the police service and that this was integral to their move to the YOT. One explained, "I have nothing in common with young policemen. They're different animals … I don't get on well with police officers generally".

Consequently, it is a paradox of multi-agency work that collaborating staff are likely to be unrepresentative of their parent agencies (Sampson *et al.*, 1988; Crawford and Jones, 1995). As Crawford and Jones (1995) argue, in practice this can boost relationships within the partnership: where conflict is anticipated, relations may be smoothed by staff who appear somehow atypical of their respective agencies. As a social worker on the Midlands YOT said, "we're very lucky with the police officer we've got. He's thoughtful, more intelligent than most". However, by bringing into focus the ways in which staff are distanced from their home agency, multi-agency work puts at issue practitioners' sense of occupational belonging.

Professional cultures or professional confusion?

In addition, the development of multi-agency practice prompts us to question whether agencies truly have distinct occupational approaches. Multi-agency practitioners are required to put aside accustomed ways of working and explicitly engage with fundamental questions about the aims and scope of their work. In so doing, it can reveal not only conflicts in agency approaches, but the similarities and confusion within and between them as well.

For example, the first new, multi-agency programme developed in the Midlands YOT was the establishment of group work with young offenders. In setting up the groups, staff had to consider whether attendance should be compulsory, and, if so, whether young people should be returned to court ('breached') if they did not come. Underlying these apparently procedural issues were core questions about the values and purpose of work with young people. Were young people responsible for their offending? Should the team punish young people, or try to help them? And what did this mean? Consequently, practitioners found themselves debating the fundamental purpose and values of work with young offenders. But, as a result, it became clear that no agency had a clear position on these issues. Instead, there was wide disagreement and confusion among staff from all agencies. As the education officer said, "we all disagreed on what we should do.... There's a lot of different philosophies out there about what the team is, punitive approaches, and welfare approaches". Moreover, the confusion in practitioners' own views became apparent, as the education officer described: "I mean I'm very welfare based ... I *thought* I was very welfare ... but I think they have to comply. I know that if it was one of my young people on the group and I had to breach them I would hate it, but I think we have to do it".

Towards a common approach?

The development of multi-agency practice therefore presents a number of complex challenges to practitioners' sense of professional identity. By moving beyond the established practices and boundaries of participating agencies, multi-agency work puts at issue what it means to be a member of a given profession. Staff may find themselves becoming distanced from the skills and expertise claimed by their occupation. In addition, it is no longer possible to see practitioners as straightforward representatives of a distinct occupational ethos and approach. Instead, multi-agency work may expose ambiguities in practitioners' relationships with their parent agencies and confusion over the aims and values of work with young people. Of course, these complexities were always present in the work of the various former youth justice agencies. However multi-agency practice brings them to the surface. But for practitioners, the experience can be deeply unsettling. In the Midlands YOT, staff felt that the multi-agency team had 'disintegrated' and that the members were 'in chaos'.

This calls into question the central assumption of multi-agency practice, namely that drawing together staff from diverse agencies will straightforwardly result in a pooling of skills, expertise and approaches, and therefore bring about a 'common approach' to practice (Home Office, 1997). Experiences in the youth justice system suggest that the process is more complex. Rather than easily consolidating diverse approaches, multi-agency work instead exposes their underlying uncertainties. However, while experiencing such uncertainties can be uncomfortable, acknowledging them can be a crucial basis on which to build a shared, multi-agency approach. The central challenge for multi-agency teams, therefore, is to tackle these issues in a constructive and open manner which allows the conflicts and uncertainties within and between agencies to be recognised and addressed (for example, Sampson *et al.*, 1988; Crawford, 1994).

Finally, this raises a further question about the development of multi-agency work: to what extent is the development of a 'common approach' to practice desirable? Experiences in the youth justice system indicate that it is crucial for practitioners to maintain a sense of their distinct professional identities in order to feel integral parts of a multi-agency organisation. Moreover, the benefits of multi-agency practice derive from the diversity of multi-agency teams. The mix of professional skills, approaches and backgrounds is the key to the emergence of a coherent, holistic and creative approach to practice, and to overcoming traditional barriers to interagency cooperation.

In other words, and paradoxically, it appears that a central aspect of a shared, multi-agency approach to practice is the acceptance and incorporation of difference.

References

Audit Commission (1996) *Misspent Youth*, London: Audit Commission.

Burnett, R. (2005) 'Youth Offending Teams', in T. Bateman and J. Pitts (eds) *The RHP Companion to Youth Justice*, Lyme Regis: Russell House Publishing, pp 106–112.

Burnett, R. and Appleton, C. (2004) 'Joined up services to tackle youth crime: a case-study in England', *British Journal of Criminology*, vol 44, no 1, pp 34-55.

Crawford, A. (1994) 'The partnership approach: corporatism at the local level?', *Social and Legal Studies*, vol 3, no 4, pp 497-519.

Crawford, A. (1997) *The Local Governance of Crime: Appeals to Community and Partnerships*, Oxford: Clarendon Press.

Crawford, A and Jones, M. (1995) 'Inter-agency co-operation and community-based crime prevention: some reflections on the work of Pearson and colleagues', *British Journal of Criminology*, vol 35, no 1, pp 17-33.

Farrington, D. and West, D. (1990) 'The Cambridge study in delinquent development', in H.J. Kerner and G. Kaiser (eds) *Criminality: Personality, Behaviour and Life History*, Berlin: Springer-Verlag, pp 115-38.

Feeley, M. and Simon, J. (1992) 'The new penology', *Criminology*, vol 30, no 4, pp 452-74.

Foster, J.A., Newburn, T. and Souhami, A. (2005) *Assessing the Impact of the Stephen Lawrence Inquiry*, Home Office Research Study 294, London: Home Office.

Geertz, C. (1973) *The Interpretation of Cultures: Selected Essays*, New York, NY: Basic Books.

Gilling, D.J. (1994) 'Multi-agency crime prevention: some barriers to collaboration', *Howard Journal*, vol 33, no 3, pp 246-57.

Goldson, B. (2000) 'Whither diversion? Interventionism and the new youth justice', in B. Goldson (ed) *The New Youth Justice*, Lyme Regis: Russell House Publishing, pp 35-57.

Graham, J. and Bowling, B. (1995) *Young People and Crime*, Home Office Research Study 145, London: Home Office.

Holdaway, S., Davidson, N., Dignan, J., Hammersley, R., Hine, J. and Marsh, P. (2001) *New Strategies to Address Youth Offending: The National Evaluation of the Pilot Youth Offending Teams*, Home Office Research Study 69, London: Home Office.

Home Office (1997) *No More Excuses: A New Approach to Tackling Youth Crime in England and Wales*, London: The Stationery Office.

Home Office, Department of Health, Welsh Office and Department for Education and Employment (1998) *Establishing Youth Offending Teams*, London: The Stationery Office.

Hood, C. (1991) 'A public management for all seasons?', *Public Administration*, vol 69, no 1, pp 3-19.

Huntington, J (1981) *Social Work and General Medical Practice: Collaboration or Conflict?*, London: Allen and Unwin.

Labour Party (1997) *Tackling Youth Crime: Reforming Youth Justice: A Consultation Paper on An Agenda for Change*, London: Labour Party.

Martinson, R. (1974) 'What works? Questions and answers about prison reform', *The Public Interest*, vol 35, pp 22-54.

Muncie, J. (2009) *Youth and Crime* (3rd edn), London: Sage Publications.

Nacro (National Association for the Care and Resettlement of Offenders) (1987) *Time for Change: A New Framework for Dealing with Juvenile Crime and Offenders*, London: Nacro.

Northampton Juvenile Liaison Bureau (1985) *First Annual Report*, Northampton.

Pearson, G., Blagg, H., Smith, D., Sampson, A. and Stubbs, P. (1992) 'Crime, community and conflict: the multi-agency approach', in D. Downes (ed) *Unravelling Criminal Justice*, London: Macmillan, pp 46-72.

Pitts, J. (2000) 'The new youth justice and the politics of electoral anxiety', in B. Goldson (ed) *The New Youth Justice*, Lyme Regis: Russell House Publishing, pp 1-13.

Pratt, J. (1989) 'Corporatism: the third model of juvenile justice', *British Journal of Criminology*, vol 29, no 3, pp 236-54.

Reiner, R. (2000) *The Politics of the Police* (3rd edn), Oxford: Oxford University Press.

Sampson, A., Smith, D., Pearson, G., Blagg, H. and Stubbs, P. (1991) 'Gender issues in inter-agency relations: police, probation and social services', in P. Abbot and C. Wallace (eds) *Gender, Power and Sexuality*, Basingstoke: Macmillan, pp 114-32.

Sampson, A., Stubbs, D., Smith, D., Pearson, G. and Blagg, H. (1988) 'Crime, localities and the multi-agency approach', *British Journal of Criminology*, vol 28, no 4, pp 473-93.

Schein, E.H. (1985) *Organizational Culture and Leadership*, San Francisco, CA: Jossey-Bass.

Schwartzman, H.B. (1993) *Ethnography in Organizations*, London: Sage Publications.

Souhami, A. (2007) *Transforming Youth Justice: Occupational Identity and Cultural Change*, Cullompton: Willan.

Thomas, T. (1986) *The Police and Social Workers*, Aldershot: Gower.

Youth Justice Board (2004a) *Sustaining the Success: Extending the Guidance, Establishing Youth Offending Teams*, London: Youth Justice Board.

Youth Justice Board (2004b) *The Provision Of Health, Education and Substance Misuse Workers in Youth Offending Teams and the Health / Education Needs of Young People Supervised by Youth Offending Teams*, London: Youth Justice Board.

Ten

Childcare social work: perspectives on the professional

Andy Rixon

Introduction

There is a substantial sociology of professionalism analysing how and why certain occupational groups have professionalised. One common conception is that of the 'professional project' (Larson, 1977) in which such occupation groups gradually come to define and lay claim to areas of expertise, developing regulatory and educational structures to support it. Since 2005 the term 'social worker' has been a protected title (2000 Care Standards Act, 2001 Regulation of Care Scotland Act), joining the ranks of those such as 'nurse' and 'occupational therapist' which had already been protected for several years. The same legislation also established regulatory bodies and a registration process with accompanying codes of practice. Combined with the introduction of the degree-level qualification for social work in 2003, and proposals such as the creation of a Royal College of Social Work (DCSF, 2009), these trends could be interpreted as reinforcing the distinct, and more professionalised, status of social work. They place it more on a par with other professional groups such as teachers, while practitioners in other fields including early years and youth work have been undergoing similar debates about their relationship to professionalisation (Osgood, 2006; Bradford, 2007). This chapter starts by discussing the context of professionalisation in social work and some of the forces acting on its construction, specifically in relation to social work with children and families.

The introduction of the degree and other post-qualifying awards and qualifications are arguably particularly significant, as education and training are always central to discussions of both professionalism and a profession's claim to knowledge and expertise. This chapter goes on to discuss in more detail how some of these issues of professionalism and knowledge are played out within the framework of continuing professional development. This exploration draws on a series of interviews conducted with social workers who were undertaking an example of this further professional development – a post-qualifying award in childcare – and who were asked to reflect on the impact of undertaking this award on their practice. Their responses give some insight into the range of social workers' perceptions of both professionalism, particularly in the multi-agency context, and of the tensions between forms of knowledge and the role of experience in professional practice.

A professional project under pressure

If the professional project is a useful framework within which to consider the development of the social work 'profession', then the project has been far from smooth. Social work has shared a similar pathway with other occupational groups that have been seen at some point as 'semi-professional', but has also been subject to influences peculiar to its history and place in society.

Of course the very meaning of being a professional is contested, including within social work itself, and in reality its boundaries are increasingly blurred, as all workers in the childcare workforce are expected to act with 'professionalism', even though in policy terms demarcations are still frequently made between qualifications that are professional rather than vocational (DfES/DH, 2006).

If some of the developments noted in the introduction are attributes of aspiring professionalisation, these changes have not necessarily been 'successful'. Many commentators have observed the opposite – that they fit into a long-standing trend towards deprofessionalisation, with an increased emphasis on management, regulation, targets and the resultant bureaucratisation and proceduralisation. Arguably it is then possible to more easily portray social work as requiring 'technical' knowledge, rather than the 'professional' expertise and creativity needed in the 'indeterminacy' of complex situations (Eadie and Lymbery, 2007). These pressures can also be seen as impinging on areas that social work had always seen as central to its identity, such as the skills (and time and space) required for forming relationships with children and families. However, the emphasis on relationships and the importance of communication complicates the argument over professionalism. Lymbery suggests that social work has remained in a double bind between claiming 'a particular monopoly of skill' while wanting to present itself to service users 'in terms which could be readily understood' (Lymbery, 2004: 52).

Social work also maintains an uneasy and uncertain place in society, operating as it does in highly emotive and contentious areas such as the abuse of children. Crucial to the public perception of this 'place' has been the role of the media. Periodically various areas of social work receive the media spotlight, but none are quite so exposed as those working specifically in safeguarding and child protection. A series of high-profile public inquiries over several decades have reinforced negative perceptions of the profession. The case of Baby Peter for example (a 17-month-old child, whose death was caused or allowed by his mother, her boyfriend and a lodger, despite being on the child protection register) revealed clear failings but also demonstrated that photographs of individual social workers appearing on the front page of tabloid newspapers under headlines demanding their sacking is not an apocryphal story (*The Sun*, 2008). Lymbery argues that rather than the advent of the degree, the creation of social services departments after the Seebohm Report in 1971 marks the peak of social work's professional project as the last point at which it had a 'clear agreed and recognised role' in society (Lymbery, 2004: 51).

Even within the profession itself there has been a history of uncertainty: the Barclay report investigating social work 'roles and tasks' concluded with three different reports as the committee were unable to agree (NISW, 1982). In England the report of the Social Work Task Force (DCSF, 2009) still saw the need to clarify the role of social workers, including, as will be discussed later, their training and skills requirements. Some traditions within social work itself have seen professionalisation and the role that social workers should be playing in society as incompatible. For them traditional professionalism, its codes of conduct and illusions of specialised knowledge, would distance social workers from the families they work with and the true cause of their problems – social inequality:

> Professionalism is a particularly dangerous development specifically because social workers look to it for an answer to many of the problems and contradictions of the job itself i.e. being unable to solve the basic inadequacy of society through social work. It must be fought at every opportunity. (Bailey and Brake, 1975: 145-6)

Overtly radical voices have become much less evident and the government has also ensured that the 'official requirements' of a professional qualification in social work have gradually reduced the commitment to ideas of social justice and anti-discriminatory practice (Dominelli, 2002). Social work should be 'free of unnecessary ideological influences' (DH, 1998: para 5.15.)

Childcare social work has become perceived by many as being in a demoralised state, even crisis, with high rates of vacancies, turnover and levels of dissatisfaction (ADSS, 2005; DCSF, 2009). A Scottish review of social work found 'a social work profession lacking in confidence in its own skills and unclear about its distinctive contribution' (Scottish Executive, 2006: 14).

Some local authorities have even found it necessary to promote the 'reclaiming' of the social work profession in relation to work with children and families, summarised by Lord Laming as:

> Observing that social work as a profession has lost its way, lacks confidence, expertise and gravitas, is over bureaucratised and risk averse they suggest that whilst assessment should remain central to planning and decision making, more time should be spent on direct intervention with families to effect positive change. In order to achieve this, they state that clear professional accountability, clinical support and high calibre practitioners are fundamental. (Laming, 2009: 48)

Despite or perhaps because of these pressures there have been calls for social work to search for a new and different form of professionalism, one which tries to build on different forms of relationships with service users – a 'new professionalism' (Edwards, 2004) or a 'progressive and democratic professionalism' (Davis and Garrett, 2004), and one which can recreate itself for the postmodern world (Fook, 2004).

The cognitive dimension

A key element in the claim to professional status is the 'cognitive dimension' (Larson, 1977: x), the body of knowledge, expertise and skills necessary for that area of work and the training required to master it. Consequently, references to training, education and qualifications are usually central to discussions of professionalism within any group of practitioners. Project 2000, for example, saw a shift to university-based education for nursing and an increasing emphasis on degree-level qualifications, arguably reinforcing nursing's own professional project (McDonald et al., 2006); the path to graduate-only entry has already been signalled. The introduction of the degree for social workers was to 'transform the status, image and position of social workers' through putting their training 'on a level with other professions' (DH, 2002a: 1). Training for social work, and with it some of the first moves towards professionalisation, is not a modern phenomenon but can be seen as early as 1900 with the first courses established at universities (Lymbery, 2004). Over a century later one response to the death of Baby Peter was a recommendation that all childcare social workers undertake a postgraduate qualification with some urgency (Laming, 2009).

For social workers the nature of qualifications reflects some elements of the contradictory trends of professionalisation discussed above. Although potentially strengthening professional status, the formal requirements laid down restrict the scope of what counts as social work. These requirements also assume that competence in social work, including complex interpersonal professional activity, can be described by measurable competency outcome-based statements – an assumption questioned by many (Cooper, 2009). The nature of what social workers need to know varies according to how the role is perceived. The balance between the 'practical' and the 'theoretical', for example, has also been a constant tension, with the government occasionally finding it necessary to spell out the balance between the two:

> Social work is a very practical job. It is about protecting
> people and changing their lives, not about giving
> fluent and theoretical explanations about why they
> got into difficulties in the first place. (DH, 2002b)

There has been a growing expectation that social workers will continue their professional development and acquisition of qualifications beyond their diploma or degree. Post-qualifying routes have long been in place across the UK and, even if the achievement rates have been slow (GSCC, 2005) and their shape and structure subject to continual change, the principle of an even more highly qualified workforce is well established. Specific knowledge, values and practice requirements were identified for childcare social workers in the creation of the first childcare-specific awards. The General Social Care Council (GSCC) has claimed that these awards 'make a significant contribution to the professional development of workers in their specialist fields' (GSCC, 2006: 24). In fact, evidence for their impact is limited, although there is some indication that they can contribute to enhancing social workers' practice and confidence in their professional role (Brown *et al.*, 2008). At the same time Galpin proposes that post-qualifying awards have become 'explicitly linked to the modernisation agenda, standards and inspection drives' and focus on enabling practitioners to meet the demands of 'statutory duties, performance assessment and regulation' (Galpin, 2009: 73).

In exploring this dimension of knowledge and expertise, the following sections will draw on interviews with childcare social workers in a range of roles who were undertaking a post-qualifying childcare award (PQCCA) in an English local authority. They were interviewed before and after the programme as part of a qualitative evaluation study conducted between 2005 and 2007. The questions related to the impact on practice of undertaking this award; the answers illuminated some of the continuing tensions and debates within the concept of professionalism in social work.

The interprofessional experience

The increasingly interprofessional working environment is evident in all areas of social work with children, young people and their families. The demand for professionals to work more closely together is long-standing, especially in the area of child protection where numerous inquiries over several decades have called for improvements in communication between the range of different agencies involved. Integrated teams have long been familiar to social workers in hospital teams and Youth Offending Teams (YOTs) but an even greater impetus towards integration was given by policy developments such as that in community schooling.

> New Community Schools will bring together in a single team professionals from a range of services. Improved coordination of existing services is not enough to achieve the fundamental improvement in children's lives which the Government is seeking. Integration of services is essential, and the school is an excellent site for this to become a reality. This will require radically new approaches (Scottish Office, 1998: 1).

Replication of this theme across services for children has led to a corresponding call for 'workforce reform at all levels of the system, including embedding a culture of integrated working' (DCSF, 2007: 152).

Such integrated working has increasingly brought challenges as the different perspectives, cultures and knowledge bases of practitioners are brought into close proximity mixed with the associated issue of professional status. The challenges of this are not unique to social work; it is an interesting time of conflict and compromise for everyone in this area of practice.

One aspect of this issue of working with other professionals proved, in the evaluation study, to be a significant feature of the responses of the childcare social workers in their first and second interviews. One social worker in particular believed that, relative to other professionals they engaged with, social work still had an essentially semi-professional status and that this was a problem in terms of the relative 'weight' of their views in multiprofessional decision-making forums:

> "Social workers describe themselves as professionals
> but I never have done – if I go to a professionals'
> meeting I think professionals and me."

> "I always feel a professional is someone who has
> a good amount of knowledge about research –
> whereas social workers by and large just wing it
> most of the time … reacting to this and that."
>
> (nine years qualified)

The idea that social workers might "wing it" most of the time would not be well received by the government or social work's regulatory bodies. However, they would support this social worker's stated priority of developing their research knowledge through the PQCCA. This social worker's second interview reflected higher levels of confidence and included an example of bringing a specific piece of research – 'the risk associated with the numbers of children born into a household' – into a multiprofessional discussion about the level of risk to a child. Although no other social worker expressed this view of social workers' relative lack of research knowledge quite so starkly, the idea that the teaching on the PQCCA had contributed to their confidence *in relation to other professionals* was mentioned repeatedly:

> "Because you're going away and researching
> theories and stuff that would make you a bit
> more confident – that makes you more confident
> in working with other professionals."

> Interviewer: "… any specific areas?"

"Yes, quite a few topics – child development, drugs …"

(two years qualified)

In fact 'increased confidence' was possibly the most frequently cited impact of the PQCCA, often in relation to work with families – for example, making decisions about risk – but equally to the interprofessional arena. This confidence was drawn from a number of sources including, as suggested above, a firmer grounding in theory, but the area most often referred to was feeling 'up to date' with research. As one social worker commented in relation to a risk assessment that was being conducted jointly with probation:

"I just felt more confident in what I was actually saying – I felt that I could back up what I was saying with research … research about risk, research on the risks associated between drugs and domestic violence." (three years qualified)

Research, with an emphasis on its potential to support 'evidence-based practice', was a significant feature of the PQCCA they were undertaking. This emphasis on evidence-based research and practice has been seen in other areas of the social professions as a potentially important element of relative professional status. Newman and Nutley (2003) identified a trajectory within the probation service which may well have parallels in social work. Their study showed many probation officers initially resistant to the introduction of evidence-based practice (known organisationally as 'what works'), seeing it as undermining of professional autonomy, yet gradually coming to see it as a source of expertise that could be laid claim to. Eventually, contrary to expectations most managers and some practitioners saw 'what works' as enhancing professional status:

Knowledge is no longer seen as a source of professional power over the client but as a source of professional legitimacy vis-à-vis other stakeholders in the criminal justice system. (Newman and Nutley, 2003: 560)

This is not to say that all probation officers in the study nor all childcare social workers in these interviews fully embraced this approach. The significance of this and the role played by evidence-based research and practice will be returned to in the next section.

The perception of a lack of professional security among childcare social workers is not universal; some of the social workers interviewed clearly felt that there were aspects of the work in which they had expertise and greater levels of confidence than fellow professionals. In more serious safeguarding work, for example, social workers were aware of the reluctance among some other practitioners to get involved and therefore would take the lead in initiating interagency working:

> "One thing I've started to do more of is bring other agencies in to help with that assessment ... it depends who it is and what their focus is, some agencies have their own thing and aren't always able to work jointly and put the child at the centre but it's something you need to ask or you don't get them on board. But some agencies are quite scared to get involved or do one-to-one work because they are worried about the impact that has on them.... (three years qualified)

However, confidence in this instance did not seem to be drawn from a claim to specific research knowledge, but rather from the day-to-day experience of working with complexity in difficult and emotive situations and the knowledge and expertise drawn from that.

Other experienced social workers shared this confident perspective on their day-to-day work with other professionals but still felt that the standing of the social work profession was exposed when they were in the court arena. Here other professionals' views still carried greater weight despite (from the social workers' point of view) their limited knowledge of the family concerned. Interestingly, while drawing on research evidence seemed to be enhancing social workers' perception of their knowledge base, this did not extend to the courts, where they were discouraged from using it:

> "I did a court report recently and we were told not to put theories and research in ... because when you're on the witness stand when you've looked at different bits of research and where you could say I know this because I've looked at such and such research they would counteract you and chuck a piece of research at you that says different." (three years qualified)

On a particular aspect of practice, interviews before and after their award also tended to reinforce the lack of space practitioners felt they had for relationship-based work, particularly direct work with children.

While the importance of this work was acknowledged, it frequently seemed to lose out in the time-pressured environment:

> "I don't really do any direct work with children. If
> I thought it was really necessary I would set aside
> some time but, nine times out of ten, something
> comes in on duty or something ... so it would be
> letting the child down." (three years qualified)

For one social worker the role itself – working directly with children – seemed to be no longer even necessarily central to the social work professional role but could be done by others in the professional network:

> "There is much less planned work [than in the
> past]. Where planned work seems to take place is
> more professionals such as a CAMHS [Child and
> Adolescent Mental Health Service] worker or so forth,
> so I might ask other people to do the work without
> actually doing it myself." (nine years qualified)

What you know and how you know it

Typically in the development of professions this 'cognitive dimension' has not been just any sort of knowledge but status has been given to the 'rationality of science and ... the rationality of scientifically oriented experts' (Larson, 1977: 137). What is unique about the knowledge and expertise of social work, ranging as it does across disciplines, has always been difficult to clearly establish and has led to unfavourable comparisons being drawn with other professional knowledge bases. The issue of what are the most appropriate sources of knowledge for social workers to draw on remains contested.

The attraction of drawing more explicitly on a scientific approach re-emerged strongly in the championing of 'evidence-based practice'. This approach is most commonly summarised using Sheldon *et al.*'s definition:

> Evidence–based social care is the conscientious,
> explicit and judicious use of current best evidence
> in making decisions regarding the welfare of
> those in need. (Sheldon *et al.*, 2005: 16)

In emphasising the need for social work to actively draw on current research knowledge it also promotes a hierarchy of research, from that using the most rigorous scientific methods downwards.

The adoption of evidence-based practice as central to modern social work was encouraged by the 'modernising agenda' of the New Labour governments from 1997 onwards, where concerns were raised about whether the social care workforce (and in particular 'professionally' qualified social workers) had the appropriate skills and knowledge to deliver quality services:

> As in other professions, it is important that professionally qualified social workers base their practice on the best evidence of what works for clients and are responsive to new ideas from research. (DH, 1998: section 5.32)

The new emphasis placed on research in social work was reinforced by the creation of bodies such as the Social Care Institute for Excellence (SCIE) to disseminate best practice of what is 'effective' in social care, and the advent of the Scottish Institute for Excellence in Social Work Education (SIESWE), with the goal of 'strengthening the evidence base for practice and education for practice'. Nevertheless the debate has continued about how narrowly or broadly the parameters of what counts as evidence can be drawn, the appropriateness of the approach for social work and the nature of knowledge itself (Smith, 2004). Where, for example, to place the 'expertise' that service users have about their own situation? Parton and O'Byrne (2000) argue that the role of the social worker is not to make an expert assessment and apply a 'scientific' solution but to construct solutions through dialogue with service users. Fook emphasises the degree to which social work practice is characterised by uncertainty and the complexity of contexts in which it operates, which calls into question 'the possibility and desirability of certain and unchangeable knowledge' (Fook, 2004: 34).

In addition, what value can be placed on the accumulated 'practice wisdom' or 'tacit knowledge' that some social workers may have built up from many years of experience? Practice wisdom is difficult to research and analyse; it can even be difficult to categorise, portrayed both as 'unreliable, personal, idiosyncratic knowledge' and enabling practitioners 'to make sound judgements in difficult, complex and uncertain situations' (O'Sullivan, 2005: 222). Smith suggests that a reflective practitioner uses research evidence 'but she also treats her experience as itself a source of evidence ...' (Smith, 2004: 13). A depth of experience interacting with practice to generate new knowledge may also be an important element of being a professional:

> ... professionals are constantly engaged with situations
> in such a way that they are not just modifying
> existing knowledge but are in fact creating new
> knowledge which is relevant to newly experienced
> and often changing situations. (Fook, 2004: 35)

As highlighted above, the interviews suggested that some social workers were very keen to utilise 'evidence-based' research, and that this could bolster their position as confident practitioners. The very experienced social workers who were interviewed also acknowledged the value of being exposed to new research but it was apparent that the process could equally be undermining. The idea that reflecting on and questioning your practice can be an unsettling one is not unusual and is rightly promoted within social work training and education. The question remained, however, of whether a value could also be placed on their knowledge and skills drawn from experience. Although not unique to the social workers who had been qualified for the longest, this uncertainty did seem to be a particular issue for them:

> "I think – one of my frustrations … is a bit of me
> felt that I have been in practice quite a long time and
> this kind of assessment – and doing this course is an
> assessment of me – I felt somehow it was a bit late in the
> day, if somehow I wasn't competent somebody should
> have worked that out by now." (24 years qualified)

> "It sounds a bit – but I already had the skills in a way
> and I'm not sure I gained an awful lot. Maybe I've been
> in the job too long, you know...." (22 years qualified)

It was noticeable that the social workers in the evaluation study portrayed length of experience as something that might be viewed negatively within the learning environment, as though they would be seen as being 'out of date' or 'long in the tooth' rather than having experience or expertise:

> "There was [an exercise] … those who have been in
> practice for three years over there, those who have been
> in practice seven years over there, those who have been

in practice for over 20 years – and there was about three
of us and you thought, 'Oh God'." (22 years qualified)

Another social worker questioned why the main measure of 'credit'
was always in terms of what they perceived to be more 'academic'
qualifications:

"I can see that being better qualified is good for the
credibility of social work as a profession but rather than
yet more academic qualifications why can't there be
credit for expertise in more practical skills maybe like
really skilled interviewing or counselling?" (16 years
qualified, did not complete post-qualifying programme)

While post-qualifying courses strive to achieve the integration of
theory, research and practice, succeeding in this integration remains
problematic. When asked what the impact of the post-qualifying
programme had been in terms of face-to-face skills in work with
families, the same long-standing difficulties of integration were
apparent, and again pertinent to professional identity:

"I don't get a strong sense that that is something that
is being promoted – *how you work with families* – it felt
to me to be about how to be professional in terms
of your role – you know, making comprehensive
assessments, evidence based, increasing your knowledge
base." (12 years qualified; emphasis added)

The connection between professionalisation and academic
qualifications perhaps touches on the question of who the social work
profession is aiming to attract. The requirement that related experience
was required before applying for a social work qualification was
dropped with the introduction of the new degree and such changes
have had an impact on the nature of the student intake. In England the
proportion of students aged between 18-25 rose from 18% in
2001-02 to 34% in 2005-06 and these students overall had a higher
level of qualification at the point of entry, while that of students
over 35 declined (Evaluation of Social Work Degree Qualification
in England Team, 2008). While this evaluation report argues that
this has resulted in an increase in the 'quality' of applicants, it agrees
that there remains a tension for the profession between striving for
higher academic qualifications and attracting a broad range of people

with non-traditional educational backgrounds. There is little research on how this affects post-qualifying education, although within this evaluation it appeared to slightly skew – whether positive or negative – the range of childcare workers coming forward to undertake a PQCCA towards younger and more academically confident practitioners.

This debate is not designed to polarise the positions of competence, evidence-based knowledge and experience or 'practice wisdom' but to highlight some tensions between them within social work education. Several writers have proposed frameworks in which differing models could be reconciled (Smith, 2004; Gould, 2006), or attempts might be made to 'break down the epistemological and pedagogical barriers separating knowledge construction and theory from actual professional practice' (Bickham, cited in Cooper, 2009: 147). And of course, in practice, various sources of knowledge and values do not in the end remain distinct but are subject to complex interactions (Scourfield and Pithouse, 2006).

Conclusion

Childcare social workers are subject to many forces acting on the status of their profession. What they 'should be doing' is still repeatedly under review, a debate reignited after each high profile instance of concern about children. The need for social workers to be autonomous professionals is frequently stressed while the possibilities of their role remains constrained. Equally the nature, level and content of social work qualifications in the UK and the competencies against which they are measured have grown and seem likely to continue to do so in the future.

What the interviews with social workers above suggest is that the nature of continuing professional development in social work directly affects social workers' perceptions of their profession and their professionalism. For some, confidence is drawn from a more certain knowledge base, particularly in relation to other professionals. For others, while striving for higher academic levels and appreciating the new theory and research to which they are exposed, the place of experience and accumulated knowledge, skills and values within their own definition of professionalism is uncertain.

Acknowledgement

Thanks to those social workers who participated in the evaluation.

References

ADASS (Association of Directors of Social Services (Cymru)) (2005) *Social Work in Wales: A Profession to Value*, 'The Garthwaite Report', Cardiff: ADASS.

Bailey, R. and Brake, M. (eds) (1975) *Radical Social Work*, London: Edward Arnold.

Bradford, S. (2007) 'The "good youth leader": constructions of professionalism in English youth work 1939-45', *Ethics and Social Welfare*, vol 1, no 3, pp 293-309.

Brown, K., McCloskey, C. and Galpin D. (2008) 'Evaluating the impact of post-qualifying social work', *Social Work Education*, vol 27, no 8, December, pp 853-67.

Cooper, B. (2009) *The Problem of Assessment in Social Work: Practice, Education and Continuing Professional Development*, Saarbrücken: VDM Verlag.

Davis, A. and Garrett, P.M. (2004) 'Progressive practice for tough times: social work, poverty, and division in the twenty-first century', in M. Lymbert and S. Butler, *Social Work Ideals and Practice Realities*, Basingstoke: Palgrave Macmillan, pp 13-33.

DCSF (Department for Children, Schools and Families) (2009) *Facing Up to the Task: Interim Report of the Social Work Task Force*, London: DCSF.

DCSF (2007) *The Children's Plan: Building Brighter Futures*, London: The Stationery Office.

DfES (Department for Education and Skills)/DH (Department of Health) (2006) *Options for Excellence: Building the Social Care Workforce of the Future*, London: The Stationery Office.

DH (Department of Health) (1998) *Modernising Social Services*, London: The Stationery Office.

DH (2002a) *Requirements for Social Work Training*, London: DH.

DH (2002b) 'New social work degree will focus on practical training', Press release, 22 May (www.dh.gov.uk/en/Publicationsandstatistics/Pressreleases/DH_4014188).

Dominelli, L. (2002) 'Anti-oppressive practice in context', in R. Adams, L. Dominelli and M. Payne (eds) *Social Work: Themes, Issues, and Critical Debates* (2nd edn), Basingstoke/Maidenhead: Palgrave/Open University Press, pp 3-19.

Eadie, T. and Lymbery, M. (2007) 'Promoting creative practice through social work education', *Social Work Education*, vol 26, no 7, October, pp 670-83.

Edwards, A. (2004) 'The new multi-agency working: collaborating to prevent the social exclusion of children and families', *Journal of Integrated Care*, vol 12, no 5, pp 3-9.

Evaluation of Social Work Degree Qualification in England Team (2008) *Evaluation of the New Social Work Degree Qualification in England. Volume 1: Findings,* London: King's College London, Social Care Workforce Research Unit.

Fook, J. (2004) 'What professionals need from research: beyond evidence based practice', in D. Smith (ed) *Social Work and Evidence-based Practice*, London: Jessica Kingsley Publishers, pp 29-48.

Galpin, D. (2009) 'Who really drives the development of post-qualifying social work education and what are the implications of this?', *Social Work Education*, vol 28, no 1, pp 65-80.

Gould, N. (2006) 'An inclusive approach to knowledge for mental health social work practice and policy', *British Journal of Social Work*, vol 36, pp 109-25.

GSCC (General Social Care Council) (2006) *Social Work Education in England: Listening, Learning, Shaping. The 2006 Social Work Education Quality Assurance Report*, London: GSCC.

Laming, Lord (2009) *The Protection of Children in England: A Progress Report*, London: The Stationery Office.

Larson, M. (1977) *The Rise of Professionalism*, Berkley, CA: University of California Press.

Lymbery, M. (2004) 'Responding to crisis: the changing nature of welfare organisations', in M. Lymbery and S. Butler, *Social Work Ideals and Practice Realities*, Basingstoke: Palgrave Macmillan, pp 34-56.

McDonald, R., Campbell, S. and Lester, H. (2006) 'Practice nurses and the effects of the new general practitioner contract in the English National Health Service: the extension of a professional project?', *Social Science & Medicine*, vol 68, no 2009, pp 1206-12.

Newman, J. and Nutley, S. (2003) 'Transforming the probation service: "what works" organisational change and professional identity', *Policy & Politics*, vol 31, no 4, pp 547-63.

NISW (National Institute for Social Work) (1982) *Social Workers: Their Role and Tasks*, London: Bedford Square Press.

Osgood, J. (2006) 'Rethinking "professionalism" in the early years: perspectives from the United Kingdom', *Contemporary Issues in Early Childhood*, vol 7, no 1, pp 1-4.

O'Sullivan, T. (2005) 'Some theoretical propositions on the nature of practice wisdom', *Journal of Social Work*, vol 5, no 2, pp 221-42.

Parton, N. and O'Byrne, P. (2000) *Constructive Social Work: Towards a New Practice*, Basingstoke: Palgrave.

Scottish Executive (2006) *Report of the 21st-century Social Work Review: Changing Lives*, Edinburgh: Scottish Executive.

Scottish Office (1998) *New Community Schools Prospectus*, Edinburgh (www.scotland.gov.uk/library/documents-w3/ncsp-02.htm).

Scourfield, J. and Pithouse A. (2006) 'Lay and professional knowledge in social work: reflections from ethnographic research on child protection', *European Journal of Social Work*, vol 9, no 3, pp 323–37.

Sheldon, B., Chilvers, R., Ellis, A., Moseley, A. and Tierney, S. (2005) 'A pre-post empirical study of obstacles to, and opportunities for, evidence-based practice in social care', in A. Bilson, *Evidence-based Practice in Social Work*, London: Whiting & Birch, pp 11–50.

Smith, D. (2004) 'Some versions of evidence-based practice', in D. Smith (ed) *Social Work and Evidence-based Practice*, London: Jessica Kingsley Publishers, pp 7–28.

Sun, The (2008) 'Failing Baby P staff must be sacked', 28 November.

Eleven

'To see a world in a grain of sand' or how supervision changed my working life

Mary Robson

This chapter attempts to illuminate my practice in arts in health and education with particular reference to professional supervision, reflection and leadership. While this appears a very particular niche, it has relevance to professionals and volunteers working with children and young people in a variety of settings, for example as teachers, sessional youth workers, children's service managers, social workers and children's centre workers.

Beginnings

I have always held a desire for shared experience, never wanting to be a singular artist. As a teenager, I was drawn to the theatre as a performer, until a teacher pointed out that I could combine my interests in literature, art, drama and history by training as a theatre designer. My ideal of the production of a play was one in which the roles of designer, actor, stage manager *et al.* were entirely interdependent, and yet comfortably set within a framework created by the director's vision. Theatre projects are usually intense experiences that last for a few weeks with teams that may be assembled for the purpose. Sometimes my ideal was realised, but I was confounded on occasions when I found myself in a dysfunctional working situation.

Subsequently, I have worked in community-based arts, variously in theatre, health and education, for over 25 years. My work is small scale, often celebratory and nearly always collaborative and communal; I can't do it on my own. My work now is in the field of arts in health and education. Having almost always worked as a freelancer, I have moved through being an employee, an artist/designer employed to contribute to a project, to being a director of projects, a facilitator of events and the chairperson of two organisations. As an autodidact,

I have learned through experience about various styles of working, about the nurturing of the next generation of workers in a field that is still emergent, and about leadership.

Freelance arts practitioners have long been offered help with their business needs and with professional development that is concerned with time management and how to prioritise what is urgent and/or important and suchlike. It is only within the last few years that reflection, professional supervision, mentoring and co-mentoring have become available. For example, in 2006, The Sage Gateshead was funded to conduct Reflect, a national programme in cross-sectoral co-mentoring between emerging leaders in creative and cultural organisations and schools. Previous strategic initiatives in education had been increasingly underpinned by different models of mentoring and coaching; a shift towards more collaborative practice was acknowledged as central to the delivery of the government's creativity agenda.

Supervision

From 2000 to 2004 I was the director of a programme called Common Knowledge, bringing together 250 health workers, artists, educators, local authority and voluntary sector personnel and community participants across the Tyne and Wear region. Individually and together, through Common Knowledge and subsequent pilot projects, the participants helped initiate new ways of working informed by practice that promoted health and well-being, and always involved the arts. Its long-term goal was to improve the health and well-being of all those involved in the initiative and to help reduce health inequalities. One of its key aims was to change the way that people work through their shared learning.

Common Knowledge helped to crystallise many of my views on healthy ways of working. In leading what was an innovative programme, I had of course to face criticism, for which I was ill prepared. One particular incident in 2000 left me dwelling unhealthily on what I perceived were my professional failings. I dwelt only on the negative aspects of the incident and found it increasingly affected my professional self-confidence. I realised I needed support that was different from that proffered by friends, family and colleagues. I needed to be able to articulate challenging issues for myself; I wanted to grow and learn professionally while contending with the nature of the work, and I wasn't looking for therapy.

Professional supervision was suggested by two colleagues, both adherents of its benefits. My only knowledge of it to date was as clinical supervision for counsellors and psychologists. Here was someone offering supervision to freelance arts professionals. I signed up and have been seeing a supervisor ever since. Within the first 18 months I noted an increase in self-confidence, I had changed some unhelpful thinking processes as a result of the sessions and had found and attended a training course with ICA:UK[1] on ways to bring about group consensus through purposeful and productive conversations.

I attend supervision for an hour-and-a-half every month. My supervisor is trained as a counsellor, psychotherapist and drama therapist. What follows is based on my experience with her and on the methods she employs, informed by the work of Carl Rogers (1961, 1983) and some concepts from Transactional Analysis. Such professional supervision is a positive and challenging experience. Based on a 'person-centred' approach, the core elements of the relationship between supervisor and practitioner/s are congruence (where words are in line with feelings), unconditional positive regard (that there is respect and liking for each other) and empathy (that the supervisor understands the essential feelings of the supervised).

In such a safe and congenial space, I am able to look closely at what I do and how I do it. I can explore problem solving and work through difficult practice-based issues; explore the interface between personal and professional; plan and develop professional practice; and recognise the emotional implications in the work.

Supervision has had a profound impact on my professional practice and actively contributes to my ability to lead effectively. My thinking processes have changed for the better. I no longer take things too personally and am a more confident decision maker. As a result, I am much more help to my colleagues.

Reflective practice

Supervision has encouraged me to continually reflect on my working practice and change has inevitably happened as a result. I began to seek out everyday opportunities for reflection as a life skill, not only for my own benefit, but also for colleagues and the children and young people with whom I work.

> By developing the ability to explore and be curious
> about our own experience and actions, we suddenly
> open up the experience of purposeful learning – derived
> not from books or experts but from our work and
> our lives. This is the purpose of reflection: to allow the

> possibility of learning through experience, whether that
> experience is a meeting, a project, a disaster, a success,
> a relationship, or any other internal or external event,
> before, during or after it has happened. (Amulya, 2004: 1)

One of my current roles is director of Roots and Wings, a project based in Chickenley Community Primary School for two days a week throughout the school year. Chickenley is a larger-than-average primary school with just over 300 pupils on the roll, on the outskirts of Dewsbury in West Yorkshire. The area served by the school is socially and economically disadvantaged and nearly half of the pupils are eligible for a free school meal. Eight years ago the school was in special measures, but by 2008 Ofsted inspectors agreed with the school's self-evaluation that 'it now provides a good and improving education for its pupils and has some outstanding features'. The staff of Roots and Wings work with pupils, their families and the wider community to foster social and emotional development and encourage cultural change through the arts and new traditions that mark significant moments in the life of the community.

Children reflect at the end of every Roots and Wings session. Using a structured conversation method, every child gets the opportunity to voice fact, feeling and opinion and to make decisions based on their experiences of the project that day.

> "This is good because I'm setting my own targets."

> "I just feel wonderful when I've got a piece of work in front of me and I'm like – whooaa I an't done that! I'm just shocked at how good it is. It feels like I've just hit the sun!"

> "I'm facing my temper. I think if I have this [his drawing] in class and I could look at it, it might help."

'Day-to-day books' are used to record all of the information: one of the project's artists always scribes while the children talk, and staff document their own reflective sessions. Some artists also maintain their own personal journals. Consequently, the project has built a considerable library of information. The books are the 'family albums', a chronological, reflective record of the project's development that is referred to by staff and participants alike and that has proved useful to its evaluation.

A reflective session for workers at the 'Roots and Wings' project, Chickenley Community Primary School (Mary Robson is second from left)

Systemic reflection breaks down what Rogers (1977) termed the 'jug/mug' approach of the teacher/facilitator as giver and the child/young person as taker of information. We are all learning together and the child has opportunities to contribute and help set an agenda for further learning.

This seedbed of supervision and reflection is a nurturing environment for the professionals involved in Roots and Wings. Our practice places at the heart of everything we do a belief that curiosity is the fuel of development. Modelling congruent behaviour is constant and is crucial to its success. While some professional talk will be of attainment, resilience, attendance and expectations, the quality of such projects as these is in the relationships they foster, and in the creation of a fund of memories, both individual and collective, that is helping to redefine perceptions of the community. Many of our children need different choices for adulthood, and some need better memories of childhood. Here are two 11-year-olds, fresh from their first day at high school, reflecting on how taking part in the Roots and Wings Carnival Transition Parade back at the end of the summer term helped them through the experience:

> Chloe: "It boosts your confidence in a way, because everyone is looking at you. It prepared me for today because I expected people to be looking at me. In a way you feel a bit special when they look at you."

Courtney: "Before I went, I were nervous. I think I
would have been panicking a lot more if it hadn't been
for carnival because it helped us to see what to expect.
It comforted us. It made us know who we really are.
It helped us see and understand it's going to be all
right and there are other things to worry about."

Chloe: "When we got to high school we could
talk to other people with more confidence
because we already know who we are."

Leading by example

Roots and Wings was initially project-funded for three years by the
Children's Fund. It has sought and was awarded further funding and
is now in its seventh year, currently coming to the end of two years'
funding from NHS Kirklees. My role is now somewhat more than the
relatively straightforward job of directing and delivering a one-off and
finite project. Roots and Wings has grown organically, and while based
within a supportive school and with significant funding for two-to-
three-year periods, is a project, not a company. We are defined by our
partnerships and exist in the spaces between initiative and institution.

Leadership in such an environment is inevitably complex and in
constant development. My role has grown along with the project,
and includes the overall vision, planning, budgeting for and delivering
the work; recruiting, contracting, managing and nurturing staff; and
developing partnerships with other organisations and practitioners.
Given the project's success, further fundraising and organisational
development are added to the list. In common with successful
initiatives from other sectors, we are at a stage where decisions must
be made about the future of the project. Shall we become a charity,
a limited company? Should we stay on the school site or branch out
into the community? What will our focus be and where shall we
find further funding? Maintaining a balance between such strategic,
long-term issues and the continuance of the high-quality everyday
experience for children and the community makes significant
demands. I give the cohort of committed freelance staff, who are
steeped in the culture of the project, opportunities for development
and in turn this frees up my time to further the strategic development.
At the same time, I have to ensure that the work is adapting to the
changing needs of the children and the community. I try always to
clarify my thinking to staff and take opportunities to pass on relevant

literature and examples from other areas of my working life to enrich their professional experience. I am constantly on the lookout for chances that will simultaneously identify and address need, often in seemingly complex ways.

Here is one such example: one of our arts practitioners initially came to the project as a 16-year-old volunteer, the elder sister of a Year 6 pupil. Five years on, she is now in the third year of a Fine Art degree and is employed by Roots and Wings to run a project with reception children and their families. Her assistant is another student with aspirations to work with children and community. Here is development from every angle – the project, the practitioner, the sustainability of the practice.

In preparation for the writing of this chapter, I asked the project's coordinator to give some honest thoughts and feedback on my leadership style:

> "You are very calm – except on Parade Day! If there is a crisis you can be relied on to be calm and to be as objective as possible. You encourage consensus but aren't afraid to overrule us.... On the whole, you are very clear. You walk the talk and model everything – with children and other adults – and we get that from you." (Lisa Jagger, development coordinator)

While this perspective is gratifying, my point in including it here is that it illustrates the culture of the project that I feel emanates from leading by example. I must continuously and actively walk the talk, no matter that I might feel pressured and over capacity.

For example, I will always positively and unequivocally challenge prejudicial language. That will involve the session with children being interrupted in order to hold a conversation with the whole group about the origin and meaning of the vocabulary used and reasons why it may be considered offensive. Consequently, project staff are more confident about instigating such challenges themselves. Such confidence cuts through political correctness and replaces it with informed debate. It promotes thinking and conversation as real options for children as opposed to simply emulating others' behaviour.

It is crucial that staff become accustomed to a working environment where they feel valued and very much part of the picture. It is important that it isn't simply the 'how', but also the 'why' that is passed on in such a culture. As a consequence, the very strong ethical core of the project is one to which everyone – not only the project staff – actively subscribes, as can be noted from the following statement:

> "Seeing how Mary and her team deal with the children I've learned that a raised voice is perhaps not the most effective way of managing things! When you've got an angry, stressed-out child, shouting at them and telling them off makes them more angry and stressed. I realised I had come into the school and adopted a 'survival-of-the-fittest' approach – you win by shouting louder than the children. So, yeah, watching Mary give them time to calm down, explaining what went wrong and then asking people to make choices has been a revelation. It's very powerful. Now, I just don't get angry. I try not to remonstrate. I wait till they're calm and I listen, and usually the problem is diffused. Before I wasn't solving problems, I was capping them, and when they erupted again it was worse. I go into other schools now and I see that 'teacher-anger-meets-child-anger' all the time, and it just makes things worse. In a way, I've completely changed my whole approach."
> (Dean Tombling, a former Year 6 teacher at Chickenley)

Sustainability

Dean has taken his new approach to his latest role, as deputy head of another primary school. I don't define sustainability as simply financial. Change inevitably happens and needs to be recognised. Who knows, the work at Chickenley might end next year or in three years' time, but the energy of it will have been taken somewhere else, a gift freely given and passed on in the lives of the children, in the work of staff, artists and teachers.

> When a gift passes, it becomes the binder of many wills. What gathers in it is not only the sentiment of generosity but the affirmation of individual goodwill, making of those separate parts a spiritus mundi, a unanimous heart, a band whose wills are focused through the lens of the gift. Thus the gift becomes an agent of social cohesion, and this again leads to the feeling that its passage increases its worth, for in social life at least, the whole is greater than the sum of its parts. (Hyde, 2007 [1979]: 36)

I believe gifting to be an essential, ethical construct of my work. I don't dispense, I give, with strength and trust and confidence. I like to think of it as a set of fractals, curved or geometric figures in which the same patterns repeat endlessly within themselves. The closer you look, the more you will see the same gift repeated at different scales, with no qualitative difference between them. They just go on and on, ad infinitum.

Conclusion

When I look over my shoulder, the journey from my first experience of supervision to leading today's complex model of reflective practice at Roots and Wings seems clear and straightforward. I can't see the twists and turns and course corrections I had to make to get me here. Nor can I see what is round the next bend. I consider it a strength that I never reach a plateau from which there is a clear and uninterrupted view.

I know that reflection is a life skill, not only for the children I work with but also for me and my colleagues. It helps us cultivate thinking skills that help us flourish as citizens, as professionals, as people.

Note

[1] The Institute of Cultural Affairs (ICA) (www.ica-uk.org.uk) is a global network of research, demonstration and training organisations 'concerned with the human factor in world development'. It aims to act as a catalyst for people in a variety of contexts and circumstances to take active responsibility for their own personal, community and societal development.

References

Amulya, J. (2004) *What Is Reflective Practice?*, Cambridge, MA: The Center for Reflective Community Practice, Massachusetts Institute of Technology (www.itslifejimbutnotasweknowit.org.uk/files/whatisreflectivepractice.pdf).

Hyde, L. (2007 [1979]) *The Gift: How the Creative Spirit Transforms the World*, Edinburgh: Canongate.

Rogers, C.R. (1977) 'The politics of education', *Journal of Humanistic Education* vol 1, no 1, pp 6-22. (Also published in Rogers, C.R. (1983) *Freedom to Learn for the 80s.* Columbus, OH: Charles E. Merrill Publishing Company, and in H. Kirschenbaum and V. Land Henderson (eds) (1989) *The Carl Rogers Reader,* Boston, MA: Houghton Mifflin.)

Twelve

Men wanted? Gender and the children's workforce

Martin Robb

Introduction

Recent years have seen a succession of initiatives aimed at increasing the number of men working in services for children. Prominent among these has been a series of campaigns to recruit more male workers in early years childcare, the most recent at the time of writing being the 2009 drive by the Children's Workforce Development Council (CWDC, 2009). There have also been parallel initiatives in primary education, prompted by concern at an apparent decline in the number of male teachers. These policy developments have been accompanied by a vigorous debate about men's role in work with children, together with a number of research studies examining the issue (Cameron *et al.*, 1999; Cameron, 2001; Owen, 2003).

This chapter offers a critical perspective on these developments, posing the question as to why this issue has become so important to policy makers and practitioners, and examining the range of discourses that come into play when men's role in work with children is discussed, as well as the ambivalence and unresolved tensions that surround the topic.

Gendered division of labour in children's services

Work with children and young people has been marked throughout its history by a gendered division of labour. As in the wider world of work, some professional roles have been coded as more suitable for men, while others have been viewed, explicitly or implicitly, as 'women's work'. Traditionally men have been better represented in work with older children, and in professions that involve elements of instruction, or discipline and control: examples would be youth justice, youth work and secondary education. By contrast, services for younger children, and roles that foreground care and nurture, such as early years childcare and infant teaching, have until recently been the almost exclusive preserve of women.

Teaching in junior and middle schools is something of a liminal area, where the proportions of male and female teachers have fluctuated over time, with some evidence of a recent decline in male representation. Surveys in early 2009 revealed that almost a third of primary schools in Northern Ireland, and a quarter in England, do not have a male teacher (BBC, 2009; *The Daily Telegraph*, 2009), although some commentators have questioned whether there was ever a 'golden age' of high male representation in primary teaching (Harnett and Lee, 2003).

Attempts to explain this gendered division of labour have advanced a number of theories, all linked to unequal gender relations in the wider world of work and in society generally. Some explanations focus on the ways in which professions with greater social status and reward have been the preserve of men, while women have been disproportionately represented in areas of work (such as childcare) which are low paid and low status. Of course, the reverse can be argued: that some jobs are poorly regarded and rewarded *because* they are seen as 'women's work'. Writing about the supposed absence of men from primary teaching, Penelope Harnett and John Lee state:

> In one important sense the concern for the recruitment of males is part of the general concern over recruitment. Teaching like other public service professions is relatively low paid. One explanation for the dominance of women may simply be that historically women are more likely to accept lower pay. The record shows that female work roles are worse paid and enjoy lower status than those deemed to be male. (Harnett and Lee, 2003: 85)

Another possible (but not incompatible) explanation is that the workplace tends to reflect and reproduce gendered roles within families, where 'care' has been seen largely as the mother's role, while fathers' conventional role has focused more on knowledge transmission and discipline. Following on from this, the framing of care for children as 'women's work' has meant that it has been seen as effeminate. As a corollary, hegemonic masculinity (Connell, 1995), at least in the modern west, has come to be associated with a distancing from the direct care of children. In a survey carried out in schools in North Lanarkshire, boys gave the following reasons for the low numbers of men working in childcare:

■   Men should be "doing physical work", and "getting their hands dirty".

■   Women are seen as "more loving, caring, and playful". Women are seen as "better with children" and having "a special bond with children".

■   The work was also seen as low paid and low status. "It's a soft job". Men could get 'better' jobs than those available in childcare – "women are accustomed to it" and "men are needed for other jobs".

(quoted in North Lanarkshire Council, 2006)

However, it should be noted that the exclusion of men from the care of children is historically and culturally relative. There is some evidence that before the Industrial Revolution men were more closely involved in the care of children within families, and also that the pattern of gendered care for children varies across cultures and historical periods (Lamb and Tamis-Lemonda, 2004).

Why so much concern about recruiting men?

How can we explain the recent upsurge in initiatives aimed at increasing men's involvement in children's services? Most obviously, these developments are part of the wider reappraisal of gender roles in western societies, in the wake of sweeping social changes and the impact of feminism. As more women have entered the workforce there has been a renewed focus on the gendered division of labour both in the workplace and in the family. In a context in which an increasing number of women are in paid work, the question of sharing childcare within families has become increasingly urgent (Fine-Davis *et al.*, 2004). As an Irish study of men and childcare argued:

A recurring obstacle to the full participation of women in employment is the fact that women have the dual burden of work and domestic care. The traditional view is that childcare is 'women's work' and is something men cannot or do not do. Encouraging men into childcare challenges these prejudices and promotes equality in roles between men and women, both at home and in the workplace. (Fine-Davis *et al.*, 2005: 1)

Social pressures, backed by government initiatives, have encouraged men to take a greater share in childcare within families. At the same time, the entry of women into traditionally male professions, and the erosion of some gender divisions in the workplace, has encouraged a reappraisal of what is meant by gender-appropriate work. If women can take on roles traditionally reserved for men, the argument runs, then why shouldn't men move into professions that have in the past been the province of women?

Alongside these practical changes, the influence of feminism since the 1960s has prompted a shift in popular perceptions of gender. There has been a movement away from an essentialist view of gender roles as immutable, and towards a more dynamic view of masculinity and femininity as culturally conditioned and capable of change. Debates about men's role in work with children and discussion of fathers' roles in families have been mutually reinforcing. In both cases, a new orthodoxy about what constitutes 'good' masculinity is emerging, which emphasises men's capacity for care and emotional expressivity (Robb, 2004a, 2004b).

Increasing men's involvement in family life has been a key emphasis in recent social policy

However, if we are trying to understand why there has been such intense concern about men's role in relation to children, it would be a mistake to overlook another important strain in the debate. Recent decades have witnessed a rising anxiety in popular discourse about the absence of men from family life and the increasing number of children being brought up by lone mothers. Concerns about the departure of men from areas of work with children where they have traditionally been fairly well represented, such as primary teaching, reflect these anxieties. Stirred into the mix are worries about the decline of male influence in the family and in the wider society. Some analysts have argued that campaigns to increase fathers' involvement in family life, and the numbers of men working with children, should be seen as part of an attempt to reinstate male power (Pringle, 1992, 1995; Martino, 2008). Along similar lines, concern about men's role in the upbringing of children can be seen as stemming in part from a broader concern about boys' supposed under-achievement and the state of young masculinities. According to Harnett and Lee (2003: 84), 'demand for more male teachers might be interpreted as a moral panic; more male teachers would serve as appropriate role models for young boys and act as stabilising influences'.

Men, sexuality and children: the discourse of risk

Paradoxically, calls for more male workers in children's services have run alongside rising anxiety about child sexual abuse, much of which has focused on men. The two debates have been almost contemporaneous, with the moral panic about child abuse having its beginning in the late 1980s at about the same time as the first organised campaigns to recruit more male childcare workers (Campbell, 1997).

Anxieties about the risk of child sexual abuse, both within families and in institutional settings, have led to increased regulation and monitoring of those working with children, and arguably this has been more intense for male workers. In the public imagination, the debate about the risk to children has been influenced by prominent media stories about (mostly male) nursery workers, teachers and voluntary leaders. Cameron and colleagues (1999) have suggested that discussion of men's involvement in childcare is marked by two equally powerful discourses: a discourse of equality and a discourse of risk. Media representations of men as childcare workers have oscillated between the two and have been characterised by a deep ambivalence. A similar tension can be seen in representations of fathers, which are polarised between stories of heroic and irresponsible dads.

In policy discussions, the two discourses tend to be kept rigidly separate. One set of policies is instigated to diminish the risk of abuse to children in care and education settings, while a separate raft of initiatives aims to change the gender balance in the children's workforce. In debates about how to recruit more men to work with children, it can be argued that a discourse of equality has suppressed discussion of risk. Issues of male sexuality have become the 'unspoken' in the discussion about men and work with children.

In popular representations, male sexuality is often portrayed as more predatory than that of women, and as a result men tend to be seen as a greater risk to children. Although feminists rightly argue that women are sexualised in our culture, they tend to be sexualised as passive objects of desire. By contrast, popular discourse characterises men's desire as active and uncontrollable. At the same time, childcare environments tend to be seen not only as feminised, but also to some extent as desexualised environments, and more broadly, childhood and sexuality have traditionally been regarded as mutually exclusive fields (Stainton Rogers and Stainton Rogers, 1992). One of the unspoken anxieties around recruiting more men into childcare may be that the arrival of men risks sexualising the environment. This is not to fall into an essentialist view of male sexuality, but rather to acknowledge that in a society in which gender inequalities have been deeply rooted, there will inevitably be an impact on the ways in which men's sexualities are constructed.

Another way in which sexuality lurks beneath the surface of debates about men and childcare is in the association between care work, effeminacy and homosexuality. Since hegemonic western masculinity has been predicated on separation from the feminised space of home and children, men who traverse this boundary, by expressing a desire to care for children, have risked being labelled effeminate. Since effeminacy is closely linked with homosexuality in popular discourse, men who work with children have often been assumed to be gay.

In her study of male childcare workers in California, Susan Murray argues that 'gay' remains a sexualised identity in the popular imagination. As a consequence, she suggests that gay men are at greater risk of being suspected of a sexual interest in children, citing examples from her research of gay male workers accused of abusing girls, even when the men's sexuality was well known. Thus the coding of male childcare workers as likely to be gay only intensifies the popular, if mostly unspoken, sense of male workers as a sexual risk to children in their care (Murray, S.B., 1996).

Two discourses

Two contrasting discourses inform campaigns to increase male involvement in work with children: a progressive discourse and a conservative discourse. Although they display distinctive features, it would be a mistake to see these two discourses as completely sealed off from each other. Instead, I want to suggest that they often overlap, and that ultimately they converge in reinforcing a conservative construction of gender identities.

A progressive discourse of gender equality has dominated official policy statements and has been the source of most of the explicit arguments in favour of recruiting more men to children's services. It can be found represented in policy documents issued by the UK government and the European Union, and in the arguments of campaigners for greater male involvement (EC Childcare Network, 1994). This egalitarian discourse assumes that men and women are equally capable of working effectively with children, and should be treated equally in recruitment to professional roles in children's services. Gender roles are assumed to be fluid and malleable, so there should be no rigid notions of what is regarded as men's and women's work. Furthermore, recruiting a more gender equal workforce will contribute to greater gender equality in society, in part by providing a model of gender equality to the next generation.

The conservative discourse, by contrast, is not often directly reflected in official discussion of the issue, but surfaces in the rhetoric of those campaigning for fathers' rights and traditional family values. It has its origins in the work of New Right social commentators (Murray, C., 1996; Dennis and Erdos, 2000) and assumes that gender roles are relatively fixed, and that complementary and contrasting male and female influences are needed in a child's development. Consequently, its proponents are concerned about the absence of fathers from family life, and about any blurring of traditional gender roles within families. They argue that the lack of male influence in children's lives, and the growing number of families headed by single mothers, is a contributory factor in rising crime and social breakdown. Whereas the progressive discourse is grounded in feminist analysis and campaigns for gender equality, the conservative discourse on men and children can be seen as part of a backlash against the influence of feminism and an attempt to stem the tide of the gender revolution.

'Male role model' discourse

At the heart of both progressive and conservative arguments for greater male involvement in children's services is the assumption that children, and especially boys, need the influence of strong male role models if they are to develop into well-adjusted adults. There are both progressive and conservative versions of this discourse in circulation, but although they begin from different starting points and have different goals, they tend to overlap and converge. I want to suggest that arguing from within the male role model discourse is ultimately counter-productive and a rhetorical dead end, and that both versions inevitably end by reinforcing a conservative position.

The progressive version of the male role model discourse argues that children in general, and boys in particular, benefit from seeing male workers modelling alternative ways of being a man: for example, by caring for young children. The implication is that this will have a positive, transformative effect both on children's own gender development, which in the long term will contribute to transforming gender relations more widely. Kevin, a young nursery worker who I interviewed as part of a study of men in childcare, suggested it was important to have male workers "so that children grow up thinking that it's not only mummy that looks after baby, that daddy can do it as well – or a male can do it as well"(Robb, 2001: 236).

By contrast, the conservative version of the discourse does not look forward to a world of transformed gender relations, but rather looks back to a world of fixed gender roles. The conservative argument is that children need strongly differentiated male and female role models in order to learn about supposed gender differences. Boys, in particular, are at risk of not developing a strong masculine identity if effective male role models are absent from their lives.

Although seemingly distinctive, there are a number of ways in which the two versions of the discourse converge. Advocates of a greater role for men in childcare can often be found switching between the two arguments. Perhaps surprisingly, my own research found examples of male childcare workers themselves voicing the conservative version of the argument. Here is Kevin again:

> "I think the children get more out of having a male and a
> female role model than not, because some of the nurseries
> I've been in you get children from the age of three months
> left five days a week, about five to eight until quarter past
> six with just a bunch of women and not their parents."

And referring to his own upbringing by a lone mother, Kevin added:

> "My father wasn't around – I was never taught how to
> mend a car or anything that the male does. I was never
> taught a male's role, whereas a male in a day nursery, OK
> they wouldn't be mending a car or anything like that, but
> there was a male role model there for little girls and little
> boys, to see what the difference is in a man and a female."

This argument was reflected in interviews with other male workers.
It suggests that arguing from the male role model discourse leads
inevitably to searching for a distinctive male contribution to work with
children. Moreover, this tends to result in an implication that women's
care for children, whether mothers in the domestic context or
women-only staff groups in institutional settings, is inadequate: Kevin's
"just a bunch of women". In addition, having to argue that male
workers bring something 'different' or 'special' to the workplace means
that even progressive proponents end up falling back on essentialist
notions of gender differences.

Challenging the male role model discourse

So far I have criticised the male role model argument for its *effects*, for
the way in which progressive and conservative versions of the argument
tend to converge in the mistaken endeavour of trying to identify a
distinctive contribution for men. Now I want to take issue with the
underlying assumption behind both versions of the argument: that boys
need strong male role models for healthy development generally and
specifically for the development of stable gender identities.

Both progressive and conservative arguments for greater male
involvement with children tend to overlook the influence of women
in general and mothers in particular. Not only does the male role
model discourse propose a rather simplistic social learning model, in
which gender roles are transmitted in a straightforward way by adults,
but there is an assumption that this learning has to be from a parent or
adult of the same sex as the child. There is a need for a more complex
model of how gender identities develop, in which the multiplicity of
relationships in which young people are situated is taken into account,
and which includes the possibility of cross-gender identifications.

In the context of primary teaching, Harnett and Lee suggest that the
argument that boys' under-achievement and disaffection stem from
a lack of male role models 'oversimplifies the issues involved' (2003:

85). Instead they argue for more nuanced analysis of boys' motivation, citing studies that argue that 'what motivates and interests boys is actually what motivates and interests all children' (2003: 85). They conclude: 'Not only was there no golden age of male teachers but new work suggests that the gender of the teacher is much less significant than is currently assumed by many commentators' (Harnett and Lee, 2003: 85; see also Martino, 2008).

One of the interesting findings from my own research with young male childcare workers was that many had either been brought up by single mothers, or had experienced particularly close relationships with maternal figures early in their lives. A number of the young men mentioned this as a direct influence on their decision to work with children. Kevin, who was raised by his mother and grandmother, said:

> "I suppose with being brought up by two women I've
> not been sort of taught how to go and mend a car or
> how to lay bricks or anything like that, so it wouldn't
> have occurred to me to go and do a job like that anyway,
> whereas I've always been taught how to care for people,
> so it was just the natural thing to go into really."

In my later research with 'hands-on' fathers, a number of participants claimed that their mothers had been a more decisive influence than their fathers on their parenting style. This was how Sean expressed it:

> "I think that my mum, certainly in the sense of emotional
> connection for, or practical needs being met, I would
> certainly perceive those as coming mostly from my mum.
> And, you know, the fact that I might have to get my
> young daughter up and wash her and give her a meal
> and make that some kind of experience that's nurturing,
> I wouldn't really be able to recollect a memory from
> having had that from my father. So I would be using
> memories or experiences from my mother to remember,
> you know, how that was accomplished and what that
> felt like and what might be nice about it and so on."

These findings suggest that, in contradiction to the 'progressive' version of the male role model argument, women might be at least as important an influence as men in the development of 'caring' masculinities. Other studies have supported this hypothesis. Jane Reeves' research with socially excluded young fathers found that, among young men who opted to stay with their partner and involve themselves in the care of the child, a common factor was a close supportive relationship with their mothers or grandmothers (Reeves and Rehal, 2008).

My own secondary analysis of interviews with young men (which were conducted over a 10-year period as part of a longitudinal study of the transition to adulthood: see Henderson *et al.*, 2007) also suggests a correlation between maternal relationships and attitudes to the care of children. For example, Khattab, a young British Asian man who enjoyed a particularly close relationship with his mother, said that he "can't wait till I'm a father", and when asked how he will bring up his children, replied "Like my mum" (quoted in Robb, 2008).

In their different ways these findings suggest that the influence of male role models in young men's lives may have been overstated, and conversely that the role of mothers, and women generally, in boys' development has tended to be overlooked. A strong maternal or female influence, even in the absence of effective male role models, far from having a negative influence on boys, may in fact contribute to the development of more caring and expressive masculinities.

The work of psychoanalytic feminist writers would appear to support this thesis. Jessica Benjamin has argued that boys tend to lose 'a vital source of goodness inside' in the transition to adulthood, as they come under pressure to repudiate their identification with their mothers:

> The denial of identification with the mother … tends to cut the boy off from intersubjective communication that was part of the primary bond between mother and infant. Emotional attunement, sharing states of mind, emphatically assuming the other's position, and imaginatively perceiving the other's needs and feelings – these are associated with cast-off femininity, emotional attunement is now experienced as dangerously close to losing oneself in the other; affective imitation is now used negatively to tease and provoke. Thus the intersubjective dimension is increasingly reduced, and the need for mutual recognition must be satisfied with mere identification of likeness…. The devaluation of the need for the other becomes a touchstone of adult masculinity. (Benjamin, 1988: 170-1)

Benjamin's argument should not be read as reinforcing an essentialist view of gender identities, or as leading to a pessimistic assessment of men's capacity to 'care'. A psychoanalytic feminist perspective, while arguing that gender differences are 'real', sees these as the result of unequal gender relations, which become embedded in personal behaviour and relationships. Benjamin goes on to argue that the shifting pattern of gender relationships in our time holds out the hope that the conventional pattern might be broken, and she suggests that 'the changing social relations of gender have given us a glimpse of another world, of a space in which each sex can play the other and so accept difference by making it familiar' (1988: 169).

Building on Benjamin's work, Wendy Hollway has highlighted a crucial distinction between renunciation and repudiation in a boy's process of coming to terms with the inevitable loss of closeness to his mother. The evidence from the research studies cited here would seem to offer support for Hollway's conclusion that where boys retain 'their positive identifications with maternal capacities to care for them' (2006: 99), they are more likely to develop into the kind of men who have the capacity to take on caring roles, particularly in relation to children.

The arguments currently advanced for employing more men in the children's workforce, whether from a progressive, egalitarian perspective or from a conservative, traditionalist perspective, make both too much and too little of gender differences. In endeavouring to identify a distinctive masculine influence on children's development, these arguments end up both essentialising men's contribution and overstating it. Progressive advocates in particular tend to underestimate genuine differences that are the residue of historical structures of inequality: for example, they overlook the ways in which male workers tend to assume positions of power within staff groups. The value of the perspective represented by the work of Benjamin, Hollway and others is that it makes it possible to understand how such inequalities become embedded at the level of personal identities, and at the same time how they could be transcended under different kinds of gender relations.

The debate on men's role in work with children is in need of a more nuanced psychosocial understanding of men's capacity to care. This will include paying attention to the meanings that children have for men (and for women too), meanings that are shaped by social structures but played out at the level of the personal and affective. More work is needed to explore the diversity of distinctive meanings that children possess for men in the contemporary context, and the implications for men's caring relationships with children.

Conclusion

This chapter has suggested that recent initiatives to achieve a more gender-equal workforce in children's services have been characterised by a deep ambivalence about men's relationships with children, and by unresolved tensions between progressive and conservative perspectives on gender and childhood. The debate about men's role in work with children has also been dogged by simplistic and uncritical approaches to issues of gender and sexuality. If genuine equality in the childcare workforce is to be achieved, and both men and women enabled to play a full part in the care and education of children, then a more critical understanding of gender inequalities and how they can be overcome will be needed.

Thus the answer to the question posed in this chapter's title might be: 'It depends'. It depends what kind of men, or more accurately, what kind of masculinity. And it depends what kind of relationships those men will have with the children in their care, and with the women with whom they work. Finally, it is too simplistic to claim that recruiting more men will be the answer to concerns about boys' well-being and achievement. The danger of focusing on the supposed shortage of male workers is that it risks diminishing the vital role played by women (both mothers and female workers) in nurturing young men. What both boys and girls appear to need is strong and caring adult role models of either gender.

References

BBC (2009) 'Primary schools need more men' (http://news.bbc. co.uk/1/hi/northern_ireland/7988897.stm).

Benjamin, J. (1988) *The Bonds of Love: Psychoanalysis, Feminism and the Problem of Domination*, New York, NY: Pantheon.

Cameron, C. (2001) 'Promise or problem? A review of the literature on men working in early childhood services', *Gender, Work and Organization*, vol 8, no 4, pp 430-453.

Cameron, C., Moss, P. and Owen, C. (1999) *Men in the Nursery: Gender and Caring Work*, London: Paul Chapman.

Campbell, B. (1997) *Unofficial Secrets: Child Sexual Abuse – The Cleveland Case*, London: Virago.

Connell, R. (1995) *Masculinities*, Sydney: Allen & Unwin.

CWDC (Children's Workforce Development Council) (2009) (www. cwdcouncil.org.uk/whats-new/1591_parents-demand-more-male-childcare-workers).

Daily Telegraph, The (2009) 'More than a quarter of England's primary schools have no male teachers' (www.telegraph.co.uk/education/educationnews/5033012/More-than-a-quarter-of-Englands-primary-schools-have-no-male-teachers.html).

Dennis, N. and Erdos, G. (2000) *Families Without Fatherhood* (3rd revised edn), London: Civitas: Institute for the Study of Civil Society.

EC (European Commission) Childcare Network (1994) *Men as Carers: Towards a Culture of Responsibility, Sharing and Reciprocity Between Women and Men in the Care and Upbringing of Children*, Brussels: EC Equal Opportunities Unit.

Fine-Davis, M., Fagnani, J., Giovannini, D., Hojgaard, L. and Clarke, H. (2004) *Fathers and Mothers: Dilemmas of the Work–Life Balance – A Comparative Study in Four European Countries*, Dordrecht, Boston, MA and London: Kluwer.

Fine-Davis, M., O'Dwyer, C., McCarthy, M., Edge, G., O'Sullivan, M. and Wynne, K. (2005) *Men in Childcare: Promoting Gender Equality in Children – Evaluation of a Pilot Project*, Dublin: National Flexi-work Partnership (www.tara.tcd.ie/bitstream/2262/23660/1/Men+in+Childcare+Report,+final+in+pdf+(printer's+version).pdf).

Harnett, P. and Lee, J. (2003) 'Where have all the men gone? Have primary schools really been feminised?', *Journal of Educational Administration and History*, vol 35, no 2, pp 77-86.

Henderson, S., Holland, J., Mcgrellis, S., Sharpe, S. and Thomson, R. (2007) *Inventing Adulthoods: A Biographical Approach to Youth Transitions*, London/Milton Keynes: Sage Publications/The Open University.

Hollway, W. (2006) *The Capacity to Care: Gender and Ethical Subjectivity*, London: Routledge.

Lamb, M.E. and Tamis-Lemonda, C.S. (2004) 'The role of the father: an introduction', in M.E. Lamb (ed) *The Role of the Father in Child Development* (4th edn), Hoboken, NJ: John Wiley, pp 1-31.

Martino, W.J. (2008) 'Male teachers as role models: addressing issues of masculinity, pedagogy and the re-masculinization of schooling', *Curriculum Inquiry*, vol 38, no 2, pp 189-223.

Murray, C. (1996) *Charles Murray and the Underclass: The Developing Debate*, London: Civitas: Institute for the Study of Civil Society.

Murray, S.B. (1996) '"We all love Charles": men in child care and the social construction of gender', *Gender and Society*, vol 10, no 4, pp 369-85.

North Lanarkshire Council (2006) 'Men into childcare: where have all the good men gone?' (www.northlan.gov.uk/Your+Council/facts+and+figures/education+and+training/ey+men+into+childacare.html#intro).

Owen, C. (2003), *Men's Work? Changing the Gender Mix of the Childcare and Early Years Workforce*, London: Daycare Trust.

Pringle, K. (1992) 'Child sexual abuse perpetrated by welfare personnel and the problem of men', *Critical Social Policy*, no 36, pp 4-19.

Pringle, K. (1995) *Men, Masculinities and Social Welfare*, London: UCL Press.

Reeves, J. and Rehal, F. (2008) 'Contextualising the evidence: young fathers, family and professional support', in J. Reeves (ed) *Interprofessional Approaches to Young Fathers*, Keswick: M&K Update Ltd.

Robb, M. (2001) 'Men working in childcare', in P. Foley, J. Roche and S. Tucker (eds) *Children in Society: Contemporary Theory, Policy and Practice*, Basingstoke/Milton Keynes: Palgrave/The Open University, pp 230-8.

Robb, M. (2004a) 'Men talking about fatherhood: discourse and identities', in M. Robb, S. Barrett, C. Komaromy and A. Rogers (eds) *Communication, Relationships and Care: A Reader*, London/Milton Keynes: Routledge/The Open University, pp 121-30.

Robb, M. (2004b) 'Exploring fatherhood: masculinity and intersubjectivity in the research process', *Journal of Social Work Practice*, vol 18, no 3, pp 395-406.

Robb, M. (2008) 'Mummy's boys? Young men, masculinity and maternal relationships', Unpublished paper.

Stainton Rogers, R. and Stainton Rogers, W. (1992) *Stories of Childhood: Shifting Agendas of Child Concern*, Hemel Hempstead: Harvester Wheatsheaf.

Part Three
Personal and professional contexts

Thirteen

The making of a good teacher in the 20th century

Jane Martin

'We take pride in the name of our paper, *The Woman Teacher*. Just as the woman teacher is known and respected and her influence felt in the tiniest hamlet as well as in the large town, so will this her paper do its work in helping to knit together the great forces that go to make a consolidated womanhood. We shall now be in a position to proclaim from the housetops our judgement on things that matter initially to the work of education and to the progress of civilisation'. (Agnes Dawson, first President of the National Union of Women Teachers, *The Woman Teacher*, 26 September 1919: 2)

The vocabulary of feminism gives expression to the idea of a radical tradition in English education, which links educational reform to social advance. The daughter of a carpenter who was often out of work, Agnes Dawson trained as a pupil teacher before entering residential training college, subsequently teaching young children and girls in working-class areas in East and South London. She later headed an elementary school and, more unusually, helped found the first feminist union in England, the National Union of Women Teachers. For her, as for many others, teaching was a way of moving into another class and a new way of life. In this chapter I introduce a historical perspective on teaching as a vocation, suggesting that there is much value in understanding professional cultures of the past and tracing how the present and future resonates with both continuities and changes.

From the 1870s and 1880s, the systematisation of compulsory elementary schooling offered new opportunities for working-class children to get an education and become teachers. Agnes and her contemporaries were among the first cohort of British teachers to have received their own schooling and subsequently their training within a mass system of state education, organised under the 1870 Education Act. By 1900, roughly three quarters of those employed to staff public elementary schools in England and Wales were female (Oram, 1996: 228-31). This account of teachers' lives draws on the findings of a three-year research project examining the relationship between work, identity formation, reproduction and change over the past 100 years, as part of the Economic and Social Research Council (ESRC)-funded 'Identities and Social Action' programme. Methods of life history work, historical and comparative analysis were used to explore intergenerational changes and gender differences within and between workers from banking, railway work and teaching, in the North West of England and the South East. In examining the experience of those beyond the reach of memory, the team used a range of public records and life documents, including letters and diaries. For this chapter, I focus on teacher texts and testimonies.

In making sense of the changing character of work in schools in a range of historical moments, I draw on the influential work of Pierre Bourdieu (Bourdieu, 2001). Drawn together with the concept of the 'habitus' and most centrally 'capital', Bourdieu understands the social world as made up of different but overlapping fields of power which function according to their own tacit logic or set of rules and help explain intergenerational reproduction through historical time. Acceptance as a legitimate player of the game within a specific field of action is achieved by access to different types of capital – economic, social, cultural and symbolic.[1] The individuals profiled here are similarly located in terms of their common experience of a specific field of action constituted by their shared participation in schooling processes. Embedded within everyday actions, much of which is subconscious but socially constructed, I use Bourdieusian notions of 'habitus' to illuminate teachers' accounts of durable, transposable dispositions in a female-dominated education field. Learned more by experience than by teaching, 'habitus' relates to a way of seeing and being within the world as it is mediated through, for example, linguistic competence, lifestyle, politics and prestige, combined with particular dispositions, attitudes and tastes.

The work of Gerald Grace (1987) is of real conceptual utility for mapping the contours of the teachers' lives/policy interpellation in England. This can be understood as the moment and process of recognition of interaction with the policy at hand, within which the teacher self can be constituted. Grace identifies four broad phases of teacher–state relations, extending from 1900 to the 1980s, intended to be indicative of policy trends. The use of a precise historical chronology would, however, be far too monolithic and deterministic because formations of 'professionalism' are historically contingent, and depend on the sector within which they emerge and the relations that underpin that sector. Grace characterised the early part of the 20th century in terms of a politics of confrontation. Class cultural condescension was the hallmark of government policy, allied to inspector pressure and low wages. Teachers were ranked and classified first on the basis of gender, seniority and then merit (qualifications plus experience), and state intervention and regulation increased. In the 1920s and 1930s some teacher associations worked toward the acquisition of empowering identities as trusted professionals, while radical movements in the state sector presented perspectives for reform based on direct popular control of education. By 1939, state school teachers had achieved respectable white collar/white blouse security as one of the accepted lesser professions associated with what Grace called an *ethic of legitimated professionalism*.

The third phase of teacher–state relations he identified was 1940 to the mid-1970s. Then, under the influence of war, new political and intellectual groupings forged a settlement around planning, state intervention and universal forms of social provision that began to assert the importance of education. With regard to teachers' construction of professionalism, this was the supposed heyday of teacher autonomy albeit generally confined within the limits of their own classrooms, since they often had little control over school goals and administration. Furthermore, the examination framework to meet the needs of universities and employers traditionally exerted a significant check on teacher agency at secondary level. If we consider Grace's final period, from the late 1970s/early 1980s, we can see how, with reformist 'welfare' solutions widely questioned, teachers saw the breaking of this social democratic and professional consensus and the return of a politics of confrontation in terms of the trajectory of government policy. The development of increasingly demanding systems of public accountability was a clear move in this direction.

Since the election of a New Labour government in 1997 there has been some softening of 'rhetoric' tempered by continuities regarding a culture of naming and blaming teachers for declining standards. Increased levels of public spending have accompanied further years of mandated reform, and promotion of change implementation by external interest groups (including government agencies and corporate bodies) as opposed to educator groups. What does this mean, then, for the temporal constitution of perceptions of the 'good teacher' in

20th-century England? Gendered discourses of vocation, career and professionalism become the point of entry for historical analysis.

Central to the ESRC project, in terms of methodology, was a set of 40 semi-structured interviews, with female and male teachers in both the primary and secondary sector, from both rural and inner-city schools. They all volunteered to take part and represented a broad spectrum of professional and biographical profiles in terms of age, experience, personal history, levels of the promotional structure and domestic arrangements. The work-life histories point up working lives of paradox, ambiguity and contradiction. Thickly layered descriptions reflect the complexity of several realities that our participants simultaneously balance. For example, gender identities are confirmed repeatedly, as part of the reproduction of social and sexual divisions in the family and labour market within capitalist society. Male teachers were more likely to self-identify as career teachers, whereas women's unpaid labour in the home often broke the paid work narrative for female teachers. This was the norm for the overwhelming majority of married women teachers beyond our reach, as most local authorities operated a marriage bar in the inter-war years that prevented them working other than as supply teachers.

The first section of this chapter uses documentary sources to examine the working life of someone active in the early 20th century. In the second section I focus on a cohort of male and female retired city teachers, both primary and secondary, ranging in age from 58 to 78. The third section ranges across the testimonies of our last two generational tiers, to listen to the voices of those who became teachers during and after the final phase of teacher–state relations that Grace identified. All of these teachers experienced the structural changes imposed on their profession in the late 1980s with the implementation of the national curriculum, and associated introduction of testing, inspections and league tables started by the Thatcher government and continued more recently by New Labour.

Narrative analysis of these work-life histories, recorded using oral history methodology, shows the impact of the past continues in the present. Conventional qualities of the 'good teacher' persist with emergent themes of caring, commitment, dedication, selflessness and respect. However, teachers' talk suggests a dissonance surrounding the emergence of new occupational identities that support Martin Lawn's (1996) post-1980s understanding of the 'good teacher' as a competent employee experiencing a diminishing sense of agency or control. Lawn's ideas take us beyond the 'modern times' charted by Grace, suggesting that there are continuities in teacher vocation, but that the meaning of a 'good teacher' is reconfigured within successive policy settlements. Individual biographies are used to make narrative sense of this conjunction of continuity and change within the broader context of their situation as public sector employees.

Narratives of the good teacher

'Moral missionary'

The London School Board appointed Clara Bulcraig head of Monnow Road Girls and Infants School in 1871. There she stayed until she retired in December 1911. Clara started her working life in the 1860s as a pupil teacher in London, having attended the Home and Colonial Institution in the Gray's Inn Road, a proprietary school run on joint stock principles for the education of the lower middle classes. Although only in her twenties when she became a headteacher, Clara's early career advancement was relatively common during the rapid expansion of mass schooling. In 1891, the publication of the first of Charles Booth's social surveys of *Labour and Life of the People in London* (1891) revealed a close correlation between a growing residential segregation in the city and a hierarchical gradation of schooling. The story of Monnow Road School well illustrates this

Monnow Road School: A showcase building, © City of London, London Metropolitan Archives

dynamic. In a place of abject poverty, its location in a not-too-bad street meant that in 1875, when elementary school fees ranged from 1d to 9d a week, it was the only 4d school in Bermondsey. From inauspicious beginnings in temporary premises lit by lamps donated by the ironmonger in the shop next door, Clara presided over its transformation into a School Board higher grade school, responding to the demand for post–elementary schooling. In 1900, the school moved into a new showcase building with gas lighting.

Evidence in the school magazine, dating from 1909, captures an elementary school world organically and integrally connected to the local community. The school and its head fostered an ethos, which the school motto epitomised. The challenge to pupils was to 'fight bravely against difficulties', be 'fair and square' and avoid 'everything mean and underhand'. 'Stick to this', they were told and 'it will bring you honour'. The school's habitus prepared working-class girls for immediate employment in the locality while shoring up a set of explicitly gendered subject positions. Witness Clara's homily, as some girls entered in the Bermondsey Swimming Competitions for the first time: 'A boyish girl is even more objectionable than a girlish boy is and you know what your brothers think of such boys. Do what you do, swimming included, in the very best way, but always let your aim be worthy and upright' (quoted in *The Monnow*, October 1911: 137).

Experimental science prep at Monnow Road School, © City of London, London Metropolitan Archives

Caring for the children and caring for each other was crucial to
the workplace culture. In an affectionate valedictory address, Clara's
colleagues declared: 'All those with whom you have been associated
in your life's work hold you in the highest esteem; and on many
occasions those responsible for the welfare of London education have
not only consulted you on important matters of school administration,
but have borne eloquent testimony to your experience, wisdom and
integrity' (quoted in *The Monnow*, January 1912: 2). These, then, were
the qualities officials valued in those who taught in the pioneering
days of London's education service.

Agent of state welfare

In this section we move out of the archive into living history, by
examining the oral testimony. The narratives show that caring
remains an important part of school work. Gerald is a retired primary
headteacher in his late sixties. His social origins were working class
and he was one of the successful children who passed the 11+ exam
and went to a boy's grammar school. He recounts an act of teaching
that provides a special instance of a moral and ethical relationship,
showing one past teacher's commitment to his pupils' advancement.

Having moved up into the top form for French, Gerald's teacher
felt that he would benefit from a school exchange and told the head
of department so. Knowing the cost was prohibitive for his parents,
Gerald told the teachers he did not want to go, but they insisted that
he take the letter all the children took home, anyway. In fact, the head
of department had already paid his mother a home visit and advised
her that a "trip to France would do me a power of good". If she
would accommodate a "French lad" and give Gerald some spending
money, "he would be prepared to pay or to see the trip was paid".
Gerald's parents agreed and to his surprise, "they both asked me, did I
think it would be any good to me, a trip abroad, and they thought it
was a good idea ... needing no second bidding, I said I thought I could
benefit from it and it was arranged". No one told him the full story
until after the teacher's death and his mother wrote him a letter with
an article from the local press.

This grammar school practitioner combined a morality of care with
a morality of justice. He accomplished teaching as caring through
writing a series of language textbooks and imploded the dichotomy
of academic subjects and interpersonal relationships. He tried to
nurture the children and teacher–child relationships extended beyond
the classroom. The way in which he 'lived' languages in his daily life

was one of the reasons Gerald went into teaching. On French day, for instance, he had French newspapers delivered to his home, he and his family spoke nothing but French and his French scholars would join them for a meal and play such games as the French version of Monopoly. Gerald's belief was that he was a good teacher who cared for children and cared for his subject area.

Other teachers extend the foundational bases of caring discourses. A common theme was male primary teachers who articulated a care perspective sustained through a self-sacrificing giving of their time, attention and commitment to school sports. This reinforces socio-historical analysis of loving or caring about children as being a mainstay of the teacher self. Take Roy and Susan, for example, a married couple who became primary teachers in the 1950s and 1960s respectively. Now retired, Susan remembered her working-class parents were ambitious for her. They encouraged her to become a teacher and were proud of her educational achievements. A preference for connectedness, said to be more characteristic of women than men, was at the centre of Susan's account. She consolidated her teacher self through her relations with older women teachers who "sort of mothered you".

Typically, Roy devoted Saturday mornings to school "football teams and whatnot", weekday evenings to school cricket and was at pains to emphasise that he saw this as "the only way of doing the job". Roy's caring activities derived from his teacher identity, expressed as values of care, dedication and self-investment, which he believed in. Observing the intersection between teaching and valued community activities, Roy emphasised the need to develop a rapport with parents as well as children. He explained "you've got to educate the children, but at the same time you've got to bear in mind that the parents have a role in this and if you can talk to parents as if they're human beings on your level, then you get on far better and your results are far better with the children". He saw this aspect of his work as crucial to the respect afforded teachers, enabling them to convert their limited economic and cultural capital into social capital in the public sphere of civil society. This can be understood as an example of the co-production of professional identity (see also Jane Franklin, Chapter Six, and Jayne Osgood, Chapter Fifteen, this volume).

What angered retired teachers the most, when remembering a life in education, were the new contracts and conditions of service imposed by the Thatcher government re-elected in 1987. For example, Roy thought the policy changes of the late 1980s had deprofessionalised teachers, making them "slaves to the system" in contrast to the autonomous professionals of his generation. The metaphor powerfully reflects a sense of disempowerment among teachers.

The competent employee

In the 1980s and 1990s state teachers had to make sense of a set of reforms that did not fit, at least on the surface, with long-held beliefs about the discourses of teaching as a vocation or calling. With this new welfare settlement, public services became increasingly defined as market commodities. The move to market accountability in education gave rise to a reorientation of the concept of vocation and this was integral to the teachers' testimonies. For instance, many expressed a sense of loss with regard to past educational arrangements. They spoke to a 'golden age' where vocation, care and dedication characterised and defined what it meant to be a teacher. The career story of secondary teacher Richard encapsulates this and is worth quoting at length. In his sixties and close to retirement, he began: "I came from a working-class family and a working-class area and the only, if you like, professionals that I saw, as part of my life, were teachers and occasionally doctors. So I didn't realise that there was a much wider scope than that. Even so, I had a push to be a teacher". Teacher identity intersects with other dimensions such as gender and ethnicity, but also class. Richard's experience turns on such coordinates. Told as a journey through time, his account combines past, present and futurity.

Richard decried the effects of education policies that had resulted in a new stress on efficiency, the growth in management systems and audit accountability and an attack on moral systems, such as child-centredness. He felt that these revised education's priorities and purpose and thereby affected representations of the good teacher and teachers' positioning in the field. Here follows an extract where he described how he witnessed the start of these changes at teacher training college in the early 1970s:

> "I think, piecemeal, we are going to get to that training centre position where, you know, teachers ... are told what to deliver and they are told how to deliver and then they are assessed on their ability to deliver and the kids in much the same way, are told this is what you've got to learn, this is the time frame you've got and you're going to be tested on it before you can go on and I think that ... we're going to go from what was liberal education to something which is closer to training."

What is also pertinent to this discussion is the paradox of teacher status. If pay was "a measure of the way people are seen in society, we are seen in a more favourable light, but I think that, as I said before, the main thing is a lack of trust. You know, we need to supervise what is going on because if we don't supervise what's going on people are going to be lazy".

The open espousal of central regulation redefines teachers' work through an emphasis on output as opposed to input. According to Richard, teachers "used to think of children as being people that we wanted to help grow into adults and as part of that there'd be … things like character building and social responsibility". Whereas now, "we're not really so interested in that … in them as a whole person, we are just interested in the skills that they are going to take to the workplace". Richard finished his interview by saying that the national curriculum, testing and inspection prevented him from teaching in the way that he thought was best for his pupils. Nonetheless, two former colleagues revealed that he has a reputation as a "saint" among many of the staff in this school for his way of always being calm with the pupils and willing to help colleagues.

Martin Lawn argues that the ideology of the market in education marks the end of modern times in teaching. New discourses, seen in the competitive nature of the reforms, began to redefine teacher professionalism. Under postmodernity, classroom teaching becomes 'a form of competent labour, flexible and multiskilled: it operates within a regulated curriculum and internal assessment system in a decentralized school market. The dominant version is now a notion of individual responsibility and incentive reward legitimated by the Citizen's Charter idea of efficient service and performance incentive' (Lawn, 1996: 12-13).

James, deputy head of an inner-city secondary school, articulated this: "What's happening to teaching? I think we've got a post-Fordist approach to teaching which is squeezing excellent teachers out, bringing in … a career teacher who actually is squeezing, squeezing the career up-ways just to see how quickly they can get right up to the top and beyond, out of schools into consultancy". He categorised the people who were becoming teachers now, as "Thatcher's children". The difference between his teaching generation and these new entrants was that "they don't argue politics and politics of teaching…. The argument is why have you given me this form, whatever?". He drew a contrast with the days of the Inner London Education Authority, for whom he worked before its abolition in 1990, when "there was an idea that you were playing with ideas". Politicised reflexivity was an aspect of his teacher self, a way of seeing schooling in the light of history concerned with the direction and subtext of educational change. Seen in this way we can perceive a mismatch between a teacherly habitus constituted around enduring notions of 'the good teacher' and an evolving institutional habitus within which neoliberal values of individualism and performativity dominate new managerial discourses and developments.

Rooted in societal and institutional constraints, the residue of teaching as a vocation, rather than a job, remains. Harriet, a primary school teacher in her early fifties, reckoned that "most people who are teaching, certainly in primary schools … do it because they enjoy it, and they get a lot out of it". When she reflected on the quality of commitment from a personal perspective, she described "feeling you're doing something worthwhile.…You can actually see, as well, physically sort of, what you have done over time. Because a lot of the children I have for two years and you can see a huge difference in, in how they've sort of matured and grown and advanced in two years". This links to an earlier comment, which extends the metaphor of teaching as care in gendered ways: "I think there's an awful lot of females go into it thinking that they're lovely little children, and that's what they want to do".

This is not to recourse to an essentialist equation of women with caring. Another participant, Dave, spoke passionately of his working-class social origins, as constitutive of his teacher self. "I went into teaching for the kids", he said. "I believe in teaching, I believe in it. I believe in what I'm doing, I believe, I believe in the kids." So Dave chose to work in an inner-city secondary school in a deprived area. The educator as change agent was part of his very identity and practice. There are clear parallels here with Harriet in her primary setting. Speaking about why she taught, she said "I think I do it as first, you know, a social sense, for the whole of society, I personally get something out of seeing the children develop". All of which suggests that deep personal and emotional investment characterises the caring activities of teachers, not just those teaching young children.

Making connections: the 21st-century teacher

Ivor Goodson (2003: 126) defines practical and reflexive professionalism as a body of knowledge 'concerned with the intricate definition and character of occupational action'. Those becoming teachers since the 1988 Education Reform Act must accept new governmental guidelines and national objectives and curriculum. However, their accounts suggest that, in defining their own occupational identities, they have sought to reappropriate the official discourse in order to incorporate their sense of vocation. A major plank of their rhetoric builds on the standards agenda pushed for by central governments but reworks this in terms of a commitment to active *care* for students, and a belief in social practice and moral purpose.

Some took up the language of Christian rescue to express their belonging and commitment to elements of their work. Nina, a young English teacher in an inner-city secondary school in the North West, spoke of her charismatic evangelical church as constitutive of her current identity and practice as a teacher. In her words, "it is a massive part of who I am as a teacher and I try to, like I do try to pray about the school and pray for the kids that I meet and I try to kind of show them the good side of being a Christian, you know". She loved teaching, because it satisfied her need to feel that "you can make a difference". Curriculum development and professionalism is the driving force in this situation, albeit powerfully informed by deeper roots in her religious faith. Her belief propelled her towards teaching and extra-mural welfare work with the homeless and destitute.

Max, a primary school teacher in his mid-twenties, revealed how he had quickly become disillusioned with the ideology of the market, with input replaced by output as the key evaluative rule of education. "It's becoming a lot more, I don't know … it feels more like a business. It feels more like it's some sort of company and you're reaching your quota and you're reaching your target rather than a school." Contrary to the dominant performance indicators in the opening decade of the 21st century, he believed teaching to be an intuitive act and placed great emphasis on the school as an organic entity. Inseparably linked with memories of the past, the legacy of his own experience of primary education enabled him to compare the current system with a time when the schooling pedagogic process placed more emphasis on the child.

An historical approach to thinking about professional identity alerts us to successive 'stages' in policy development. It also reminds us that institutions and organisations are socially constructed, not given, and are in an ongoing process of transformation. New policy settlements produce a value shift that is troubling for many (but not all) who work in the welfare field and participants described the challenge of intergenerational communication between professionals.

A continuum of caring discourses ranging between the more specific definitions of caring (such as caring as parenting) and the most inclusive (caring as commitment) was a common feature in this investigation into the making of the good teacher in the 20th century. Sometimes this was couched in child-centred professional discourses. Emma, a newly qualified female primary teacher in her early twenties, proffered some insights into the situation. As a girl growing up in the 1990s, she loved her favourite primary teacher and she loved playing schools:

> "I used to write all my teddies' and my dolls' names down on an A4 piece of paper and I would just do the register, then pretend it was a new day, and do the register again.... The children have found me a bit, not maternal, because obviously I'm not their mother but really approachable and you know, I love hearing their wacky stories and you can't help but become part of their family for that time you're teaching them really.... I can tell them what to do and the results they produced from what I told them to do, it's just a great sense of satisfaction for me, a sense of achievement."

In an important sense, then, the teacher habitus rests on a nurturing, familial vocabulary. These reminiscences suggest how teachers forge a 'teacherly' self in interaction with children, and maintain and amend this over the course of a career and beyond. There were clear generational differences in the storylines but the continuities in vocation that come through the oral histories can provide us with both the insights and the inspiration to reassert collective strategies that give strong impetus to the expanded conceptions of social education and democracy articulated here.

Acknowledgements

'Does Work Still Shape Social Identity and Social Action?' was supported by the ESRC, award number RES 148 25 0038. The other members of the research team were Steve Jefferys, John Kirk, Tim Strangleman and Chris Wall.

Note

[1] 'Economic capital' refers to income, wealth, financial inheritances and monetary assets. Cultural capital, defined as high culture, can exist in three forms: embodied cultural capital, objectified cultural capital and institutional cultural capital. The last is the product of investment in formal education. Social capital is the product of sociability, which speaks of investment in culturally, economically or politically useful networks and connections. When valorised in a given field of practice, the different forms of capital take the form of symbolic capital.

References

Booth, C. (ed) (1891) *Life and Labour of the People in London. Vol. 1*, London: Williams and Norgate.

Bourdieu, P. (2001) *Practical Reason*, Cambridge: Polity Press.

Goodson, I. (2003) *Professional Knowledge, Professional Lives*, Buckingham: Open University Press.

Grace, G. (1987) 'Teachers and the state in Britain: a changing relation', in M. Lawn and G. Grace (eds) *Teachers: The Culture and Politics of Work*, Lewes: Falmer, pp 193–228.

Lawn, M. (1996) *Modern Times? Work, Professionalism and Citizenship in Teaching*, Lewes: Falmer.

Oram, A. (1996) *Women Teachers and Feminist Politics 1900-39*, Manchester: Manchester University Press.

Fourteen

Feminist Webs: a case study of the personal, professional and political in youth work[1]

Janet Batsleer

The Feminist Webs archive held at Manchester
University and online at www.feministwebs.com

This chapter presents a case study of critical
reflective practice: the Feminist Webs project. Its
aims are twofold: to present an account of the
interconnections between a political perspective –
feminism – and a professional practice – youth work;
and to go beyond a micro-account of reflective
practice by locating that professional practice in a
wider social, historical and political context. In a youth work context,
feminist ideas have primarily influenced work with girls, as well as
informing an approach to work with young men that challenges
sexism and sees boys as people first rather than as a social problem
to be tackled. The account given here of the relationship between
youth work as a profession and feminism as a politics is situated,
partial, not innocent, as is the way with all reflective practice. Nor is it
linear. The chapter begins with an exploration of the web metaphor
employed by the Feminist Webs project. Secondly, the nature of
the intergenerational professional reflection captured in this web is
presented through a Question and Answer (Q&A) format, which is

itself available on the Feminist Webs website (www.feministwebs.com). Thirdly, and in a more conventional argument, the implications of the Feminist Webs project for other professionals and for discussions of reflective practice are explored.

The web

Before the internet made the web an everyday cliché of communication it was used by women peace campaigners associated with Greenham Common as a metaphor for the threads of association and activism that would be able to subvert the linear hierarchical power of the military. 'It's not just the web, it's the way that we spin it; it's not just the world, it's the women that's in it; that's what gets results', as the song went. The more threads, the stronger the web. Women, after all, are spinsters. This metaphor has re-emerged to communicate the practice of an intergenerational project aiming to revive the connection between feminism and youth work.

The project

Feminist Webs is an intergenerational enterprise to design and produce an online 'women and girls work space' that will act as both an archive and a resource for practitioners, volunteers and young women involved in youth and community work with young women. Our bias is toward work that encourages participation and is from a feminist, 'rights-based' perspective.

Young people have been working alongside older women who have been active in feminism and in youth work to come up with a set of exercises we have also made into a pocket-sized poster/leaflet that youth workers can use in sessions.

Go to the *feminist webers* (www.feministwebs.com/about/feminist-webers/) page for mini-biographies of the people involved in creating the project to date.

Young people have helped to design the site and booklet, and create new activities and resources. If our second-stage funding is successful the young people will be trained in oral history and will act as roving reporters to collate older women's stories and advice and archive material to create the online archive section.

Other groups and people involved include both academics and practitioners who have contributed to the content of the resource section and who also provide materials/loan materials to be uploaded onto the site. Partners and supporters include: ICA:UK, Manchester Metropolitan University, the University of Manchester, The Young Women's Health Project, The Women's Resource Centre, Stockport Young Women's Forum, Lancashire Youth Service, The Young Advocate for the North West and the North West Regional Youth Work Unit.

The Feminist Webs project is a place of connection and debate between practitioners and academics, girls, young women, recent graduates, middle-aged women, older women.

Source: Taken from www.feministwebs.com

Some of the girls and young women involved in the project come from established Young Women's Forums across the North West, which have their roots in the earlier moment of feminist organising. Young Women's Forums were established as a form of positive action, giving young women a voice in youth work dominated by fears of and for young men. Participants also come from lesbian and bisexual youth projects, now able, in contrast to the situation in the 1970s and 1980s, to organise openly and attract public and charitable funding. A third route to involvement has been through mainstream participation initiatives such as the UK Youth Parliament. Some participants made contact with the project directly through their involvement with other feminist political networks and others who have become involved through family and friendship networks.

Feminist Webs are:

> about forwardness
> about interconnectedness
> full of spaces
> and also lines that are the connections and the stories
> they hold people together like a net
> points of understanding across generations
> a way of representing what feminism is and making links
> with other social justice movements
> sticky: they hold people together
> but people can also get stuck in them

not unusual
not innocent: ask the fly!
(Feminist Webs Oral History Residential, November 2008)

The threads of this web are made by using new communication media including Web 2.0 and Twitter as well as older forms of organising recognisable to previous generations. They are interpersonal, organisational and political. Youth work methods, such as small group work and residential, reappear in contemporary virtual form. Links from the website can take the reader to detailed designs for group work sessions, international feminist websites such as The F-Word and announcements of public actions such as 'Reclaim the Night' marches and a march organised by Mothers against Violence challenging gun and knife crime. Contemporary feminist youth work speaks a different language from the language of the 'five outcomes' and of *Every Child and Young Person Matters*, while undoubtedly affirming the intrinsic worth of young women and contributing to the desired 'outcomes' of policy. The threads of the web are personal, political and professional.

Speaking about feminism enables practitioners to resist the bureaucratised languages that characterise current initiatives. This attests to the sources of inspiration for the Feminist Webs project outside of the policy mainstream in an attempt to recover and archive something that was being lost. The artefacts and papers from the Girls Work Movement, the cartoons of Jackie Fleming, the poems and music now stored in the archive (both physical and virtual) are the sparks for storytelling and focused conversations which weave the threads of the web. The places where the threads join are shared events and shared actions, new memories and new stories to be told in future.

Imagine the conversations provoked from this archive item found in Box 7 of the physical archive.

Archive item

A Q&A session about Feminist Webs

Question: Can you explain something about the relationship between feminism and youth work?

Answer: There has been a long tendency for youth work to be dominated by the concerns that society has about boys, and for girls to be seen as the solution to the problems boys are thought to be. Good youth work has always tried to challenge this and instead to start from where young people are and from a sense of their potential, whether the young people are male or female, whatever their class or community background. It does not do this 'starting from strengths' by taking a gender-blind or 'colour-blind' approach, however. This is how the current National Occupational Standards for Youth Work explain this:

> It respects and values individual differences by supporting and strengthening young people's belief in themselves and their capacity to grow and change via a supportive group environment.
>
> It is underpinned by the principles of equity, diversity and interdependence.
>
> It recognises, respects and is actively responsive to the wider network of peers, communities, families and cultures that are important to young people, and through these networks seeks to help young people achieve stronger relationships and collective identities, through the promotion of inclusivity.

In other words, good youth work cannot deny the ways in which significant social divisions, such as those associated with class and racism as well as gender, have an impact. At the same time, good youth workers do not assume they know the meanings of these divisions to young people ahead of focused conversations with them.

Question: So feminist youth work is just good youth work then?

Answer: That's what some of its practitioners would argue, as would practitioners of Muslim youth work, and Christian youth work, and Jewish youth work, and cooperative humanist youth work of course! Feminism and youth work can find common cause in a variety of ways though. This is how the definition of youth work just mentioned begins:

Young people choose to be involved, not least
because they want to relax, meet friends, make new
relationships, to have fun and to find support.

The work starts from where young people are in
relation to their own values, views and principles
as well as their own personal and social space.

It seeks to go beyond where young people start, to
widen their horizons, promote participation and invite
social commitment, in particular by encouraging
them to be critical and creative in their responses
to their experience and the world around them.

It treats young people with respect, valuing each
individual and their differences, and promoting
the acceptance and understanding of others, while
challenging oppressive behaviour and ideas.

Feminist practice in youth work is all about enabling young people
to be critical and creative in response to the world around them.
Feminists have historically been concerned to make visible and
challenge the violence and oppression that can limit women's
opportunities and all good youth workers seek to contest the limits
that are placed on young people reaching and fulfilling their potential.

Question: Why did feminism and youth work have such a strong
connection in the late 1970s and early 1980s? And why are young
women interested in it again now?

Answer: The memories of the 'Girls Work Movement' are
exhilarating. The notion that 'the personal is political' led to a
transformation in understandings of what is a suitable agenda for
politics and therefore open to change. And youth work as social
education always started from the everyday personal concerns and
happenings of life. Alongside other movements, the Women's Liberation
Movement made the body political and the site of potential democratic
transformation. Violent and abusive marriages ceased to be seen
as a matter of 'bad luck'. Decision making about childbearing and
childrearing was possible and could be supported by public resources
in health services and nurseries. The cultural representations of women,
including the representations of women as sex, were open to re-
invention and change. Seeking sexual pleasure was not something
women were to be denigrated for. Women imagined themselves in

places and positions they had previously been denied: making the films and the music; riding and repairing the motorbikes and racing cars; flying the planes; raising hopes and expectations for excitement and adventure beyond the limitations of the private and domestic sphere. Women also demanded recognition of the work and the value of the work involved in mothering and investigated the persistent sources of women's poverty. This transformation of the sphere of the 'personal' into a site of political struggle is a lasting achievement of that movement. This is how the connection with youth work, which also starts from young people's personal everyday concerns, came to be made.

Feminist campaigns now – such as Object – are focusing their attention on the ways in which misogynist, sexualised representations of women are controlling women's opportunities in the workplace, in leisure spaces and in the public domain, while the issue of the 'Beauty Myth' and body image has become a significant concern to many young women. Resistance to both public violence in war and street violence, and to interpersonal domestic violence and rape is once again a focus of younger feminists' attention.

Youth workers and feminists (often the same people) in the 1970s and 1980s were asking questions about what the life of adult women might be like in the context of equality of the sexes and this led to questioning the 'femininities' on offer to girls growing up and to offering them the wherewithal to challenge the limitations placed on them because of their gender by adults such as teachers, parents and other relatives, including cousins and brothers. The Girls Work Movement flowered only briefly. As the wider political movement all but disappeared in the 1990s, its remnants and traces could be found in continued 'separate provision' for girls and young women, but this largely ceased to be feminist space. It became seen either as a space for 'culturally sensitive' work with Muslim girls, 'the ultimate separatist cage', or a feminised space for various kinds of pampering or arts and crafts, with political passion and vision seemingly lost. It was this state of affairs that led the young women who initiated 'Feminist Webs' to ask the question: 'Done Hair and Nails? Now What?', the title of the first resource pack produced by the project.

Question: Are there any difficulties about the connections between political agendas and professionalism for feminist youth workers?

Answer: Of course and it is for this reason that many youth workers who promote 'Work with Girls and Young Women' have chosen not to identify their work as feminist. They see it as raising issues of political indoctrination, in a similar way to the ways in which the term 'Christian youth work' raises fears of evangelisation. When youth work is understood as an educational process raising critical questions these fears can be addressed. There are many advantages to the use of the 'F' word. It challenges ways of drawing professional boundaries that rely on more apparently neutral terms such as 'gender', 'inclusion' or 'mainstreaming'. It is the very unsettling nature of the F word that rapidly enables a context of critical conversation to occur.

Feminism is a strong word, associated with being critical and discontented with received ideas of what it means to be a woman or a man. As a political term, it contains the possibility, and perhaps the necessity, of forging links with other rights-based social movements. It is also a word that provokes fear, misunderstanding, and has in itself been misrepresented in order to diffuse its power: it has been read as 'man-hating', 'lesbian', 'white and middle class'. It is certainly true that it puts people's backs up, particularly the backs of people who believe there isn't a problem in the realm of sexual equality. For feminists working together in Feminist Webs, the word is also an affirmation of commitment to women, to women's space and women-centred practice. But this too raises problems: there is no consensus about the value of this practice among feminists, many of whom now work alongside pro-feminist men.

Question: But are there also problems about 'professionalising' a politics? Doesn't the issue become that people only engage with feminist agendas when they are paid to do it?

Answer: Yes, and it can clearly be argued that the movement fell apart in the 1980s when it was mainstreamed, became part of managerial agendas and ceased to be grounded in a political movement. The presence of the term 'feminism' is immensely valuable to the movement of ideas and practice across generations. It is itself an 'equaliser' as it challenges preconceived ideas of managerialism, authority and communication. It draws on collective storytelling; it opens up questions of pedagogy and learning which can revive understandings of the role of the educator and of the learning implicit in practice. Feminist learning cannot be one way, between the older 'expert' and the younger 'novice'. And many youth work traditions are anti-managerialist!

Question: That isn't the only story about how and why the movement fell apart though. What about the question of how feminism itself as a politics and set of practices addresses difference between women and the complicated impact of power differentials on the agendas of the movement?

Answer: Well, that story has been well rehearsed in many places and is incredibly important to the older women involved in the intergenerational oral histories project. For the younger women the issues seem less conflict ridden and it seems to be taken as read that there will be diversity of perspectives and visions about the future for women. In the poet June Jordan's words, 'When we get the monsters off our backs we may all want to run in very different directions'. Involvement with youth work means that the projects do cross class boundaries as well as engaging with young women who are marginalised from mainstream education for many reasons. There are young graduates involved in Feminist Webs as well as young women who were excluded from school; the archive is seeking oral histories from all the threads of activism that critiqued as well as engaged with the 1980s movement. There are overlaps with lesbian histories, with Black women's activisms and with disability politics.

A key shift is that instead of seeing these differences as sources of antagonism and hostility it is more possible now to seek out alliances and recognise the complexity of identities. So, for example, young feminist women are working with pro-feminist men.

Question: You imply that because youth work is an educational practice, this prevents the Feminist Webs project becoming uncritical indoctrination in feminist politics. How?

Answer: Feminist youth workers are informal educators. But there are a number of ways of understanding the educator role. All are present in the Feminist Webs project and sometimes they are in tension with each other. For example, education is thought to be about transmitting information. This starts with the idea that young women in particular are in the dark about important information, such as the fact that for every £1 a man earns, a woman earns 87.5p for doing the same job or that women own only 1% of the world's property. This ignorance denies girls choice, freedom and opportunity. The resources created through Feminist Webs will give girls knowledge. They will then be able to make well-informed decisions on the basis of having facts on women's inequality at their fingertips. The educator is an illuminator, shedding light in the darkness of ignorance and disbelief.

Another model of education sees learning as emancipatory. The ignorance we have of our own situation is a ruse of power, both a consequence of sexual inequality and a condition for it. Challenging this ignorance, therefore, involves challenging the power relationships that produce it. Feminist educational processes then become a process of critical pedagogy delving below the level of apparently discrete facts about disadvantage to find hidden connections and a systemic account of women's oppression. In this approach the role of the youth worker as educator is to support and encourage young women to make a courageous leap into a new and fuller knowledge of their own situation. During the Feminist Webs project young women have found affirmation of their courage in challenging the status quo in stories from the earlier experience of older women. Older more experienced women can say: you are not the first people and you will not be the last to feel anger, shock, hopelessness and fear in response to the facts about your situation as women. Nor will you be the last to feel exhilarated in the process of challenging these 'facts' that are social and not eternal and can be changed.

Here the role that the youth worker as educator takes is that of the scientist or grand theorist, enabling previously unenlightened girls to recognise the underlying truth of their situation. Or the youth worker is imagined as a heroic seeker after truth and justice who is passing on alternative counter-hegemonic knowledge which enables the uncovering of a system of oppression – patriarchy – which lays women low at every turn. The educator invites participants in projects both into a more truthful worldview and into a community and set of identities that enable resistance. These may be 'big' identities, such as 'campaigner' or 'activist' or 'cultural practitioner' or 'lesbian', but they may also be apparently uniquely personal stories, of finding a way to channel anger or of overcoming a lengthy and suicidal period of depression. The stories that are being recovered and passed on through the oral history project can be thought of both as the links in a chain that is a chain of a political movement over time and also as community building in themselves. 'This is what it might mean ... to advocate feminism.' It is not only stories that are passed on but also traditions of activism: the banner-making which dates back certainly as far as the suffrage movement; 'Reclaim the Night' marches; as well as re-inventing old methods – such as the postcard campaign – for a new period of internet activism. Emancipatory pedagogies have the great strength of recognising that education in women's rights are caught up in the power struggle and that for young women to be invited into such work requires an ethical stance of care on the part of the youth worker who supports the coming-to-voice and power-to-name in young women.

Lastly, there is a powerful model of youth work that sees education and knowledge as *contested* and dialogic, rooted in conversation. This model focuses on the gaps, risks, realisations and struggles and the ambivalence involved in change. In this case, it becomes important for the intergenerational work *not* to position older feminists simply as 'experts'. It becomes possible to explore the 'blind spots' and areas of misunderstanding between groups of women, including between older and younger women, as potentially fruitful sources of knowledge. So, for example, discussions of 'race' and racism, discussions of relations with men, discussions of sexuality and other 'differences that matter' have historically been the site of both painful division *and* of growth and development for feminist analysis. This is once again potentially the case when, in the current 'equalities and diversities' agenda a structural divide-and-rule is occurring with the different 'diversities' put in a position to compete for the same pots of funding. It should not surprise us therefore to hear discourses on all sides which claim that 'the other' group is prioritised: racism over sexism, or, alternatively, sexism over racism, disability over racism, everything over disability, sexuality over racism and no mention of class and so on in a terrible regress. Recognising the situatedness of knowing and the particular, historical movements into and out of positions of relative power and relative powerlessness potentially opens up a different set of conversations. One woman remembered wearing a badge that said 'We don't want the crumbs, we want the whole bloody bakery', and the image of groups fighting over the crumbs potentially reshapes the rivalrous conversations away from 'either/or' towards 'both/and' thinking.

If Feminist Webs really is a space for 'moving beyond the comfort zone', a place where older and younger women can challenge one another, then difficult questions cannot be avoided. If the role of the youth worker as educator is to create a space in which all voices can be heard, questioning, facilitating and creating their own terms for conversation, then dialogues across all kinds of division and the delineation of genuine conflicts of ideas and perspective becomes possible.

Conclusion: The implications of the Feminist Webs project for other professionals working with young people and for conceptualisations of reflective practice

Cross-generational conversations of the kind documented here could be engaged throughout the children and young people's workforce. It need not be an investigation of gender that forms the basis of critical enquiry in reflective practice. The important issue would be the potential for intergenerational learning in relation to a shared agenda.

During the period of the 'mainstreaming' of feminist ideas it was argued that commitment to gender equality should become professionally mandatory and be delivered through performance management. However, youth work which embraced an explicitly feminist approach to work with girls and young women was not in fact well protected by the ritual writing of well-intentioned commitments to anti-oppressive practice. Such statements were systematically and fiercely fought for and won and just as systematically ignored. The re-emergence of feminist activism revives the debates about whether it is possible to inscribe – for example, a commitment to feminism – as a professional requirement. The experience of Feminist Webs implicitly involves a critique of technicist models of reflective practice that seek compliance to a set of standards or norms.

However, contemporary professional practice requires an engagement with such matters as quality standards and multidisciplinary practice in ways that were unknown to an earlier generation. It may be that the opportunities for shared reflective learning in multidisciplinary teams will create new spaces for networks and webs. If this is to be so, the models of practice-based learning which are available in those teams matter enormously. So what, if anything, can we take into a model of professional learning from Feminist Webs and what models of professional learning might be most consonant with it?

The model of cross-generational learning that Feminist Webs embodies is not individual but shared and collective. Many models of 'reflection' are intensely individualised and promote problem solving. The experience of Feminist Webs reinforces the idea that reflection can move beyond this, as has been suggested by writers in critical management studies who suggest that 'critical reflection' is concerned with questioning assumptions, focused on the social not the individual, paying particular attention to the analysis of power relationships and concerned with democracy.

The experience of Feminist Webs suggests that the situated knowledges of professionals might be understood in terms of a bigger picture. 'Professional identities' are formed in ways that are always interacting with the other aspects of biographies, both personal and political. While models of collective learning which draw on ideas of 'communities of practice' may assist with understanding political learning that can occur in organisations, some critical management theorists also point to 'group relations conferences' as sources for understanding the conscious and unconscious processes at work in organisations and networks which release energy for change, or undermine it, or both (Reynolds and Vince, 2004).

Recent feminist theoretical work on the epistemological significance of emotion in organisations and networks might also offer a resource for understanding something more about the pains and joys of change (Ahmed, 2004; Davidson *et al.*, 2005).

Emancipatory values are central to youth work and informal social education but the Feminist Webs project suggests that these values can be expressed through open educational processes rather than imposed managerially. Focused conversations with groups and other well-established youth work/group facilitation tools have been used as a facilitating method throughout the Feminist Webs project.

The model of learning in Feminist Webs, while it is collective, is not (yet) institutionalised. The model of learning through communities of practice that operate at the edge of and across the boundaries of institutions potentially offers a fruitful basis for understanding this. Wenger's components of learning in 'communities of practice' – *meanings, practice, community and identity* – can be used to analyse this (1998).

Meanings – of what it means to be a woman as well as of what it means to espouse feminism – are investigated and exchanged.

Practice – that opens up the historical resources of informal social education that is youth work, of which 'girls' work' is one strand.

Community – that affirms through the public production of memories and the sharing of stories that such efforts are worthwhile and of value and that we can grow in competence in negotiating an unequal world as a result of them.

Identity (what Wenger calls 'learning as becoming') – so that the learning that occurs through involvement in Feminist Webs has the potential to shape, affirm and change our sense of who we are in the context of being a woman, within the feminist communities reflected in Feminist Webs and in our roles as women in a range of communities.

Cross-generational work suggests something about a willingness to engage in learning over time and between times which is entirely absent from most models of reflective practice which might most typically have an 'organisational year' (or much shorter period) as the time frame. Models of experiential learning that have mostly informed 'reflective practice' have tended to value immediacy and relevance (experience, observation, reflection, action) in ways that undervalue the abstraction, the distance required for criticality and the power of theorisation and conceptualising. However, it has been the shared and changing conceptualising and acting of 'feminism' over time and across age groups that facilitates learning. It is thought-provoking to wonder what it might mean to allow a longer time frame for the passing on of professional knowledge and understanding. This would clearly pose problems in a policy context that insists on perpetual change and new initiatives.

Developing a space for professional learning outside the established and legitimated framework enables creativity. The 'outsider's eye' enables practitioners who do not take their agenda directly from public policy to see new things, for example, that the phrase 'young people' in public policy very often has a gendered reference which is not investigated. The development of trust and open dialogue over time within the cross-generational context is also suggestive for the use of 'critical friends' in professional learning which enables dialogues across difference and the opening up of power relationships to exploration and change, so that critical reflection involves not only the backward look but also the forward projection: the model of 'making histories' and 'feminist futures'.

Finally, there is a lasting sense of the limitations of professionally based understandings in all of this. "Without inspiration and passion and a big heart for the work, it will not happen", says Marie Brookfield, one of the older activists recorded in the archive. There can only be a 'critical feminist youth work' because there is a wider feminist movement made up of women and girls and their male allies who wear the t-shirt 'this is what a feminist looks like' and who chant confidently 'we're here, we're queer and we're not going shopping'.

Note

[1] This chapter was written by Janet Batsleer based on discussion with Alison Ronan and Amelia Lee.

References

Ahmed, S. (2004) *The Cultural Politics of Emotion*, Edinburgh: Edinburgh University Press/Routledge Edinburgh.

Davidson, J., Bondi, L. and Smith, M. (eds) (2005) *Emotional Geographies*, London: Ashgate.

Reynolds, M. and Vince, R. (eds) (2004) *Organizing Reflection*, London: Gower Ashgate.

Wenger, E. (1998) *Communities of Practice: Learning, Meaning and Identity*, Cambridge: Cambridge University Press.

Fifteen

Professional identities in the nursery: contested terrain

Jayne Osgood

Introduction

In this chapter I propose that the professional identitics of nursery workers are politically and socially constructed. I begin by mapping the discursive landscape in which nursery workers are located, suggesting that they are pathologised through dominant policy and media narratives. Nursery workers' constructions of professionalism are explored to offer insights into the ways in which ideas of social class and professionalism are closely interwoven, and how the successful performance of professionalism are co-produced, depending on contextual factors such as parental recognition and managerial support. I also explore the ways in which classed, 'raced' and gendered subjectivities intersect with notions of professionalism in nursery work. In effect, my aim is to demonstrate that professionalism is personal, shaped and inflected by autobiography, and professional identities are malleable and shift according to the social context in which they are located. It is my intention to contribute to critical understandings of the ways in which identities are discursively produced performances and offer suggestions for the ways in which narrowly prescriptive constructions of professionalism might be problematised.

My approach is informed by Foucault's idea of discursive (re)positioning to explain how professional identities are constructed and (re)negotiated when hegemonic and counter discourses intersect. Foucault describes power as:

> Never localised here or there, never in anybody's hands, never appropriated as commodity or a piece of wealth. Power is exercised through a net-like organisation. And not only do individuals circulate between its threads; they are always in the position of

simultaneously undergoing and exercising this power.
They are not its inert or consenting target; they are
always also the elements of its articulation. (1980: 98)

The nursery workers in this study were variously positioned through
discourse as more or less professional at different times, in different
contexts. By taking into consideration the social milieu in which
they are located at any given moment, I provide insights into the
complexity of 'doing professionalism'.

The discursively constructed nursery worker: policy discourses

Nurseries play a crucial role in the web of services and occupational
groups that work with children and their families. Over the past
decade nurseries (and the staff within them) have undergone an
intense process of politicisation (Dahlberg and Moss, 2005). Never
before have nursery staff encountered the degree of (political, media
and public) attention than has been the case since the election of a
New Labour government in 1997. Commentators have observed
that nurseries have taken on a central role politically, economically
and within educational/welfare policy (Levitas, 1998; Randall, 2000).
Increasingly, nurseries are looked to by government as the means to
reach its goals of greater labour market participation (that is, working
mothers) and providing social/educational opportunities to children
(that is, school readiness) (Rahilly and Johnston, 2002).

Shortly after taking office, New Labour extensively outlined
concerns about the quality of nursery provision, as well as issues of
accessibility, availability and affordability (DfES, 1997). *The National
Childcare Strategy* (DfES, 1997) proposed a 'crisis in childcare', laying
the ground for a decade of sustained reform. While 'quality' remains
a contested concept (Dahlberg and Moss, 2005; Osgood, 2008), prior
to *The National Childcare Strategy* this term was generally taken to
encompass physical environments: health and safety, nutrition, adult/
child ratios and so on. However, within the policies produced by New
Labour concerns with 'quality' were extended to include the staff
working in nurseries and their claims to professionalism:

Our goal must be to make working with children an
attractive, high status career and to develop a more skilled,

> flexible workforce ... improve the skills and effectiveness
> of the children's workforce.... (DfES, 2003: 10)

Throughout *The National Childcare Strategy* (DfES, 1997) the
workforce is constructed as 'neglected' (p 3); as 'lagging behind' (p 10);
'failing to meet the needs of children' (p 10); 'under-qualified' and not
of 'the right calibre' (p 11).

> For too long the UK has lagged behind in developing
> good quality, affordable and accessible childcare ...
> the quality of care can be variable. (DfES, 1997: 5)

Within policy documents (for example, DfES, 1997, 2003, 2005) it is
clear that the nursery workforce is deemed to lack 'quality' in terms
of pedagogical practices and professionalism. An entire chapter of *The
National Childcare Strategy* (DfES, 1997) is devoted to 'Raising quality',
which carries the implicit assumption that nursery provision lacks
quality.

Media constructions of the nursery worker

Nurseries 'risk creating a generation of Vicky Pollards' claimed *The
Guardian* in August 2006. The article described how the chair of the
Professional Association of Teachers (PAT) attacked nursery workers
for failing to meet minimum standards or present positive role models
to the children in their care. Speaking at a conference the chair went
on to criticise nursery workers for dressing inappropriately, with long
nails and 'chunky' shoes, frequently complaining about hangovers
and with an inability to articulate effectively or spell beyond the
limits of text messaging. Nurseries also featured in a number of
primetime documentary-style television programmes around the
same time (for example, Panorama, Inside Out). Without exception
these programmes presented nurseries negatively, fuelling the risk
discourses that have come to shape postmodern parenting (Furedi,
2008). For example, 'Nurseries undercover', aired in August 2004
on the BBC, pathologised the nursery staff by presenting a selective
account of working practices, showing staff to be 'sleeping on the
job'. The documentary received considerable press coverage (Collins,
2004; Taylor, 2004; *The Daily Telegraph*, 2004), creating something of a
moral panic (Cohen, 1986) and further fuelling negative constructions
of nursery workers. Media coverage of nurseries and the staff that
work within them continues to attract negative press. A recent

example includes the discovery of abusive practices in a Plymouth-based nursery in 2009; such stories escalate public concerns about the trustworthiness of nursery workers.

In her research on caring work Beverley Skeggs (1997, 2003) draws our attention to how working-class women are portrayed in negative ways to serve political goals. Throughout the media attention on nurseries little or no reference is made to structural inequalities (such as low status, poor working conditions, long hours, inadequate pay, lack of professional support and development opportunities). Instead the identity of 'the nursery worker' becomes fabricated and exaggerated (Strathern, 1987) and shaped by classed prejudice and gendered assumptions.

Childcare has then become the central means through which government can achieve its political goals of increased labour market participation, lying at the heart of welfare-to-work that targets low-income families and 'work–life balance' strategies aimed at dual-income middle-class families (Williams, 1999; Randall, 2000). It is not surprising then that nursery workers have been subjected to scrutiny and critique because of what they have come to symbolically represent (a safe alternative/addition to mother care). Alongside the unprecedented policy attention nursery workers have effectively been propelled from the margins through media coverage. Parents also appear to have a keen and growing interest in the perceived shortcomings of childcare provision. A classed and gendered analysis of the discursive landscape in which nursery workers are located reveals the endemic prejudice that working-class women, engaged in care work, are subject to (Skeggs, 2003; Osgood, 2005, 2006b, 2006c; Colley, 2006).

Having set the discursive landscape I now turn to the narratives of a sample of nursery workers to unearth and problematise the taken-for-granted assumptions that shape public constructions of the average nursery worker and their (apparently questionable) professionalism. I look to the ways in which nursery workers engage with dominant discourses that discursively position them in particularly negative ways (as lacking professionalism and quality).

Normative middle-class mothering and the deficient 'other(ed) mothers'

Maternalistic discourses are in many ways embedded in discursive constructions of nursery work. Or, as Ailwood (2008: 162) asserts:

> Early Childhood Education and Care [ECEC]
> teachers continue to have their skills and knowledge
> regularly and enduringly attributed to natural
> mothering instinct ... the naturalisation of their work
> undermines their struggle for professional status.

Motherhood is a central theme to emerge in debates about ECEC
practice, professionalism and professional identities (Cameron *et al.*,
1999; Ailwood, 2008; Osgood, 2008). Yet it is 'sensitive' middle-class
mothering that is normalised within ECEC practice and policy.
For the primarily working-class women that make up the nursery
workforce, enacting middle-class normativity in their professional
conduct can be treacherous and represents a challenge to their sense of
self (Osgood, 2008). The extent to which the nursery worker occupies
a sense of authenticity in their professional performances relies on the
context in which they are located and the relationships through which
their professionalism is questioned.

The data drawn on in this chapter come from a recent study
(Osgood, 2008) with nursery staff in London. Three nurseries were
purposively selected to ensure comparability. To enable an exploration
of the classed nature of childcare consumption nurseries were included
from the private, voluntary and statutory sectors.

The statutory sector nursery was held in high regard by the local
authority and by local parents. The intake included a broad mix of
middle-class fee-paying families (believing the nursery to be aligned
to their leftist politics and a firm belief in comprehensive education)
and families from the housing estates close by, many of whom were
unemployed and/or lone-parent families. A small number of children
were statemented with special educational needs.

The voluntary sector nursery was nestled within the heart of a
high-rise housing estate and the intake reflected the immediate
urban working-class community it served; as such it was ethnically
diverse and included a significant proportion of children with specific
language and literacy needs. As a voluntary sector nursery the local
community were active in the management and direction of the
provision via a management committee.

By contrast, the private sector nursery catered almost exclusively
for fee-paying, predominantly white, middle-class children from three
months to three years old. This provided a site for highly classed and
'raced' relationships between nursery worker and mother (which I go
on to demonstrate). Compared to the private nursery, workers at the
statutory and voluntary sector nurseries were more readily constructed

as esteemed experts in child development, so that the classed relationships between parent and nursery worker became inverted. The nursery worker co-constructed a more middle-class, professional role that became increasingly pronounced in relationships with parents routinely pathologised in public discourse (that is, families under social services).

It is my contention that nursery workers occupy particular subjectivities dependent on their relationships with parents and other professionals working with young children. Identities are fluid and shifting (Butler, 1990; Francis, 2002; Osgood, 2006a) and context-specific, and nursery workers are positioned in particular ways at different times. Central to this positioning are the normalising middle-class discourses that are promoted through policy, the media and consumer parents. These discourses 'interpolate' or address the nursery worker in such a way that it has important implications for the ways in which the nursery worker understands the self, the *professional* self. The extent to which the nursery worker is positioned as more or less professional/more or less middle class becomes reliant on their social positioning at any given moment.

The nursery worker as 'esteemed expert'

The implications of classed, 'raced', gendered and aged relationships for establishing an authentic sense of professional identity in nursery work are enormous. As suggested above, the relationships between parents and staff at the voluntary and statutory sector nurseries generated generally positive professional identities among the staff. Many of the women from the statutory nursery constructed relationships with parents as founded on mutual respect, partnership and shared goals/values, which were facilitated through good lines of communication:

> "We can think that we know best because we are the
> professional but if we work well with parents, communicate
> well with them, they can see the benefits of what we
> are doing above and beyond what they do with their
> child at home and they come to respect us. It is our
> responsibility to help them understand what we do."
> (Francelle, senior practitioner, statutory sector nursery)

> "Through the classes that we run for parents they …
> recognise that we have the expertise in the area of
> child development and so on. So through training and

> experience [of using the nursery] they come to rely
> on us for expert, professional knowledge, so we have
> become classed as professional in their eyes and that wasn't
> how it was before; we now have professional status and
> standing." (Bertrise, manager, voluntary sector nursery)

Uttal (1996: 305) proposes the possibility that relations between parents and childcare provider can be 'coordinated' when the relationship is characterised by 'synchronising philosophies, values and practices'. Evidence of working towards this form of coordination existed in both the voluntary and statutory sector nurseries. Open days and parents' evenings were common practice and aimed to educate as well as inform parents about the role, scope and underlying philosophy of the nurseries. Parents were invited to participate in pedagogic activities that children did on a daily basis and to gain insights about the rationale and theoretical justifications. Both nurseries referred to 'an open dialogue with parents' with respect to strategic direction and managerial decision making. These activities fostered effective communication and raised the status and profile of the nursery staff.

But although nursery workers relied heavily on parental expectations and experiences for what can be understood as co-constructed professional identities, their accounts emphasise their independence from parental opinion. Although different groups of parents held varying expectations of their child's nursery career this bore no relation to the way that staff understood their role:

> "There are those at one end of the spectrum that think
> it is just play and then at the other end you have parents
> who want their children reading and writing, you
> know, think that we are in the business of cultivating
> little Einsteins ready for *real* school. But once we have
> educated them about what it is we are doing then they
> take it on board and accept that we know what we
> are doing and I think you can feel that they are mostly
> appreciative of our knowledge, or expertise, you know?"
> (Iesha, senior practitioner, statutory sector nursery)

Uttal (1996: 303) highlights parental acceptance of the important role that childcare providers play in their child's life:

> They [mothers] acknowledge the degree to which other
> people are caring for and influencing their children's social

and moral development … they perceived themselves
as sharing mothering with their childcare providers.

The demographic profile of the children at the voluntary sector
nursery was more mixed in social class terms than at the statutory
sector nursery, serving predominantly working-class families. However,
a strong emphasis was similarly placed on the active involvement
of parents (which was achieved through a committee structure
with elected parent representatives actively engaged in the strategic
direction of the nursery). The insights gained (into the complexities of
managing, running and doing nursery work) were heightened, which
reinforced the discursive constructions of staff as 'esteemed experts'.
The nursery staff invested heavily in this construction. Many described
the crucial role they played through their professional practice in
providing children with opportunities to both access and acquire
cultural capital from their nursery experiences. The nursery workers
in effect became the means through which middle-class experiences
become within the reach of 'disadvantaged/vulnerable' urban
working-class children.

> "We take them to the theatre, to museums, to galleries;
> they have access to a whole lot of cultural, artsy stuff,
> so their horizons are being broadened if you like. It is
> unlikely that anyone living around here would think to
> do those things with their children; it's just not on their
> radar, not an interest. It's outside their world basically."
> (Ruth, senior practitioner, voluntary sector nursery)

This demonstrates that positive constructions of the nursery worker
are readily created and become embedded through the social milieu
in which they are situated. However, positive constructions tend
to be less stable, less transferable or sustainable when taken out of a
given context. An example of this is available through the narratives
of the nursery workers when referring to their positioning in the
children's workforce hierarchy. Many of the nursery workers felt that
colleagues from statutory sector nurseries and related professionals
working directly with families (health visitors, social workers, child
psychologists etc) routinely devalued their contribution and degree of
expertise. The discursive positioning of 'esteemed expert' becomes very
fragile. The 'expert professional', the 'transmitter/facilitator of cultural
enrichment', becomes entirely dependent on contextual specificity
and the recognition of others.

The career trajectories and qualification level of the staff at the three nurseries were very similar. However, the (co-)construction of the nursery worker as more or less expert, more or less professional, more or less middle class, is shaped and determined by the discourses in which they are positioned at a particular moment. I go on to demonstrate the relational construction of the nursery staff at the private sector nursery.

The nursery worker as classed subject

The accounts gathered from staff at the private nursery were saturated with emotion (a combination of anger, frustration, offence and injustice) in respect of the relationships they had with many parents. The interactions with some of the middle-class mothers were characterised by routine processes of pathologisation:

> "They see us as part of the nursery – like the tables and chairs, we are just here. But ... we have souls, we are human, we suffer and they sit there thinking that it is okay [to treat us that way], well it's not ... so many people are leaving: no respect, why would they stay on?" (Nyesha, Level 3 practitioner, private nursery)

The study exposes the enactment of acute class distinction between professional middle-class working mothers and nursery workers in the commercially driven private sector. Vincent and Ball (2006) suggest that parents have a more diffuse and distant relationship with carers in nurseries than those located within the home, and because the focus becomes centred on the ethos and character of a given nursery rather than the individual workers. While the quote above, with references to being treated as part of fixtures and fittings, would appear to support this, the implications of diffuse/distanced relationships are significant for the sense of security and the professional identity of the nursery worker. Vincent and Ball (2006: 116) argue that the 'power in the care relationship lies with the provider and the parent has to take what is on offer'. This study reveals the nexus of power at the heart of care relationships to be more complex than this. Workers in the private sector become dehumanised and obscured from parental view where nursery provision is marketed to parents as a service. It is common practice for nurseries from all sectors to set out aims, mission statements and institutional philosophies through marketing materials. However, what marked the private nursery as distinct from the other

nurseries in this study was that the 'public face' of the nursery ethos
was embodied in the manager (Delia). She was educated to degree
level, having passed through private schooling. Her career trajectory
involved summer camp in North America and Scandinavia. She was
very well spoken, highly articulate and very sporty.

By contrast 'the girls' (as they were routinely referred to by Delia)
were in many ways her antithesis. The data indicate that many middle-
class mothers judged the working-class identities of 'the girls' in
derogatory ways. Vincent and Ball (2006) exposed class prejudice and
emotionality as central to shaping (negative) parental constructions
of childcare workers. In this setting there appeared to be a deliberate
strategy to minimise direct interaction between 'the girls' and
the mothers. The character of the nursery as 'a home from home'
(that is, middle-class environment) was achieved through aesthetic
resources such as the décor and Annabel Karmel's daily menu, and
importantly through the manager's middle-class capital. So middle-
class mothers came to construct the nursery as acceptable, based on
a discursively constructed middle-class environment and culture.
All parties – mothers, nursery workers, the manager and ultimately
the children – were embedded within this artifice. The classed and
'raced' interactions between 'the girls' and the mothers were obscured
through formal practices – some parents preferred to liaise directly
(and wherever possible) exclusively with the manager rather than the
key worker assigned to their child. Furthermore the daily interactions
between nursery worker and the white, middle-class children in her
care were ubiquitously classed and 'raced' but this was a fact apparently
conveniently overlooked by the mothers. The lack of positive
interaction between (principally working-class) nursery worker and
(exclusively middle-class) parent positioned the workers who were the
focus of this study in particularly damaging ways:

> "Some parents think that I am lower than them because I
> am looking after their child, they think that I am not clever
> … some take liberties all the time; you know turning up
> late, handing their child over with a dirty nappy … they
> can really talk down to us … like we are lower in terms
> of worth." (Ordina, senior practitioner, private nursery)

Feminist academics have highlighted the myriad ways in which
working-class women are deemed bad, insensitive, repulsive and so
on through a process of pathologisation (Walkerdine and Lucey, 1989;
Hey, 1997; Reay, 1997; Skeggs, 1997, 2003; Tyler, 2008). The coping

mechanism adopted by the mothers who handed the care of their child to (principally) working-class carers was to avoid engaging with the nursery worker wherever possible, but failing that, some mothers overtly exerted power/control over the staff through disrespectful behaviour; such as handing their child over with a dirty nappy, speaking down to the staff or engendering feelings of worthlessness.

The narratives offered to me by nursery workers throughout the course of the study provide illustrations of the powerful ways in which perceptions around social class and 'race' shape interactions between mothers and nursery workers. Where relationships were shaped by differences in class practices and subjectivities, the effects of this were pernicious on workers' sense of a professional identity. Parental constructions of nursery workers as deficient (in terms of social capital and hence 'appropriate' professionalism) were unwittingly reinforced by other important actors in the lives of the nursery worker. For example, the (white, middle-class) manager at the private nursery (while seemingly adopting a benevolent approach to her staff) was also guilty of reinforcing negative constructions:

> "The parents treat me differently to 'the girls'. The girls
> are perceived as beneath the parents. I've seen it myself
> and it's shocking how they can treat them, it's just horrible
> … I do intervene when I see it going on but it doesn't
> alter the parents' perceptions. They don't see the girls
> as being in any way equal, they see them as relatively
> uneducated, maybe it's the language that they use – strong
> London accents, and maybe their spelling … they don't
> hold themselves as well as they could … many lack
> professional confidence … it is how they are perceived
> that is the issue." (Delia, manager, private nursery)

Although Delia is protective of her staff, she nevertheless draws on and sustains middle-class normalising discourses through her identification of markers of difference such as accent and presentation of self. Class is inscribed on the self and it is repeatedly signified through distinctions in lifestyle, food, aesthetics and so on. The mothers were engaged in deploying practical signifiers to locate 'the girls' in class terms but importantly, to locate them in relation to themselves. As Bourdieu (1986: 6) contends:

> Taste classifies and it classifies the classifier. Social
> subjects classified by classification distinguish themselves

by the distinctions they make, between the beautiful
and the ugly, the distinguished and the vulgar.

'The girls' are judged on the basis of dress, accent, hair, body size and
shape; against the middle-class norm they can be understood to lack
cultural capital (Skeggs, 1997). The failure of 'the girls' to embody
middle-classness marked them as deficient, worthy of suspicion and
regulation. Delia argued that some parents were sceptical of their
professional capabilities, making judgements on the basis of their
embodiment of classed identity rather than their professional conduct.
Consequently parents liaised directly with "somebody like us" (that
is, white, middle-class, professional; see Ball, 2003). The discursive
construction of the staff at the private nursery clearly echoes the
comments about 'long nails' and 'clunky shoes' made by the chair of
PAT referred to in the introduction to this chapter.

Taking on the care, nurturance, regulation and 'love' of other
people's children places nursery workers in a highly precarious
position. Vincent and Ball (2006) write about childcare as a 'market
in love', signalling the highly emotive and emotional nature of the
relationships between carer and child, and parent and carer. The
terrain that nursery workers must negotiate in providing 'quality' care
and remaining within professional boundaries is treacherous. Not
only must nursery workers negotiate 'risk' discourses and implicit
assumptions of ill intent (Cameron, 2006) but the relationship with
parents must be carefully managed so that territorial boundaries
remain intact. A nursery worker must be caring but not loving,
nurturing but not motherly, professional but not austere (Osgood,
2008) – a complicated juggling act to perform as a project of the self
(Lawler, 2008).

As this discussion has demonstrated, the way that nursery workers
become socially constructed as more or less professional depends in
large part on the assumptions that are drawn on by those involved in
the co-construction of a professional identity. The subject position of
the parent, health visitor, child psychologist, policy maker, journalist
and so on, and the context in which judgements are made about
professionalism have a profound bearing on the degree to which a
nursery worker is viewed professionally.

Conclusion

The study on which this chapter is based demonstrates professionalism is a performance that is shaped and determined by powerful actors, so that it manifests in myriad ways, and is dependent on context and on recognition by an audience. Therefore contextual specificity is crucial to understanding the discursive construction of professional identities. Classed assumptions and prejudices are central to understanding professional subjectivity. The discursive positioning within and through normalising middle-class discourse can undermine the efforts of nursery workers to 'do professionalism' in ways that are instinctive, intrinsic to the nature of the work and foundational to providing appropriate emotional nurturance and regulation to young children in nurseries. In this study, the nursery workers constructed professionalism as 'emotional labour' requiring empathy, compassion, intuition, love, relationality and commitment. These 'insider constructions' tended to run counter to neoliberal discourses that promote standardised, individualised, competitive approaches said to ensure effectiveness, quality and professionalism (Rose, 1999).

Clearly, policy and media representations of professionalism have a significant impact on the ways in which nursery workers are understood. Further, the narrow ways in which nursery workers are constructed in public discourse is in large part based on the partial and subjective experiences of middle-class actors (the consumer parents of private nursery provision). Where conditions exist for nursery workers to take up the identity of 'esteemed expert' and form part of the legitimate authoritative framework for children's services, they come to believe in their professional capabilities and become active in promulgating and sustaining alternative, more positive constructions. The classed and gendered nature of the relationship between mothers and carers has important implications for the security of the nursery worker's sense of professionalism. The contextual specificity and fluid nature of identities mean that where nursery staff are encouraged/permitted to construct themselves as esteemed experts (as was the case in the voluntary and statutory nurseries), identities become more stable. Performing professionalism with confidence then becomes possible, and others working in children's services are able to view nursery staff more positively.

References

Ailwood, J. (2008) 'Mothers, teachers, maternalism and early childhood education and care: some historical connections', *Contemporary Issues in Early Childhood*, vol 8, no 2, pp 157-64.

Ball, S.J. (2003) *Class Strategies and the Education Market: The Middle Class and Social Advantage*, London: Routledge Falmer.

Bourdieu, P. (1986) *Distinction: A Social Critique of the Judgement of Taste*, London: Routledge.

Butler, J. (1990) *Gender Trouble: Feminism and the Subversion of Identity*, London: Routledge.

Cameron, C. (2006) 'Men in the nursery revisited', *Contemporary Issues in Early Childhood*, vol 7, no 1, pp 68-79.

Cameron, C., Moss, P. and Owen, C. (1999) *Men in the Nursery: Gender and Caring Work*, London: Sage Publications.

Cohen, S. (1986) *Folk Devils and Moral Panics. The Creation of Mods and Rockers* (2nd edn), New York, NY: St Martin's Press.

Colley, H. (2006) 'Learning to labour with feeling: class, gender and emotion in childcare education and training', *Contemporary Issues in Early Childhood*, vol 7, no 1, pp 15-29.

Collins, B. (2004) 'My nursery nightmare', *Daily Mail online*, London, 13 August (http://www.dailymail.co.uk/health/article-313849/My-nursery-nightmare.html).

Dahlberg, G. and Moss, P. (2005) *Ethics and Politics in Early Childhood Education*, London: Routledge Falmer.

DfES (Department for Education and Skills) (1997) *Meeting the Childcare Challenge: The National Childcare Strategy*, London: The Stationery Office.

DfES (2003) *Every Child Matters* (Green Paper), Cm 5860, London: The Stationery Office.

DfES (2005) *Children's Workforce Strategy: Building a World-class Workforce for Children, Young People and Families*, London: The Stationery Office.

Foucault, M. (1980) *Power/Knowledge: Selected Interviews and Other Writings, 1972-1977*, London: Routledge.

Francis, B. (2002) 'Relativism, realism and feminism – an analysis of some theoretical tensions in research on gender identity', *Journal of Gender Studies*, vol 11, no 1, pp 39-54.

Furedi, F. (2008) *Paranoid Parenting. Why Ignoring the Experts May Be Best for Your Child*, Chicago, IL: Chicago Review Press, Independent Publishers Group.

Guardian, The (2006) 'Teachers fear Vicky Pollard nursery
nurses', 3 August (http://education.guardian.co.uk/earlyyears/
story/0,,1836046,00.html).

Hey, V. (1997) 'Northern accent and southern comfort: subjectivity
and social class', in P. Mahoney and C. Zmroczek (eds) *Class Matters:
Working-class Women's Perspectives on Social Class*, London: Taylor &
Francis, pp 140–51.

Lawler, S. (2008) *Identity: Sociological Perspectives*, Cambridge: Polity
Press.

Levitas, R. (1998) *The Inclusive Society? Social Exclusion and New Labour*,
London: Macmillan Press.

Osgood, J. (2005) 'Who cares? The classed nature of childcare', *Gender
and Education*, vol 17, no 3, pp 289–303.

Osgood, J. (2006a) 'Professionalism and performativity: the paradox
facing early years practitioners', *Early Years*, vol 26, no 2, pp 187–99.

Osgood, J. (2006b) 'Editorial: Rethinking 'professionalism' in the early
years: English perspectives', *Contemporary Issues in Early Childhood*, vol
7, no 1, pp 1–4.

Osgood, J. (2006c) 'Deconstructing professionalism in the early years:
resisting the regulatory gaze', *Contemporary Issues in Early Childhood*,
vol 7, no 1, pp 5–14.

Osgood, J. (2008) 'Narratives from the nursery: negotiating a
"professional" identity', PhD thesis, London Metropolitan University.

Rahilly, S. and Johnston, E. (2002) 'Opportunity for childcare:
the impact of government initiatives in England upon childcare
provision', *Social Policy and Administration*, vol 36, no 5, pp 482–95.

Randall, V. (2000) *The Politics of Child Daycare in Britain*, Oxford:
Oxford University Press.

Reay, D. (1997) 'The double-bind of the "working class" feminist
academic: the success of failure or the failure of success?', in P.
Mahony and C. Zmroczek (eds) *Class Matters: Working-class Women's
Perspectives on Social Class*, London: Taylor & Francis, pp 18–29.

Rose, S. (1999) *Powers of Freedom: Reframing Political Thought*,
Cambridge: Cambridge University Press.

Skeggs, B. (1997) *Formations of Class and Gender*, London: Sage
Publications.

Skeggs, B. (2003) *Class, Self, Culture*, London: Routledge.

Strathern, M. (1987) 'Out of contexts: the persuasive fictions of
anthropology', *Current Anthropology*, vol 28, pp 251–81.

Taylor, R. (2004) 'Four nursery staff sacked after BBC documentary',
The Guardian, 13 August (http://www.guardian.co.uk/uk/2004/
aug/13/schools.children)

Tyler, I. (2008) '"Chav mum, chav scum": class disgust in contemporary Britain', *Feminist Media Studies*, vol 8, no 1, pp 17-34.

Uttal, L. (1996) 'Custodial care, surrogate care and co-ordinated care: employed mothers and the meaning of childcare', *Gender and Society*, vol 10, pp 291-311.

Vincent, C. and Ball, S.J. (2006) *Childcare, Choice and Class Practices*, London: Taylor & Francis.

Walkerdine, V. and Lucey, H. (1989) *Democracy in the Kitchen: Regulating Mothers and Socialising Daughters*, London: Virago.

Williams, F. (1999) 'Good-enough principles for welfare', *Journal of Social Policy*, vol 28, no 4, pp 667-87.

Sixteen

Holistic practice in children's nursing: the personal, professional and maternal

Sue Higham

A children's nurse, towards the end of a busy night shift, stops by the bed of a seven-year-old patient who is crying quietly. The nurse has no clinical task to perform for that child but stays a while, reads a story, gives the child a hug, chats. The child does not have a parent with her; the nurse has a child of her own of a similar age. The nurse's colleagues continue with the routine early morning tasks.

Introduction

Decades ago nurses were expected to leave their non-nurse selves at the door of the ward (Redwood, 2003), although the reality is that that was never really possible. This expectation is in contrast to other fields of practice such as social work where a conscious use of self is promoted (Reupert, 2009). All professionals bring a personal hinterland to their practice, replete with knowledge, skills and values from their lives before and outside their professional practice, just as service users do to their experience. In this chapter I explore the tensions that arise at the interface between the professional and the personal for practitioners working with children, young people and their families. Holistic practice is examined and the value of reflection for practice with children, young people and their families investigated, particularly in relation to professional socialisation. The association between 'maternal care' and professional practice with children and young people is considered and the relationships between professionals who are mothers and mothers who are service users examined.

Holistic practice

Holistic practice has been encouraged within nursing for many years, but while many clinical units cite holistic practice in their unit philosophies, McEvoy and Duffy (2008) argue that individual nurses may struggle to verbalise the concept.

Holistic healthcare practice may be understood as:

> A philosophy of nursing practice that takes into account total patient care, considering the physical, emotional, social, economic, and spiritual needs of patients, their response to their illnesses, and the effect of illness on patients' abilities to meet self-care needs. (Strandberg et al., 2007)

Children's nurses are concerned with understanding and responding to the needs of the child as a whole person and practise a form of care that is child- and family-centred. This approach recognises the centrality of family to the child, and provides professional support to family members to empower their participation and partnership in the child's care (Smith and Coleman, 2010). So the focus of the care that children's nurses give is on the child's symptoms, limitations, feelings, behaviour and lifestyle changes as a result of a health problem rather than on the problem itself, as well as the challenges that the family experiences in caring for the child (Casey, 2006). While holistic family-centred care is a children's nursing concept, early years practitioners also approach children holistically (Manning-Morton, 2006), the concept of holistic practice is evident in social work (Kelly and Horder, 2001), and the value of this form of personal connection is recognised in teaching (for example, Shoffner, 2009).

Holistic care is predominantly presented in the nursing literature as unproblematic, with the nurse using professional knowledge to gain a rounded picture of the patient and family while the patient and family know nothing of the nurse. Yet the nurse philosopher Gadow has argued that 'regarding the patient as a "whole" requires nothing less than the nurse acting as a "whole" person' (Gadow, 1980: 90, cited by Darbyshire, 1994: 136). Building on this insight, I propose an alternative form of holistic practice, in which the practitioner consciously uses the whole self to enhance and enrich the care of children, young people and their families. In order to operate in this way, the practitioner needs to bring their personal, non-professional knowledge to their conscious knowing, and reflection may be the means to do this.

Reflection

In their discussion of different types of knowledge Rolfe *et al.* (2001) identify experiential practical knowledge, a form of know-how that can only be gained from direct experience, the value of which is shown in schemes such as the National Childbirth Trust's (NCT's) breastfeeding counsellors. Women who have breastfed successfully are trained to support others; women cannot be counsellors without having breastfed (NCT, 2009). This raises the question as to who could better support the new mother struggling to feed her baby, the midwife who can cite the latest evidence but who has no personal experience or the counsellor who has direct experience *and* training. But what if the midwife had herself breastfed successfully? Would she know what was professional knowledge and what was personal? Would it matter? How might a mother respond if the midwife disclosed her personal experiences to her?

Practitioners in many fields use experiential practical knowledge often with little conscious awareness, but they also use personal knowledge. Eraut (2007) argues that professional work, regardless of the specific discipline, deals with complex situations for which the practitioner uses complex knowledge that defies representation. Consequently, practitioners often struggle to identify and express the personal and experiential knowledge they use. Skilled reflection may enable them to bring it to their own awareness and possibly articulate it.

Reflection and reflective practice have been seen as positive and empowering (Fejes, 2008), but challenging; involving commitment and intellectual effort and possibly leading to powerful and painful emotions (Duke and Copp, 1994). It has been argued that reflection leads to increasing self-awareness and a critical appraisal of the social world leading to transformation (Fitzgerald, 1994) and increased competence (Yip, 2006). There are a plethora of models to enable practitioners to reflect and develop their practice, individually or in groups or in clinical supervision, in which they critically analyse their own practice through discussion with another, usually more senior, practitioner. A crucial component to any reflective activity is the articulation of thoughts, either verbally or in writing (Fitzgerald, 1994).

Empirical evidence for observable differences in practice as a result of reflection has proved elusive. The value of reflection has been questioned on a number of grounds: as memory is flawed, the notion of returning to and analysing events must also be flawed (Burnard, 2004); thinking about practice while doing it often results in de-skilling, causing the practitioner to become hesitant and less proficient particularly in psycho-motor skills (Burnard, 2004); reflective activity can be destructive, bringing to the surface unresolved personal conflicts or leading to over self-criticism which undermines confidence (Yip, 2006); reflective models are too rigid, confusing and have mystical connotations (Horan, 2005). Fejes (2008) has suggested that reflection could be seen in Foucauldian terms as a confessional technology of the self, creating new forms of governmentality rather than 'truths' about practice.

Producing written reflective accounts of practice forms part of pre-qualifying education for students in early years practice (Goodfellow, 2004), social work (Taylor, 2006, Yip, 2006), teaching (Shoffner, 2009) and nursing, and is also an aspect of continuing professional development. Burnard (2004) questions whether students' reflective writing can and should be assessed and that you have to consider what the student is trying to achieve. For example, Taylor (2006) argues that while student social workers' reflective accounts are seen unproblematically as providing access to their practice and related thoughts and feelings, in fact in choosing incidents or situations and presenting the accounts, students are concerned with constructing and displaying an identity for and of themselves as competent, if fallible, practitioners. My experience of nursing students' reflective writing is that they often claim to have used propositional knowledge to inform their practice, yet would not have cited this knowledge at the time of the incident. In stark contrast to the holism proposed by Gadow (1980, cited by Darbyshire, 1994), the reflections on practice generated by contemporary nursing students appear to be shaped by a culture which emphasises evidence-based practice and values the technical-rational model over the personal and subjective. Similar tensions between the technical-rational and holistic have been discussed within social work education (Kelly and Horder, 2001).

Although the value of assessing reflective writing may be questionable, there is recognition that practice is a rich source of knowledge and theory (Jones, 2009). Rolfe *et al.* (2001) argue that reflection *can* enable practitioners to access, develop and refine their experiential knowledge – which may be from professional *and* personal experience. My contention is that reflection can do more than facilitate the articulation of personal knowledge; reflection can enable practitioners to recognise and challenge the process of professional socialisation which leads to a devaluing of the personal and understand when and where they might consciously use aspects of their life knowledge, skills and identity in a therapeutic way with children, young people and families.

Process of professional socialisation

Students setting out in professional programmes bring with them their own understanding of people and the profession they have chosen. Eraut (1994) found that pre-entry understandings influenced teachers' practice more than the theory they learned during their course, a finding mirrored in Gallagher's (2007) study of nursing students who used their preconceptions about the profession to judge the theory and practice on their course. New entrants to nursing frequently hold an idealised image of nursing, drawn from knowing other nurses, experience of nursing through their own or others' illness and from media representations (Price, 2009). There is some evidence to suggest that many nursing students find the reality of practice does not match their preconceptions, for example, students in Pearcey and Draper's study (2008) were surprised at the dominance of documentation, tasks and routine in clinical practice while Mackintosh's participants expressed disillusionment and increased cynicism towards the end of their pre-registration programme (Mackintosh, 2006).

Student socialisation into nursing was first revealed in Melia's classic study (Melia 1998), and fitting in has been a persistent theme in the literature ever since (Levitt-Jones and Lathlean, 2009). Belonging is still important to student nurses on clinical placement, despite changes in nurse education (Levitt-Jones and Lathlean, 2008). Students experience tension arising from an educational approach that seeks to develop innovative and questioning practitioners, and a world of clinical practice which values conformity and compliance (Levitt-Jones and Lathlean, 2009). For the student, there are fears of not passing the assessment, while Farrell (2007) argues that disapproval of peers and interpersonal conflict may ensue for the qualified nurse who does not conform to workplace norms. Mackintosh (2006) argues that this process of professional socialisation mitigates individual nurses' ability to care.

While nursing espouses values of care, empathy and holism, in practice functional aspects of nursing – throughputs, predetermined pathways and protocols – dominate (O'Connor, 2007). Mackintosh (2006) has argued that a concern with professional and technical issues acts as a defence mechanism against the strong emotions to which nurses are exposed. An alternative explanation is that a female-dominated workforce prioritises the rational and distances itself from the physical and emotional in order to gain professional recognition (Manning-Morton, 2006). Manning-Morton was writing in relation to early years practitioners, but this could apply equally to children's nursing. Price found that student nurses adapt their concept of care in order to cope with the cognitive dissonance arising from their situation, from an initial concept of care as compassion towards an understanding of care as competence (Price, 2009). Shoffner (2009) suggests student teachers go through a similar process, turning away from the emotional aspects of teaching they valued as novices towards a more technical approach.

It appears that student nurses and teachers learn to achieve an emotional distance in their practice – in the context of a growing recognition that to be a professional is to be called to account publicly for one's actions (Barnett, 2009). As the student develops a professional identity and becomes more fully aware of the responsibilities and demands of professional practice, their understanding of what is of value in their chosen profession is transformed. Skilled reflection may enable them to understand what is at stake in this process of professional socialisation and to integrate their personal knowledge and values into their practice. If, as Gadow suggests, we need to use 'every dimension of the person as a resource in the professional relation' (Gadow, 1980: 90, cited by Darbyshire, 1994: 136), then the reflection that may help students through their professional socialisation may then become a habit throughout their careers.

In the final section of this chapter I examine the potential of one particular aspect of the person – motherhood – as a resource for children's nursing practice as an illustration of using the personal to enhance professional practice.

Mothers and children's nurses

Approximately 5% of children's nurses are male (Robinson *et al.*, 2006), but there is no paternal tradition within children's nursing; arguably the paternal role in relation to the sick child was ascribed to the paediatrician. There is little discussion in the nursing literature of what men bring to nursing, unlike in early years and social work. Nor is there a literature exploring the salience of a wider set of personal and family roles such as friendship, fatherhood, sibling relationships and grandparenting. While children's nurses use the term 'parent', historically the vast majority of parents accompanying their children have been mothers, although this has been changing more recently with a greater proportion of fathers staying with their child.

Children's nurses work closely with the parents of their patients and it is usual for children in hospital to be accompanied by a parent throughout their hospital stay. Several studies have revealed that relationships between parents and children's nurses can be difficult (for example, Darbyshire, 1994; Callery, 1997; Coyne and Cowley, 2007). In much of the literature these difficulties are attributed to nurses' lack of communication skills, but I suggest that this is a simplification which overlooks important social aspects of interactions between nurses and mothers, of which neither nurse nor parent may be consciously aware.

Position of the professional carer

The feminist sociologist Oakley argued that in its beginnings nursing was no more than a specialised form of domestic work in which hospital nurses were married women doing for patients what they did at home for families (Oakley, 1998). The emotional labour of nursing can be seen as the commodification of this female role, which can be traded in the form of paid work. Tschudin (1997) explores the connections between the sick person's need for nursing and nourishment and popular understandings of mothering. There is some evidence to suggest a fluidity between ideas of domestic mothering and public nursing, such as those nurses in Gray's (2009) study who spoke of 'mothering' patients in order to help them to feel safe and cared for.

If nursing, then, is closely aligned to mothering through the notions of care and nurture, what of children's nursing, the essence of which is childcare? Many children's nurses are familiar with the words of Catherine Wood, superintendent of the first British children's hospital, asserting that sick children require special nursing and sick children's nurses need special training. However, few would be aware that Wood went on to write 'the child will thrive best who is *mothered by his own nurse*' (Wood, 1888, cited by Moules and Ramsay, 2008: 618, emphasis added). Both early years practitioners and children's nurses get paid to care for other people's children. Manning–Morton's description of early years practice as 'skilled manual work that draws on a broad theoretical knowledge, a deep understanding of individual children and a high level of self-awareness' (Manning–Morton, 2006: 45) could have been written of children's nursing. Although professionalisation in this sector has occurred much later than in children's nursing, the work has strong connections with mothering; indeed the emphasis until recently was on providing substitute mothering for children whose mothers worked (Cameron et al., 2002). Recent reform has seen transfer to the education sector and efforts to increase the educational attainments of the workforce (Cameron et al., 2002) and a move away from an emphasis on maternal approaches to care towards more theory and evidence-based provision (Manning-Morton, 2006). There is some discussion of this issue within the early years literature which suggests a tension between practitioners' desire to practice in a maternal (that is, emotion-based) responsive way and a policy-driven move towards professionalism which emphasises standards and performance (Osgood, 2006; Ailwood, 2008).

The explicit discussion of maternal aspects of care has disappeared from the children's nursing literature and curricula. In contemporary practice, a parent is likely to be present while the child is nursed and the nurse will encourage the parent to care for the child. This challenges the nurse to consider whether to abandon the maternal aspect of the role and focus on the technical-rational component of care, or consider how this maternal element of children's nursing might be expressed in the situation and how mothers might respond. Furthermore the nurse's knowledge, technical competence and ability to relate to and meet the needs of the child and parents are under scrutiny by parents whenever caring for the child (Thompson et al., 2002).

Position of the mother

Mothers and professionals in all fields will be influenced, consciously or unconsciously, by the dominant construct within society of the good mother, which will be present in any interaction. Generally within the home, mothers continue to be responsible for the health of the family (Cunningham-Burley et al., 2006) and seeking healthcare for children (Jackson and Mannix, 2004). Caring for sick children in the home is a maternal role, seen by many mothers in Cunningham-Burley et al.'s study (2006) as having powerful symbolic significance and as a measure of their adequacy as mothers. The act of seeking medical advice involves the mother in making a judgement of her child's condition and experiencing validation or otherwise of her judgement. A similar issue arises for mothers when deciding whether or not to send a child with a minor illness to school in relation to teachers judging whether this is appropriate or not (Cunningham-Burley et al., 2006), and mothers' adequacy is frequently the major concern for social workers (Davies et al., 2007). Jackson and Mannix (2004) argue that 'mother-blaming' is widespread in the helping professions. The mother of a child who needs nursing care might be seen as, or see herself as, having failed to protect the child from illness or injury or as over-anxious. She is exposing her mothering practice to scrutiny by people she may perceive as experts. Her child is dependent on the knowledge and expertise of those who might judge her, in whom she therefore has to trust.

Nurses and mothers working together

Given these situational factors and that these issues may be operating beneath the awareness of both parties, it is not surprising that relationships between nurses and mothers can sometimes be strained. The nurse has scientific, medical and nursing knowledge, the mother has specific knowledge in relation to her own child, particularly of subtle behavioural cues, for example how the child normally expresses pain. Clearly the child will benefit if nurse and mother develop a trusting partnership. There is an onus on all practitioners working with children, young people and families to understand what they themselves bring to the relationship, including their own values (Pinkerton, 2001) and their conscious or unconscious expectations of the other people involved.

Family–work facilitation

Recent decades have seen increased female and particularly maternal participation in paid work. In female-dominated professions such as social work, early years, teaching and nursing, it is likely that a majority of practitioners are mothers. Some women's motherhood experiences lead them to enter the helping professions while some professionals become mothers. They therefore face the same work–family stresses and conflict as other working mothers in trying to be good employees, professional practitioners, mothers and partners. Redwood argues that midwives and nurses who become mothers experience profound alterations in their practice (Redwood, 2008). Neonatal nurses returning to work after becoming mothers struggled to reconcile their dual roles, being less flexible in relation to work patterns, and found colleagues and managers lacked understanding of their changed situation (Redwood, 2003). Similarly Sheppard (2000) describes frustration on returning to social work practice after becoming a mother when colleagues could not hear explanations of a new mother's struggles because they did not fit with their own interpretations. Yet these nurses who become mothers identified many positive changes in their practice, including being more sympathetic, having increased empathy, being a gentler person as well as having a greater insight into aspects of childcare, for example breastfeeding (Redwood, 2003). Sheppard (2000) describes how reflection on her own experience led her to seek to understand a client's private perspectives and explanations. It is this kind of fusion between personal and professional insight that underpins the idea of work–family facilitation.

The concept of work–family conflict is well known, yet the concept of work–family facilitation is relatively new in the field of work–family research, meaning:

> the extent to which participation at work (or home)
> is made easier by virtue of the experience, skills and
> opportunities gained or developed at home (or work).
> (Frone, 2003: 145, cited by Jeffrey Hill, 2005: 798)

An essential element of this concept is that both work–family and family–work facilitation can occur. Family–work facilitation may enable nurses who are mothers to better understand and meet the needs of the parents of sick children. In two major studies of parents' experiences when their children were in hospital, parents expressed a preference for the care given by nurses whom the parents knew or believed to be parents (Darbyshire, 1994; Callery, 1997). In my own current study, several fathers have echoed this (Higham, 2009). Nurses reported that being a mother themselves improved their practice, stressing the value of their being mothers in enabling them to establish partnerships with parents (Higham, 2009). And in Redwood's study, nurses associated their work with pre-term infants with their own pregnancies and used their nursing knowledge with their own babies (Redwood, 2003).

So how does being a mother facilitate professional work with children, young people and their families? Although it is tempting to say that practitioners who are parents are in a better position to empathise with the parents with whom they practice, this is not necessarily true. Sheppard (2000) points out that social workers experience very different social conditions from many of their clients even if they share the status of mother. Some client situations that are close to practitioners' own experiences may raise uncomfortable feelings, limiting practitioners' ability to practise effectively. While a greater ability to empathise may play a part, further explanations are required. Practitioners who are mothers may understand and value their own maternal knowledge and therefore place greater value on the maternal knowledge in practice. Darbyshire (1994) argues that nurses who become parents undergo an existential change – their way of being in the world is permanently changed – and it is this that results in improved practice, in spite of potential work–family conflict and the 'juggling' of the working mother.

Conclusion

Personal knowledge can inform professional practice, and in this chapter I have explored the potential of reflection as a mechanism to enable practitioners to recognise, value and share the interactions between personal and professional insight. My focus has been on the professional field of children's nursing and on the personal experience of mothering. I have pointed to the idea of work–family facilitation as a model for a two-way flow of knowledge and understanding. This is a very different model than the increasingly bounded forms of reflection that dominate professional training, and which value the technical-rational over emotional-subjective. Drawing on Gadow, I suggest a form of holistic practice, in which the practitioner consciously uses the whole self to enhance and enrich the care of children, young people and their families. Although my discussion is rooted in children's nursing it raises questions for all professional groups working with children, young people and families. It also reveals the absence of relevant research on a wider range of personal and family relationships (such as friendship, fathering, siblinghood and grandparenting) that might interface with and inform professional practice.

References

Ailwood, J. (2008) 'Mothers, teachers, maternalism and early childhood education and care: some historical connections', *Contemporary Issues in Early Childhood*, vol 6, no 2, pp 157-65.

Barnett, R. (2009) 'Willing to be professional', Conference address 'Learning to be professional through a lifewide curriculum SCEPTrE', Guildford: University of Surrey, 31 March.

Burnard, P. (2004) 'Reflections on reflection', *Nurse Education Today*, vol 25, pp 85-6.

Callery, P. (1997) 'Maternal knowledge and professional knowledge: co-operation and conflict in the care of sick children', *International Journal of Nursing Studies*, vol 34, no 1, pp 27-34.

Cameron, C., Mooney, A. and Moss, P. (2002) 'The child care workforce: current conditions and future directions', *Critical Social Policy*, vol 22, no 4, pp 572-95.

Casey, A. (2006) 'Assessing and planning care in partnership', in A. Glasper and J.A. Richardson, *Textbook of Children's and Young People's Nursing*, London: Churchill Livingstone, pp 89-103.

Coyne, I. and Cowley, S. (2007) 'Challenging the philosophy of partnership with parents: a grounded theory study', *International Journal of Nursing Studies*, vol 44, pp 893-904.

Cunningham-Burley, S., Backett-Millburn, K. and Kemmer, D. (2006) 'Constructing health and sickness in the context of motherhood and paid work', *Sociology of Health and Illness*, vol 28, no 4, pp 385-409.

Darbyshire, P. (1994) *Living With a Sick Child in Hospital: The Experiences of Parents and Nurses*, London: Chapman and Hall.

Davies, I., Krane, J., Collings, J. and Wexler, S. (2007) 'Developing mothering narratives in child protection practice', *Journal of Social Work Practice*, vol 21, no 1, pp 23-34.

Duke, S. and Copp, G. (1994) 'The personal side of reflection', in A. Palmer, S. Burns and C. Bulman (eds) *Reflective Practice in Nursing*, Oxford: Blackwell Scientific, pp 100-9.

Eraut, M. (1994) *Developing Professional Knowledge and Competence*, London: Falmer Press.

Eraut, M. (2007) 'Learning from other people in the workplace', *Oxford Review of Education*, vol 33, no 4, pp 403-22.

Farrell, G. (2007) 'From tall poppies to squashed weeds: why don't nurses pull together more?', *Journal of Advanced Nursing*, vol 35, no 1, pp 26-33.

Fejes, A. (2008) 'Governing nursing through reflection: a discourse analysis of reflective practices', *Journal of Advanced Nursing*, vol 64, no 3, pp 243-50.

Fitzgerald, M. (1994) 'Theories of reflection for learning', in A. Palmer, S. Burns and C. Bulman (eds) *Reflective Practice in Nursing*, Oxford: Blackwell Scientific, pp 63-84.

Frone, M.R. (2003) 'Work-family balance' in J.C. Quick and L.E. Tetrick (eds) *Handbook of Occupational Health Psychology*, Washington, DC: American Psychological Association, pp 143-62.

Gadow, S. (1980) 'Existential advocacy: philosophical foundations of nursing' in S.F. Spicker and S. Gadow (eds) *Nursing: Images and Ideals: Opening dialogues with the Humanities*, New York: Springer.

Gallagher, P. (2007) 'Preconceptions and learning to be a nurse', *Nurse Education Today*, vol 27, pp 878-84.

Goodfellow, J. (2004) 'Documenting professional practice through the use of a professional portfolio', *Early Years*, vol 24, no 1, pp 63-74.

Gray, B. (2009) 'The emotional labour of nursing – defining and managing emotions at work', *Nurse Education Today*, vol 29, pp 168-75.

Higham, S. (2009) 'Fathers are parents too: fathers' involvement in the care of their acutely ill children in hospital', 'Back to the Future: A Celebration of 25 Years of Children and Young People's Nursing', Royal College of Nursing, Liverpool, 11 September.

Horan, P. (2005) 'Framing the new reflection', *Nurse Education in Practice*, vol 5, pp 255-7.

Jackson, D. and Mannix, J. (2004) 'Giving voice to the burden of blame: a feminist study of mothers' experiences of mother blaming', *International Journal of Nursing Practice*, vol 10, pp 150-8.

Jeffrey Hill, E. (2005) 'Work-family facilitation and conflict, working fathers and mothers, work family stressors and support', *Journal of Family Issues*, vol 26, no 6, pp 793-819.

Jones, P. (2009) 'Teaching for change in social work: a discipline-based argument for the use of transformative approaches to teaching and learning', *Journal of Transformative Education*, vol 7, pp 8-25.

Kelly, J. and Horder, W. (2001) 'The how and the why: competences and holistic practice', *Social Work Education*, vol 20, no 6, pp 689-99.

Levitt-Jones, T. and Lathlean, J. (2008) 'Belongingness: a pre-requisite for students' clinical learning', *Nurse Education in Practice*, vol 8, pp 103-11.

Levitt-Jones, T. and Lathlean, J. (2009) '"Don't rock the boat": nursing students' experiences of conformity and compliance', *Nurse Education Today*, vol 29, pp 342-9.

McEvoy, L. and Duffy, A. (2008) 'Holistic practice – a concept analysis', *Nurse Education in Practice*, vol 8, pp 412-19.

Mackintosh, C. (2006) 'Caring: the socialisiation of pre-registration student nurses: a longitudinal qualitative descriptive study', *International Journal of Nursing Studies*, vol 43, pp 953-62.

Manning-Morton, J. (2006) 'The personal is professional: professionalism and the birth to threes practitioner', *Contemporary Issues in Early Childhood*, vol 7, no 1, pp 42-52.

Melia, K. (1998) 'Learning and working: the occupational socialization of nurses', in L. Mackay, K. Soothill and K. Melia (eds) *Classic Texts in Health Care*, Oxford: Butterworth Heinemann, pp 154–9.

Moules, T. and Ramsay, J. (2008) *The Textbook of Children and Young People's Nursing* (2nd edn), Oxford: Blackwell.

NCT (National Childbirth Trust) (2009) 'Breastfeeding counsellor' (www.nct.org.uk).

Oakley, A. (1998) 'The importance of being a nurse', in L. Mackay, K. Soothill and K. Melia (eds) *Classic Texts in Health Care*, Oxford: Butterworth Heinemann, pp 191-4.

O'Connor, J. (2007) 'Developing professional habitus: a Bernsteinian analysis of the modern nurse apprenticeship', *Nurse Education Today*, vol 27, pp 748-54.

Osgood, J. (2008) 'Deconstructing professionalism in early childhood education; resisting the regulatory gaze', *Contemporary Issues in Early Childhood*, vol 7, no 1, pp 5-14.

Pearcey, P. and Draper, P. (2008) 'Exploring clinical nursing experiences: listening to student nurses', *Nurse Education Today*, vol 28, pp 595-601.

Pinkerton, J. (2001) 'Developing professional practice', in P. Foley, J. Roche and S. Tucker (eds) *Children in Society: Contemporary Theory, Policy and Practice*, Basingstoke: Palgrave, pp 249-57.

Price, S. (2009) 'Becoming a nurse: a meta-study of early professional socialization and career choice in nursing', *Journal of Advanced Nursing*, vol 65, no 1, pp 11-19.

Redwood, T. (2003) 'Nurse and mother: is there a conflict of interest?', *Paediatric Nursing*, vol 15, no 7, pp 20-2.

Redwood, T. (2008) 'Exploring changes in practice: when midwives and nurses become mothers', *British Journal of Midwifery*, vol 16, no 1, pp 34-8.

Reupert, A. (2009) 'Students' use of self: teaching implications', *Social Work Education*, vol 28, no 7, pp 765-77.

Robinson, S., Cox, S. and Murrells, T. (2006) 'Developing the children's nursing workforce: profile, first jobs and future plans once qualified', *Journal of Child Health Care*, vol 10, no 1, pp 55-68.

Rolfe, G., Freshwater, D. and Jasper, M. (2001) *Critical Reflection for Nursing and the Helping Professions*, Basingstoke: Palgrave Macmillan.

Sheppard, J. (2000) 'Learning form personal experience: reflexions on social work practice with mothers in child and family care', *Journal of Social Work Practice*, vol 14, no 1, pp 37-50.

Shoffner, M. (2009) 'The place of the personal: exploring the affective domain through reflection in teacher preparation', *Teaching and Teacher Education*, vol 25, pp 783-9.

Smith, L. and Coleman, V. (2010) *Child and Family-centred Care: Concept, Theory and Practice*, Basingstoke: Palgrave Macmillan.

Strandberg, E.L., Ovhed, I., Borgquist, L. and Wilhelmsson, S. (2007) 'The perceived meaning of a (w)holistic view among general practitioners and district nurses in Swedish primary care: a qualitative study', *BMC Family Practice* vol 8, no 8.

Taylor, C. (2006) 'Narrating significant experience: reflective accounts and the production of self knowledge', *British Journal of Social Work*, vol 36, pp 189–206.

Thompson, V., Hupcey, J. and Clark, M.B. (2002) 'The development of trust in parents of hospitalized children', *Journal of Specialists in Pediatric Nursing*, vol 8, no 4, pp 137–47.

Tschudin, V. (1997) 'The emotional cost of caring', in G. Brykczynska and M. Jolley (eds) *Caring: The Compassion and Wisdom of Nursing*, London: Arnold, pp155–79.

Wood, C. (1888) *The Training of Nurses for Sick Children*, London: Great Ormond Street Hospital for Sick Children.

Yip, K. (2006) 'Self-reflection in reflective practice: a note of caution', *British Journal of Social Work*, vol 36, pp 777–88.

Seventeen

Troubling boundaries between the personal and professional: teachers becoming mothers

Rachel Thomson

To operate in a 'professional' manner is popularly understood in terms of putting personal feelings and investments to one side, to follow fair and transparent rules of conduct and to maintain effective boundaries between the professional arena of work and the personal arena of life. The professionalisation of work with children and young people is in historical terms a relatively recent development, led by the fields of teaching and more recently encompassing a wide range of disciplines including social work, early years, youth work and youth justice. In female-dominated disciplines the struggle for professional recognition has been tied up with claims for status, autonomy and recognition (Crompton, 1997). Yet work with children and young people also continues to be shaped by competing traditions that value informality, voluntary activity and lay rather than expert knowledge (Finch and Groves, 1983). The move towards the professionalisation of the children's workforce has been motivated by a drive towards establishing and monitoring standards yet has been associated with a loss of freedom and creativity (Hochschild, 2003). Being and acting as a professional involves emotional and ethical labour, and professional boundaries can be complicated and politicised by changes in the biography of the practitioner, such as the transition to becoming a parent.

This chapter draws on data from a qualitative investigation of the transition to first time motherhood.[1] We have conceptualised the very different circumstances in which the women in our study approached motherhood in terms of 'situations' that are the configuration of bodily, biographical and cultural trajectories (Thomson and Kehily, 2008). Work is one of the factors that shapes women's situations, but their orientations towards work vary dramatically according to their age, whether or not they are invested in a 'career' and where in their career they are at this point, as well as the kind of work that they are involved in and the extent to which the boundary between working and mothering identities is seen as permeable. Most of the youngest women in our study had not yet established themselves in the world of work, and for them motherhood could act as a catalyst for imagining future work trajectories (often in childcare or, in one case, midwifery). Older women who had been working for a period of time before pregnancy had to negotiate how to manage the competing demands of employment, mothering and the financial costs of childcare. For some women, returning to work soon after birth was a financial necessity; others felt that they had some options. The extent to which women were invested in their existing working identities depended on many things, including how long they had been working, their work status and their wider family situation.

Yet whatever their status, motherhood forces women to consider questions about care. A common lament from women in the study was that they did not 'want to work in order to pay someone else to look after their child', although some conceptualised this relationship in an entirely different way as 'working for their child'. The position of women whose work is the care and education of children is particularly interesting in this context. Seven of the 62 interviewees were involved in working with children, in teaching, social work and childcare. Here I focus on the accounts of women expecting their first child who were involved in teaching, showing how their professional boundaries were troubled by the experience of becoming mothers. The chapter begins with a discussion of the conceptual framework that we are using to think about the relationship between working and maternal identities, before moving on to explore some of the themes that emerged in pre-birth interviews and one of our case studies, suggesting the complex relationship between familiar and working identities. The aim of this chapter is to explore the interplay of personal and professional identifications for those working with children and young people and to consider how ideas drawn from the sociology of work might refresh understandings of the reflexivity that are integral to reflective practice. By listening to the accounts of teachers who are becoming mothers, I hope it will be possible to gain some insights into the hidden emotional labours involved in this kind of work.

Theoretical frameworks: permeability and transposition

Our approach to thinking about work and motherhood has much in common with the framework of the 'new sociology of work', which troubles the conceptual boundaries of what we mean by work, pointing to the permeable and often blurred spatial and temporal boundaries between the domains in which 'work' occurs: public/private, formal/informal, legal/illegal, work time/leisure time. From this perspective, 'work' is not necessarily paid and is embedded in other social relations such as family and friendship, and in wider economic processes that involve consumption and exchange (Pettinger *et al.*, 2005).

> Reconceptualising work involves bringing to the forefront of our analytical prism an appreciation of the complexity of the dynamic and interconnected character of work relations. The same activity may be paid and treated as formal employment, or be undertaken informally or on an unpaid basis; such differences have implications for how it is understood and socially evaluated. Rather than isolating work from non-work activities, the project becomes one to explore the points at which they become entangled and embedded as well as differentiated. (Parry *et al.*, 2005: 10)

If we add to this framework recent feminist appropriations of Bourdieu that suggest the importance of how meanings, skills and resources are moved or transposed between social fields, it is possible to gain a fresh perspective on what has traditionally been posed in terms of 'work–life balance' (Lovell, 2000). Rather than asking how women balance private obligations and public participation, care and employment, we want to map the resources that people draw on in this work: material, cultural, social, conscious and less conscious; how they weave these together or keep them apart; and the interplay of identifications as workers, lovers, daughters, mothers and friends.

Teaching and mothering

Teaching is generally understood to be a flexible and child-friendly career for women, in terms of school holidays and the potential to take time out without jeopardising the ability to return to the classroom (Sikes, 1997). This was a view expressed by most of the teachers in our study (several of whom were themselves the daughters of teachers), and their experiences of managing the transition from a working to maternal identity was distinctive. Teachers remarked on the significance of working in an environment in which people liked children, and where there were lots of parents who were positive and excited about their pregnancy for you. This contrasts acutely with the accounts of women working in male-dominated environments in which their pregnant body was a difficult presence, and impending parenthood and maternity leave was framed in terms of 'letting the side down' and placing a burden on colleagues or the business. Being pregnant at school or nursery may be exhausting, but the pregnant body was a source of excitement and conversation with children, parents and colleagues. The physical demands of teaching had however resulted in several of the pregnant teachers beginning their maternity leave early, whether through being signed off sick, or coinciding with the summer holiday. In one case a women had to take union advice in order to challenge a demand that she should participate in a nursery trip to the seaside when seven months pregnant. Those in senior management positions also remarked on how pregnancy could undermine their status with colleagues, finding themselves excluded from decisions. More junior staff talked of their fears that they would lose out on training opportunities if it was known that they were pregnant or were planning for it.

Yet negotiating the boundaries between working professionally with and for children, and becoming a mother, was also a complicated business. Women drew on their professional knowledge and skills in imagining motherhood for themselves, yet they also drew on informal knowledge garnered in school, through observing the behaviour and values of the parents that they encountered in their work as teachers. For example, when asked about how being a teacher might impact on her ideas about motherhood, 33-year-old Madeline, head of a nursery school, commented on how inspirational she had found meeting mothers who had stayed at home with their children until they reached the age of three, rather than placing them in childcare. She also commented on how the Bengali mothers she had encountered in another school were "really dedicated" and "committed to their families", before also adding in professional mode that "some of them needed support, so we guided them in that direction". Madeline explained that her view that young children should be at home with their mothers was a "professional belief" and felt alienated by the women in her middle-class neighbourhood who made her feel "a freak for staying home", and who, in her words, "must go back to work, childcare since birth, the children must be stimulated". Her comment that "I've done 12 years with other people's children, I think it's time to spend with my own" suggests that the relationship between formal and familiar care can be fraught. Far from enjoying permeability between professional and private realms, Madeline is keen to separate the two.

Similarly complicated feelings were evident in an interview with 31-year-old Carla, a nursery school teacher. Carla saw teaching as a family-friendly profession, enabling her to "pick it up, as I go along", "go back part-time or full-time, re-train in something else to do with sort of childcare". She also noted that teaching for six years had prepared her for motherhood:

> "… it's always easier when it's other people's kids isn't it, you know? [...] but um … and just things to do, like I know how to make cakes, and I can make play dough, [laughs] and things like that, flour and oil, you know. Um … so I mean – and I really want to get involved in toddler groups, and I feel quite confident about going out to meet other parents, and that sort of thing. So I think that's been a good preparation."

During the interview Carla showed me 'educational toys' that she had made for her baby including a sensual "treasure bag", tactile materials and a "star bag" that was "excellent for encouraging language development in children with English as a second language". Yet at the same time she was resistant to encouragement by her headteacher to return after her maternity leave and to enrol her baby in the nursery.

The star bag, using professional techniques in a personal project: Rachel Thomson

Carla's collection of pregnancy books: Rachel Thomson.

While talking me through the books that she had bought during her pregnancy, Carla talked about one on attachment parenting, *Why Love Matters*:

> Carla: "Hmm, hmm that's a fantastic one. Yeah I've seen her, she did a talk at one of the courses I was on, and that was really good, I found that quite um emotional to read actually [laughs] as well. But um...."

> Rachel: "So what do you think about childcare?"

> Carla: "Um, I want to, um – I want to have a childminder, I think. And that's why I don't want to go back full-time straight away either. Um, and I haven't really got much further than that, but I can't really – because everyone at work's saying, 'Are you going to bring the baby here?', you know, because we've got the baby facilities at work. And although the children seem really confident, and the – the child – you know, the workers are very professional, and it's fine, I just ... phew I don't know. I think it's just too young, you know. And my head did say, you know, 'Would you like to bring your baby here?' And I just kind of said, 'I'd rather be in a place away from

them, because I'd be worrying', you know, trying to say it tactfully.… I just feel really strongly that um I don't think it's a good environment for very young children."

Later on during the interview Carla returned to conflicts that she had experienced between her professional identity and her emergent identification as a mother during her pregnancy:

Carla: "I've noticed with, um – with the younger mums at work, because they've got their mums sort of on board a bit. But, um, they seem to be putting them onto solid food a lot earlier than is rec–, than I have heard is recommended. You know, I have one mum of – he's like three or four months old and, 'Oh yeah he's eating solids already, it's really good'. And I was thinking, 'I thought you had to wait for six months'. And she was like very proud of this. And she's like 20/21, I think she is. And um … and, you know, you just – because as a profession, you know, you say, 'Oh yes? Oh really, yes?' .You know, and I just sort of nodded and, you know, thinking, 'Should I be saying anything? But I don't really know exactly'. [...] I sort of thought, 'Was it really my place?' Because she was sort of just chatting, it was like a – like a little – you know, the parents had come to share a lunch with the children, you know, and she was just sort of chatting like that. And um – and I didn't know … whether – because I wasn't entirely sure myself, you know, should I be contradicting that?…"

Rachel: "And also I suppose there's the difference between you being a professional and you being another mother."

Carla: "About to be a mum, yeah. And I think, hmm, that'll probably come up quite a bit actually.You know, and, um, in one of the toddler groups they had, um – they put a load of rice, dried rice out on a tray for children to play with. And, um, there was a – I'm not sure whereabouts she was from, but she was, um, sort of like an Asian parent saying that, 'We could never do this in my country, it would be disrespectful to be wasting rice on – you know'. And we sort of hadn't really thought about it like that, that was a really interesting take on it. Because we're always like, you know, sensory play, and flour and mess, and this and that.

> And she was saying, 'No, this would feed nine people, you
> know, why would we want to waste it?' And, you know,
> and there's like other, um, parents who get really, really
> upset if their children get wet playing with the water, and
> stuff like that.... There's always a battle going on a bit....''

I am not sharing these examples to expose Carla, or to question the
quality of organised childcare, but to suggest how complicated it is to be
a custodian of a professional identity while also becoming the object of
that professional knowledge. Holding the responsibility of 'being right'
and recognising difference, Carla is not only wondering whether the
'correct' professional position is to impose her ideas about appropriate
child development, or to recognise and value cultural diversity, but she
is also placing herself as a parent in relation to these other parents, and
distinguishing herself. Like Madeline, Carla's teaching experience has
been in the inner city, and impending parenthood is leading her to
consider leaving the city for a more suburban middle-class environment.
The traffic here is all in one direction – Carla wants to draw on her
professional knowledge and training to enrich her parenting skills. She
does not want to bring her baby into the environment in which she
developed these skills. In the next part of this chapter I present data
from one of these case studies, to show the potentially troubling ways
in which teaching and mothering identities are entangled, and to give
a sense of the sources of the emotional charge that characterises these
women's reflections on care.

Heather Chapman: a case study

We met 27-year-old Heather and her husband Andy shopping in
Mothercare not long after they had discovered that she was pregnant,
something that had completely disrupted their carefully made life
plans. Both were teachers, and had come to the UK from Australia
to work for a period of five years to pay off the mortgage on a house
'back home', where they intended eventually to return to start a
family. The unplanned pregnancy had thrown them. Heather was in
a primary school teaching job that she had committed herself to for
three years. Despite her fears that the head and senior management
team at school would punish her for this, the school had been
extremely supportive of her, reassuring her that she was eligible for
maternity leave and that they would support her return to work. She
describes her colleagues as 'a family of people', which she valued
enormously, having no family of her own in the country. Although

Heather recognised that financially she would have to return to work after her maternity leave, this was "a shame", having always envisaged herself as a stay-at-home mum. She had no sense how she would manage this return to work and was struggling to imagine how to balance the school timetable with childcare, fantasising about the potential of creating a school-based crèche that could support the seven babies under two that were currently 'on staff'. We re-encountered Heather just over a year after the birth of her son Ben. By this time Heather had returned to Australia and was living in a suburb of an Australian city, pregnant with her second baby. Heather explained that she was missing the networks and sociability that characterised inner-city mothering in the UK. The extracts that I have identified here capture moments in her account where there is some symbolic traffic between teaching and mothering identities, and between work and domestic domains. These are both examples of mixing and of separation between the public and private, and between lay and professional identities.

Heather presented her birth ironically as fitting the timetable of the school day, "he was out at 3.30 so it was a school day it was 9 to 3.30, the bells rang and he was there", and her account of returning to work after her maternity leave suggests how integrated and entwined her working and parenting were at this stage:

> "I'd rock in to school at… I think I was getting in to school sometimes at about 5.50, 6 a.m. in the morning so that Ben would have his morning, he'd go back to sleep, he'd have his bottle and then he'd go back to sleep and he'd normally sleep from about 6 a.m. until around 7.30 and that's when I could get work done [...] I had all the codes, I'd chat with all the cleaners, everyone you know, Ben is here and all the cleaners would come down and see Ben in the morning and then at 7.30 once he'd wake up if I hadn't finished he'd have a little play on the carpet and tot around while I got the last bits and things, being in reception was so much easier you know. There wasn't the marking, there wasn't you know the extensive amount of programming and particularly because it was the beginning of the year, and it's still primarily free play it was fantastic, I was very lucky … so once I'd finished, I'd go in to the staffroom and everyone would come down generally, all the staff would come and have a play with Ben. If I had things to do my head would take him, I was welcome to have him

> in meetings, he always attended all the staff meetings, it was
> like … he became the school's baby, which was beautiful
> you know. Everybody knew Ben, and loved him and …
> then at 9 a.m. when school started, oh … we'd go to the
> classroom, Karen [childminder] would arrive and drop her
> daughter off at the door and she'd … you know all my kids
> would run in to the class and say goodbye to Ben and off
> Ben would go for the day, and at 3.30 he'd get dropped
> back again. So it was good. And often if I had things to do
> in the afternoon I could give him to someone to have a
> bottle down in the staff room and then I'd come down."

However, this integrated life did not last, and after two months
Heather gave her notice and returned to Australia, where it was
possible for her to stay home with Ben. She explains that she may
feel okay about day care when he was two or three and had sufficient
language to "talk back to me", noting that her teaching experience
had prepared her well for the moment of separation, when as a teacher
you "have to hang on to them and have them sob hysterically as mum
walks away". Heather says that "I know I'll do it", "every child goes
through that and he'll be fine". But at the moment he is "still too baby
baby, and I want … him to be the age where he understands why I'm
walking away". In this second interview Heather also explained that
her previous passion for teaching was slipping away. She was "nowhere
near as motivated or driven" and while being a teacher had been a
huge part of her life, "it doesn't matter anywhere near as much" now.
In fact she drew on her teaching identity as a way of explaining that
"I'm really happy to go and do painting in the backyard and I'm really
happy to sit in the sandpit for an hour, because that's what my teaching
was, to do activities". Heather also revealed some more difficult ways
in which her professional training and expertise intruded on her
mothering practice, as well as some of the ways in which her maternal
experience encouraged her to rethink familiar classroom scenarios.
Knowledge of both home and classroom incited her to translate
experiences, knowledge and her son across this boundary.

> "Andy [husband] often says he hears my teacher voice
> coming out with Ben, and I don't think that's a bad
> thing, he needs to know sometimes no, and I mean it but
> I'm sure all mothers do it but I know I use my teaching
> strategies on Ben … and I sometimes think though that I
> try, I'd never say it out loud but I catch myself, not judging

because that's a horrible word but, er … no other people,
it's generally like my sister and my sister-in-law perhaps,
their mothering styles I sort of think in my head, I'm like
… oh, I wouldn't have allowed that, or you know … but
then I think I wouldn't have allowed that in my classroom,
I almost view their … like, I think I've got to remind
myself, no, these are my little nieces and they're beautiful,
and they're at home in their environment and it's okay, but
in my head I'm thinking, 'cos they're all starting to turn
three and five and they're older and that's the age I was
teaching, and I'm thinking, oh, I wouldn't let them speak
like that but then I know the funny thing is I remember
mums coming to me at school saying, oh … he never
speaks like, the way he does to you, at me at home, [...]
oh, he's such a well behaved boy and he's fantastic, oh,
he's not like that at home. And I'm seeing the home."

I asked Heather whether studying child development had an impact
on how she thought about what Ben should be doing and what was
normal for him. She replied that this knowledge was a source of
anxiety for her and that she almost wished that she "didn't know, I
think it would be so much better, maybe I wouldn't care so much",
because "it's all well and good to have the knowledge and the
background but the actually doing and putting into practice of your
own child" is a different matter. Seeing your own child through your
teacher's eyes can be challenging, exposing uncomfortable knowledge,
including the contradictions between a disciplinary educational gaze
and an unconditional maternal perspective (Pitt, 2009). Heather shared
a number of concerns about Ben's social development in the interview,
describing her frustrated attempts to find friends for him of the same
age and sex within a highly privatised suburban neighbourhood.
The following example shows how anxiety-provoking professional
knowledge can be, but also the partial and destructive impact of its
mundane classifications:

"… it had never occurred to me that Ben could be a child
that could be isolated. I've taught in so many classes, and
you walk in to the room and you can immediately pick
the child that is the isolated, ostracised one in the room.
And either you find, or I've found that it's, the parents
will reflect the child, when you get to meet the mum
who often is a single parent, their lack of confidence and

self-esteem and it breaks your heart dealing with them because they're upset about their child or you get the opposite where, er … or you get the child who's ostracised and isolated because he's aggressive and he's angry and he's a bully and then you meet the parents and you go, oh well, that's why I said I'd never considered, it wasn't until that night seeing Ben isolated that oh my goodness he could be the one…. Andy said, don't be silly it takes an all-rounded parents to produce an all-rounded child, he'll be fine. And I said but if I was to go back to teaching now I would view it so differently, because somewhere there's a mother who every night might be feeling the way I am tonight, every night when she lays down in bed, I've only got one night of this feeling sad about Ben, being … isolated, just devastated me, I've never … and I always work hard with those kids and try and make them special and get them involved in a group you know. I make them, I give them a nickname, a cool name in the class, and try and get them involved. But I just thought, if I think back over those kids that were the isolated ones and it just devastates me that there's a mother and a father seeing their child come home upset or knowing … and that would change my teaching for ever, which I didn't understand before."

Heather's decision to step back from teaching during her children's early years needs to be understood in relation to the intensive reflexivity produced by the permeable boundary between working and maternal identities and practices. Heather narrated her pre-mothering self as able to give unconditionally to her pupils. With motherhood this generosity could no longer be afforded.

"… mum has always been 'Heather you're just a born teacher' that sort of thing, and it's just realised to me that it's not as important as I thought it was, er … this could sound so bad, but I'm sure a lot of teachers who are mothers, I hope they've gone through the same thing, of, where as I would come home, I would work for hours, my programmes in my opinion, I've worked so hard they were fabulous […] you know I would spend weekends, go round … planning and programming and putting effort in, above and beyond what I know a lot of other staff at other schools do. And it wasn't anything to do with, er

> ... I enjoyed it, I really enjoyed having fantastic lessons
> that the kids would fun out on, I enjoyed their successes.
> When it blew them away that they got something, yet
> now when I think about going back, and even when I
> did ... when I think about, yeah, going back in the six
> months that I did, I still cared about the education of those
> children, it still mattered extremely to me but I did, I did
> what was required of me, I didn't go beyond the call....."

Conclusion: Troubling reflexivity

Ideas of reflective practice within a professional context assume
processes of personal reflection, yet largely exclude the personal from
this process. It is as though reflection draws on personal resources yet
is very much a professional performance from which complicated
personal feelings and investments are excluded. Commentators have
talked about this kind of 'reflexivity' as a habit of late-modern culture,
something demanded of us in order to convincingly perform the
flexible and emotionally fluent worker increasingly demanded within
both public and private sectors (Adkins, 2003). Yet in practice, a more
profound form of reflexivity and heightened awareness is produced
by the mixing and transposing of knowledge, skills and techniques
between professional and personal across biographical fields. This
is a reflexivity that produces troubling and ethically connected
knowledge, not so easily captured and integrated. Returning to the
theoretical frameworks of the 'new sociology of work', which points
to permeability between different kinds of work, we can say yes, for
this group of teachers/mothers there is a great deal of traffic, and that
yes, it is productive of reflexivity. Yet, as Heather's case study suggests,
this can be a troubling reflexivity, which has the potential to transform
both the professional and the maternal identity. We have been struck
by the direction of traffic across the boundaries of teaching and
mothering, the tendency to take the professional into personal projects
of mothering rather than taking mothering into the professional realm
of the school and the nursery. Carla does not want to enrol her baby
at her workplace, and although Heather begins by mixing the two, this
situation does not last.

Teachers and childcare workers are a small part of our wider sample,
and represent a very particular configuration of the situation of work
and mothering. While teaching is recognised or possibly constructed as
a particularly flexible and family-friendly profession, our data suggest
that it produces some specific and challenging juxtapositions for

imagining motherhood, where the projects of work and mothering so apparently similar may be experienced as being in tension and even in competition. Our wider findings from the study suggest that the arrival of a new generation is a moment that is productive of social class distinctions – marking both the destination point for the classed journey of the daughter who is now a mother and the beginning of a new classes journey for the child (Byrne, 2006; Thomson and Kehily, 2008). As teachers working in inner-city schools and nurseries, Carla, Madeline and Heather have a heightened awareness of the ways in which education and care are implicated in projects of social mobility. Their proximity to the parenting projects of low-income families is contained within professional discourses of 'support' that are destabilised by sharing the subject position of the mother. One response that is evident in the data that I have presented today is escape and separation, and the privatisation of professional skill into an intensive middle-class mothering. Yet this also separates these women from other middle-class mothers who may maintain an investment in work and career, and who may be protected by their lack of insider knowledge of childcare settings.

Note

[1] The research project 'The Making of Modern Motherhood: Memories, Identities and Representations' (Res 148-25-0057) was funded by the Economic and Social Research Council (ESRC) as part of the 'Identities and Social Action' research programme (www.identities.ac.uk). The project was directed by Rachel Thomson and Mary Jane Kehily and involved Lucy Hadfield and Sue Sharpe. A subsequent stage of the study, 'The Dynamics of Motherhood', has been funded by the ESRC as part of the Timescapes initiative (www.timescapes.leeds.ac.uk).

References

Adkins, L. (2003) 'Reflexivity: freedom or habit of gender', *Theory, Culture and Society*, vol 20, no 6, pp 21-42.

Byrne, B. (2006) '"In search of a good mix": race, class, gender and practices of mothering', *Sociology*, vol 40, no 6, pp 1001-17.

Crompton, R. (1997) *Women and Work in Modern Britain*, Oxford: Oxford University Press.

Finch, J. and Groves, D. (eds) (1983) *A Labour of Love: Women, Work and Caring*, London: Routledge and Kegan Paul.

Hochschild, A. (2003) *The Commercialization of Intimate Life: Notes From Home and Work*, Berkeley, CA: University of California Press.

Lovell, T. (2000) 'Thinking feminism with and against Bourdieu', *Feminist Theory*, vol 1, no 1, pp 11–32.

Parry, J., Taylor, R., Pettinger, L. and Glucksmann, M. (2005) 'Confronting the challenges of work today: new horizons and perspectives', in L. Pettinger, J. Parry, R. Taylor and M. Glucksmann (eds) *A New Sociology of Work?*, Oxford: Blackwell, pp 104-15.

Pettinger, L., Parry, J., Taylor, R. and Glucksmann, M. (2005) *A New Sociology of Work?*, Oxford: Blackwell.

Pitt, A. (2009) 'Generation and the paradox of autonomy in the teaching profession', Paper presented at 'Gender and Education' Seventh International Conference, University of London, Institute of Education, March.

Sikes, P. (1997) *Parents Who Teach: Stories From Home and From School*, London: Cassells.

Thomson, R. and Kehily, M.J. (2008) *The Making of Modern Motherhood: Memories, Representations and Practices*, Milton Keynes: The Open University (www.open.ac.uk/hsc/__assets/yqwnotatstun71rdbl.pdf).

Eighteen

Shifting the goalposts: researching pupils at risk of school exclusion

Val Gillies and Yvonne Robinson

This chapter reflects on our efforts as researchers to instigate and manage an ethnographic study of challenging behaviour in the classroom. A key aim of the project was to work collaboratively and in consultation with school staff and young people to develop an holistic view of pupils identified as troubled and troublesome. Here we give a candid account of our fieldwork in one particular school, drawing out the everyday practices and personal relationships through which our research was forged. We highlight the power of research in providing a distinct, critical perspective rarely available to those with professional positions and responsibilities. Our position, as embedded, independent observers unbound by normal institutional roles, expectations and investments, generated valuable insights into taken-for-granted or normalised practices.

We begin by briefly setting the study in context, considering our motives and some of the assumptions framing the research questions. We then explore how our expectations, hopes and anxieties were reframed during fieldwork. Through our personal narratives as researchers, we illustrate how a commitment to produce detailed, situated knowledge demands flexibility and emotional investment. Emphasis is given to the central role of critical reflexivity in guiding decisions, reviewing progress and generating credible research findings. Thus, the chapter aims to demonstrate the essential place of reflexive engagement in responsible, ethical and effective practice.

Context: researching 'at-risk' pupils

The topic of youth disorder and anti-social behaviour is an emotive one. Responses range from fear, anxiety and anger over a perceived generational threat to civility, to a more liberal concern over the way young people are constructed as dangerous and treated accordingly. In particular, the issue of poor discipline in the classroom has attracted considerable comment, with opinion divided over whether pupils, teachers or parents are to blame. Our research grew out of a critical interest in this public and political context, and more specifically an awareness of how silent young people's voices are in this debate. There has been strikingly little engagement with the perspectives of those defined as displaying problematic behaviour. While there is a large body of research focusing on causes, effects and strategies for dealing with disruptive conduct in the classroom, there has been little consideration of how disruptive pupils manage their experience of the school system.

We aimed to address this gap with an intensive ethnographic study based in Behaviour Support Units (BSUs) in inner-city secondary schools. BSUs are (often self-contained) facilities in mainstream schools to address issues around conduct. Pupils are sent to the units for varying amounts of time, ranging from weeks to years. Our intention was to explore how disaffection with and disengagement from school are experienced, lived and understood. We spent time in the units, conducted group work activities and interviewed pupils, parents and teachers. Over the course of two years we were located in three schools, two co-educational and one single-sex girls' school. We worked with a total of 73 pupils, 24 young women and 49 young men.

This chapter focuses on our experiences in establishing our study in Halingbrooke,[1] the first school we approached. This school has a troubled history despite receiving a good Ofsted report in 2008. Very high numbers of students are eligible for free school meals, and many have learning difficulties and disabilities. Large proportions of pupils join or leave Halingbrooke during term time, and pupils excluded from other schools are often accepted onto the school roll. Boys heavily outnumber girls in Halingbrooke BSU; in two years, we worked exclusively with male groups.

Feeling our way and learning the ropes

Launching any substantial research project is a daunting prospect. Unforeseen complications are inevitable in fieldwork, and few studies proceed exactly according to design. In the case of ethnographic research, the embedded location and real-world demands are particularly difficult to anticipate. This was compounded for us by a lack of practical knowledge. We had little experience of working in schools or with challenging pupils. We were acutely aware that the success of our research would depend on our ability to connect with young people commonly labelled anti-social and hard-to-reach. In the early phase, we relied heavily on extensive reading and consultation to devise our methods. We approached the fieldwork with a mixture of apprehension, hope and naivety.

The gap between theory and practice soon became apparent. We knew from national policy that each institution would have a Learning Support Unit to address conduct issues. Our plan had been to establish ourselves within these units, and begin to negotiate the types of group activities to run with pupils. In practice, we found considerably more complex structures and several layers of intervention and support. All three schools had at least one dedicated area where conduct issues were dealt with, albeit in different ways. The terminology used to describe these units varied between schools, but for convenience we use the term 'Behaviour Support Unit' here.

Our initial contact in Halingbrooke was the pastoral support manager, Mr Baker, who was extremely enthusiastic and supportive. However, the school distinguished between 'troubled' and 'troublesome' pupils, the former being referred to pastoral support, the latter to a separate BSU. This split was more than organisational: the two areas were opposing factions. Bitter disputes raged over where pupils and resources were to be directed, and the philosophy behind the decision.

The antipathy between the two sides was obvious on our first visit, when Mr Baker made several disparaging and highly personal comments about the manager of the BSU, Dave Stirling. When we explained that the BSU best fitted our research, Mr Baker seemed disappointed. Warning us that the manager was "difficult", "prickly" and unprofessional, Mr Baker showed us to the BSU and ushered us into a class in session. We sat awkwardly and watched while Mr Baker tried and failed to get Dave Stirling's attention. Eventually he won a terse agreement to hold a conversation after the lesson. This was our first taste of the personal and institutional dynamics that underpin everyday school life. The contempt between the two men was barely disguised. Mr Baker left us with a suspicious and distinctly frosty Dave Stirling, whose distrust quickly abated, and we established a long-term base in the BSU with his help. Nonetheless, from the start we were clearly aligned with Dave Stirling, and this largely isolated us from pastoral support. Mr Baker stopped acknowledging our presence from this point, and we were concerned to think we had burned a bridge that might be difficult to re-build in the future.

Such fraught relationships were a defining feature of our research. Challenging behaviour in the classroom provoked particular tensions, resentments and frustrations in all three schools. We regularly encountered staff members breaking down in tears, making rude personal remarks about colleagues, pupils or parents, and even levelling serious allegations about conduct within the school. Conflicting and conflicted views about bad behaviour, its causes and solutions were the source of disagreement and ill will. Heated disputes stemmed from strong emotional commitments to pupils (both well behaved and badly behaved) and teaching as an ideal. Staff turnover was high (Mr Baker left before we did), resources were fought over, and the threat of forced closure hung heavy. This was a tense and delicate environment in which to install ourselves as outsiders conducting research.

Having established our base in Halingbrooke, we began a period of observation and discussion with BSU staff. We were given an account of the referral system and everyday running of the unit, which we used to firm up plans for our group sessions. We were assured that pupils were sent to the BSU for six weeks at a time, and that regular meetings were held between key staff to discuss allocation and progress. It soon became obvious that this description bore little resemblance to reality. Many of the pupils we worked with stayed in the BSU for years, and several came straight from primary without ever troubling the mainstream school. Few stayed for six weeks or less unless they were excluded. Decisions concerning referral, exclusion or reintegration were commonly made without consultation with Dave Stirling. Our research became a form of detective work aimed at uncovering how things really worked. As we discovered, the schools' practices were flexible, changeable and often inconsistent with written procedures.

Observing interactions between staff and students in the BSUs was a crucial precursor to our group work sessions. We became familiar with the units' cultures and routines, and with the kinds of pupils (and behaviours) we would be working with. Also, pupils began to recognise us and ask questions before they were formally invited to participate in the research. Before entering the schools, we had been concerned about what pupils would make of our presence. In particular, we worried that pupils would feel under surveillance. This anxiety quickly receded in the noisy and chaotic context of Halingbrooke BSU. Arguments, fights and pupil/staff confrontations were common. Teachers (often supply), mentors and classroom assistants came and went throughout the day. Pupils regularly moved in and out of the unit to attend different interventions and appointments with professionals, and some were allowed to attend the odd lesson in the school. We had little sense that we were disturbing or unsettling normal routines.

Explaining our role was somewhat more problematic. On our first visit, a 12-year-old boy approached us while we were talking to a teaching assistant. He extended a hand to greet us and asked who we were. The teaching assistant introduced us as "teachers who had come to see what went on in the BSU". The pupil soon wandered off, and we explained that we were researchers, not teachers. This clarification was waved away by the teaching assistant, who emphasised quite assertively that we must pretend to be teachers to gain the authority we needed. We were uncomfortable with this suggestion and wished we had been quicker to identify ourselves properly to the student. But despite our best efforts to explain our role, we found the term 'research' meant little to pupils, many of whom continued to refer to us as teachers. In fact, pupils tended to call mentors, classroom assistants and youth workers 'teachers', leading us to realise that professional distinctions are far more significant to us than to them.

Early BSU observations were particularly useful for establishing what was considered acceptable and unacceptable behaviour. It varied from pupil to pupil, and situation to situation, and depended heavily on the staff member in charge. We were impressed by the patience and commitment of staff members, and we noticed the subtle strategies used to avoid futile or inflammatory confrontation. In short, staff picked their battles. For example, chewing gum, eating sweets and swearing were not openly tolerated. Offending pupils were often challenged, sent out of the classroom or made to apologise. But there were times when staff would pretend not to notice these misdeeds. Some pupils (particularly those diagnosed with ADHD, attention-deficit hyperactivity disorder) found it difficult to control their behaviour. Peter, a 12-year-old, was a compulsive gum chewer, and frequently yelled "f★★★" at the top of his voice. While he was certainly not given free rein in the classroom, he was a persistent offender and got away with far more than other pupils. In other cases, staff would recognise that particular pupils were having a bad day (or week) and give them some leeway. Swearing and shouting at staff might also be overlooked in the context of an escalating argument, and bad behaviour would sometimes be dealt with by gently steering pupils into the office and attempting to reason with them.

Interactions between staff and students operated on a subtle and seemingly intuitive level. Dave Stirling demonstrated particularly impressive skills in managing often large groups of highly challenging pupils. A teacher for over 26 years before specialising in behaviour for seven, Dave appeared to have an instinctive knack for keeping even the most difficult pupils interested, engaged and under control. He cared deeply about the BSU attendees (and was scathing about the distinction between pupils with problems and problem pupils). As we established, almost all the students liked and respected him, as did their parents. Many other staff members were less successful in handling the volatile atmosphere, and so lessons were often chaotic and punctuated by flare ups, resentments, defiance and, at times, aggressive behaviour.

Researching challenging pupils

For our group work sessions, we were able to use a drama studio next to the BSU. With very high, small windows, it allowed ball games to become part of our repertoire. We drew up a list of introductory activities and produced pupil-focused leaflets explaining the research. We took our responsibility to gain informed consent very seriously and our intention was to talk through the research with students. At this point we came up against our first hurdle. The pupils were bored, impatient and suspicious of us – clearly they were not accustomed to having a choice in a school context. They swung on their chairs, rolled their eyes, screwed their faces up and chatted to each other as if we were not there. They glanced at our leaflets and made them into paper planes, or chewed or discarded them. Our direct questions about taking part were met with shoulder shrugs and curt nods. This felt uncomfortable and slightly shameful, as though we had failed in our ethical duties, but subsequently we realised that gaining consent was entirely for our benefit, not theirs. From the pupils' perspective, consent was conditional and given on a minute-to-minute basis. They had no intention of taking part in activities if they did not want to. Their strategies for resistance were the same practices that labelled them as disruptive in the first place, namely outright refusal, verbal abuse, ignoring us or walking out of the classroom.

   Our intention was to work as collaboratively as possible with the pupils, allowing them a say in organising our sessions and choosing activities. We began by attempting to negotiate 'ground rules' that all members of the group could agree to abide by. Encouraging pupils to set their own regulations seemed a likely way of encouraging participation. We thought it would create a sense of ownership of the research process and provide us with some legitimacy when rules needed to be enforced. In practice, it was a tense and uncomfortable experience. As we realised, ground-rule setting is a well-worn activity in the classroom, where it is generally approached as a test, not a democratic opportunity. Some pupils clearly resented the process and were irritated by the pretence. After much coaxing and coaching, we came up with a standard list that prohibited aggressive behaviour, swearing, shouting and not listening. While we were eventually able to nag and cajole students into agreement, the process felt meaningless and slightly disingenuous. When we repeated the exercise with the next group, we discovered to our embarrassment an almost identical set of pupil-constructed guidelines hanging on a wall behind us.

The futility of rule setting became obvious once we began the sessions. Several of the ground rules were completely unenforceable and so we quickly abandoned them. For example, we had to overlook the no-swearing rule because so many of the pupils cursed regularly without realising it. We necessarily had to overlook all sorts of behaviour that would not have been tolerated in a mainstream school. We drew the line at threatening, aggressive or dangerous behaviour, and often had to exclude pupils temporarily from sessions on this basis. On these occasions, we made it clear that pupils would be able to join the next session. To our relief, almost all did. Nevertheless, sessions were rowdy, unruly and loud. We comforted ourselves with the thought that our hands-off approach helped to create a relaxed space where, within reason, pupils could express themselves.

Involving pupils in planning the sessions was relatively successful in terms of participatory ideals, but resulted in us binning most of our prepared activities. Pupils were very clear about what they did not want to do, and preferred fast-moving games, particularly those involving a ball or cards. If we tried to introduce an unpopular activity, boredom or disengagement could lead to play fights, mass walkouts and requests to opt out of the research. The practical difficulties associated with researching our topic area became very evident at this point. High levels of physical energy put paid to sustained periods of sitting down, particularly for pupils with ADHD. We also found that low literacy levels precluded activities requiring even basic levels of writing. These constraints were combined with an emotionally volatile atmosphere. Impulsive actions were also common, like setting off fire extinguishers. This kind of behaviour often resulted in exclusion, meaning we lost many of our pupils at an early or interim stage of the research.

During our search for engaging activities, we struggled to target sessions strategically towards data collection. Instead, we learned how to target data collection towards sessions. We wove questions and themes around the kinds of activities pupils enjoyed. We also began to recognise some of the opportunities associated with the challenges. Low literacy was often compensated by exuberance and exhibitionism.

Despite expressing dislike of drama, the young people loved performing, and this suited their high levels of physical energy. We began to realise that volatility was commonly associated with intense emotional engagement. Excitement, enthusiasm and comedy were to the fore, alongside frustration, anger and, sometimes, tears. It was hard work managing these dynamics, but they provided a rich context for data collection and a research finding in their own right. Our project had been founded on the assumption that challenging pupils were disaffected, disengaged and hard to reach. We discovered a much more complex, personally invested reality, where pupils displayed strong emotional attachments to particular members of staff, their families, each other, and the principle of education and learning.

In establishing a connection with 'difficult' or 'hard-to-reach' young people, our time and effort paid off quickly. The Halingbrooke groups were passionate about football, so we came up with activities to tap into this enthusiasm. For us, this involved a crash course in football players and terminology. We acquired a large portable goal that we assembled for sessions, much to the delight of the pupils. The goal was awkward, heavy and difficult to put together, but it conveyed our genuine commitment to listening and understanding pupils. One of our first activities involved a penalty shoot out, requiring goal scorers to answer a question drawn from a deck of prepared cards. This generated much excitement and noise, and unfolded at tremendous speed. The frenetic atmosphere left little time for reflexivity or elaboration before moving on.

Our attempt to build on this football theme produced a very different order of data. We decided to take a risk and introduce some improvisational drama techniques, inviting pupils to take part in mock post-match interviews as on Match of the Day.[2] Realising that many questions put to footballers contain analogies with school life, we came up with our own questions ranging from the broad ('How do you feel about your performance today?') to the more probing (involving 'red card' incidents, 'fouls', 'fitting into the team' and advice to 'younger players'). This activity was enormously popular. The pupils recognised the analogy immediately and really seemed to enjoy playing along with it. Their answers referred to the 'manager' (meaning Dave Stirling), who pupils described as shouting too much, sometimes spitting by accident (something we recognised), but 'firm but fair'. Pupils were captivated by the fantasy of being a premiership football player, but their interviews were grounded in the reality of their everyday lives. For example, 13-year-old Keishawn partly attributed his fantasy football success to his love of ice skating and regular trips to his local rink (Gillies and Robinson, forthcoming).

Indulging pupils' interests in football made us popular, and while the sessions never really lost their chaotic edge, we were often struck by the kindness, warmth and thoughtfulness displayed towards us. Pupils shouted hello when they saw us in the street, confided intimate and sometimes compromising stories, and willingly passed on telephone numbers so we could include their parents in the research. We came to know many pupils as charming, funny and articulate. We had been so preoccupied in the beginning, designing strategies to engage 'difficult' young people, that we had not anticipated how much we might grow to like them.

Managing multiple perspectives

Given our aim to understand pupils' own perspectives, we became emotionally invested in the fraught undertow of school politics. We were outraged when we had to reschedule our sessions because mainstream pupils were given priority use of the drama studio. We caught ourselves expressing antipathy for teachers we had not even met. We cared deeply when pupils got excluded, our feelings ranging from sadness, frustration, anger and sometimes relief. These emotional pulls shifted and changed shape as the research progressed, particularly when the different perspectives of parents and teachers were included. We tried hard not to jump to conclusions, and found these extra perspectives could transform our interpretations or simply deepen our understandings of the context framing pupils' behaviour.

Interviews with parents were particularly illuminating, not least because they involved visits to pupils' homes, revealing to us the disadvantage and hardship framing many pupils' lives. We had gathered, from their worn, sometimes tattered clothes, and often ravenous hunger, that poverty was an issue for some pupils, but on visiting we found some lived in exceptionally poor conditions. For example, 12-year-old Rodrique, who, with his mum, dad, brother, sister and baby sister, struggled to cope with life in a damp and overcrowded bed-sit. Similarly Daniel, who lived in a crowded two-bedroom flat with his mum and five siblings. Some pupils lived on estates notorious for drugs and crime, and many had lived in a number of boroughs, travelling long distances to school. We spoke mainly to mothers, but we managed to include some fathers as well. We gained significant insights into pupils' backgrounds. Many had experienced domestic violence or family bereavements, or seen their older brothers and/or fathers sent to jail. In the case of 12-year-old Lindon, we discovered his mother was seriously ill and had been in and out of hospital. He had often mentioned his mother, and described their relationship as close, but he gave no indication that she was unwell. No one in the BSU mentioned this to us either, leading us to wonder whether the school was even aware of his situation.

Parents are often blamed for their children's bad behaviour. This view was held by many school staff, who were sceptical about the likelihood of some parents agreeing to participate in our research. We often found that school offices held outdated contact information, so tracking parents down was not always easy. Some lived in temporary accommodation and often moved, others were wary of answering the telephone to unrecognised numbers, and sometimes the language barrier caused confusion. We encountered only one refusal to participate, and more acceptances than we could keep pace with initially. Most parents were keen to be interviewed. Many articulated grievances about the school's treatment of their children, and every parent we spoke to expressed deep concern for their child's welfare, giving often poignant accounts of their struggles to address problems, and telling of their fears for the future. In some cases, we discovered pupils' behaviour was more extreme than we had realised, and included fire-starting or staying out all night.

We interviewed Daniel's mother shortly after he was permanently excluded for an altercation with the school caretaker. Layla was distraught and desperate. Daniel was very distressed too, and begged us to ask the head to reconsider. Daniel's account of the incident tallied with our observations of the caretaker as aggressive and provocative towards BSU pupils. Layla had not been informed of her right to appeal, so we put her in touch with a parents' advisory centre and encouraged her to pursue the issue. This was an ethically informed decision, but it left us feeling slightly disloyal to the school, and anxious about how staff members might respond.

While we developed a great fondness for many of the young people, talking to teachers from the mainstream school helped to undermine any sense that the pupils were simply misunderstood. At times we felt genuine horror at the extent of pupils' bad behaviour, particularly when it involved spitting at and violence towards teachers, or serious cruelty or abuse towards other pupils. It was difficult sometimes to relate behaviour to a pupil we felt we had grown to know. Consequently, we came to understand and sympathise with the frustrations many class teachers experienced. Most felt a strong responsibility towards pupils who displayed a keen desire to learn, and worried that disruptive behaviour hampered their potential. Understandably, many also felt they should not have to tolerate abusive behaviour.

Our inclusion of parents and a range of school staff provided important insights, although versions of events were not always compatible. Rather than try to establish 'truths', we sought to gain a broad overview of the shifting dynamics contextualising pupils' behaviour and trajectories. Pressures shaping pupils' experiences could also come from outside the school, to devastating effect. During our time in Halingbrooke, the government listed the school as 'failing', as part of the National Challenge strategy. Despite steadily improving SATs results and a good Ofsted report, Halingbrooke was not able to ensure that 30 per cent or more pupils left with A★ to C grade GCSEs. The school was informed the target would have to be met by 2010 or face closure. With this and the absence of national targets to reduce permanent exclusions, furious arguments raged between staff over resources for challenging conduct. We felt real empathy for overburdened, harassed mainstream staff, but alarm and despair at how many of our research participants received permanent and fixed-term exclusions. The fall-out from the government directive highlighted for us how abstract policy and practice are experiences on a very personal level.

Centring emotions

Emotionality characterised our research at every turn. Challenging behaviour is an emotionally charged topic and experience. Pupils' feelings got them into trouble, and their anger, frustration and even humour provoked often emotional responses from staff. Institutional relations were also emotionally fraught, with hostility, feuds and resentments bubbling under the surface of everyday life. Somewhat ironically, the schools were invested in the social and emotional aspects of learning (SEAL) imitative to promote the concept of 'emotional literacy'. Staff were highly committed to this agenda, believing that young people's ability to recognise and effectively handle their emotions impacts significantly on their capacity to learn. At Halingbrooke, posters in the BSU urged pupils to stay calm, identify their feelings and banish negative emotions. Regular 'circle time' activities required pupils to share their thoughts and reflect on 'appropriate' emotions. Anger management classes were a school staple, along with sessions to raise self-esteem.

There was a very evident gap between the rational emotionality embodied in SEAL and the real–life dynamics characterising the experiences of pupils and staff. For example, at Halingbrooke the anger management classes were delivered by a member of staff notorious for furious outbursts. The irony was not lost on pupils or staff. Even when sessions were facilitated by less explosive staff, their emotions could become potent, forceful and sometimes uncontainable. The disjuncture between the ethos of emotional literacy and life at Halingbrooke was not surprising, given the structural pressures, human dramas and personal investments behind everyday school life. Pupils might learn to label emotions as appropriate or inappropriate in the classroom, but this did not appear to impact on their experience and expression of feelings. More significantly, raw emotionality could be experienced by staff and pupils as a strength rather than a weakness. Stressful and difficult feelings among staff often derived from passion and commitment. Anger could be a very effective negotiating tool. For pupils, particularly boys, displays of fierce anger could earn them a formidable reputation, protecting them from threats inside and outside school. These threats were very real, as a majority of boys had fallen victim to muggings, violent attacks and, in several cases, stabbings.

But while emotions were often given free reign in the BSUs, we came to realise that many pupils had greater control over their feelings than we had first thought. Traumas, hardships and anxieties were often normalised and discussed as if they were everyday annoyances. Affect rarely featured in the telling of these experiences, as pupils preferred to present themselves as being in control. Given their circumstances, most were coping extremely well. The majority made it to school every day, and despite poor academic records and behaviour, most still hoped to gain something from education. During an interview with Lindon's sick mother, she produced a heartrending letter he had written to her in hospital. The letter conveyed just how worried he had been throughout the period when we were working with him. The normality of school may have been a welcome escape from the difficult feelings he must have been experiencing at home, but we wonder how he coped with the frequent fixed-term exclusions he received during this time.

Emotionality shaped our time in the schools. It defined our substantive topic, characterised the research process and informed our interpretations as researchers. While aware of the emotive nature of our subject matter, we had not anticipated the extent to which it would order our data. The schools' emotional-literacy agenda belied a considerably more torrid reality. Researching this affect-laden environment required us to foreground our own feelings. By immersing ourselves and building relationships in the schools, we inevitably became emotionally invested in them. Rather than see this as a challenge to validity or interpretation, we approached emotionality as a core ethnographic resource demanding a critical examination of the social and personal relationships characterising research. This reflexive voicing of an often-hidden dimension is an important step towards producing a rigorous and convincing ethnography (see Gillies and Robinson, 2010: forthcoming).

Conclusion

Our position as researchers facilitated a high level of critical reflexivity that can inform professionals working with children and young people, demonstrating the value of continuous reflection on practice. Our expectations, conjectures and hopes were reshaped during our time in the schools. Pupils did not fit the template driving our original research proposal. Although they were badly behaved, impulsive and often extremely challenging, they were not particularly disaffected. Efforts to engage pupils in our research demanded the shifting of goalposts, both metaphorically and literally. Participation was on pupils' terms, not ours, but this yielded rich and valuable data. The opportunity to include the perspectives of parents and teachers provided even greater depth of understanding, and highlighted pupils' social connectedness.

As our research progressed, anxieties about building relationships with 'hard-to-reach' youth were replaced by concerns over managing our emotional attachments to pupils. We had occupied a privileged space within the schools, gaining a detailed overview while remaining relatively detached from the everyday workings, but over time we inevitably became embedded through our relationships and concerns. Without this emotional investment and sense of connection, it is hard to imagine how we would have been able to research our topic. Importantly, our time in the schools was limited, and our withdrawal allowed us to reflect critically on our insights and experiences. By outlining the unique perspectives and knowledge generated by ethnographic research, this chapter has emphasised the value of adopting a thoughtful and self-questioning approach to practice.

Notes

[1] In this chapter pseudonyms have been used for the school, staff and pupils.

[2] Thanks to Steve Benson for this suggestion.

References

Gillies, V. and Robinson, Y. (2010: forthcoming) 'Managing emotions in research with challenging pupils: some methodological reflections', *Ethnography in Education*, vol 5, no 1.

Gillies, V. and Robinson, Y. (forthcoming) 'Developing creative methods with pupils at risk of school exclusion', *International Journal of Research Methodology*.

Index